Unlocking Potential

UNLOCKING POTENTIAL

College and Other Choices
for Learning Disabled People
A Step-by-Step Guide

Barbara Scheiber
Jeanne Talpers

ADLER&ADLER

Published in the United States in 1987 by
Adler & Adler, Publishers, Inc.
4550 Montgomery Avenue
Bethesda, Maryland 20814

Library of Congress Cataloging-in-Publication Data
Scheiber, Barbara.
  Unlocking potential.

  1. Handicapped — Education (Higher) — United States.

I. Talpers, Jeanne, II. Title.
LC4815.S33 1987   371.9   86-14205
ISBN 0-917561-29-5
ISBN 0-917561-30-9 (pbk.)

Printed in the United States of America

Figures

APPRECIATION

More than the words on this page can say, we extend our sincere appreciation to the organizations and people who believed in the purposes of this publication and helped bring it to fruition. We wish to express our deepest appreciation to the Fund for the Improvement of Postsecondary Education (FIPSE), U.S. Department of Education, for its grant to Closer Look/The Parents' Campaign for Handicapped Children and Youth, which made this publication possible, our outstanding Advisory Board, and all those who participated in the extensive interviews — professionals, parents — and, most of all, the learning disabled students and adults who so generously and openly shared their struggles and strategies for success. These interviews were the heart and soul of the project, indeed, they gave the manuscript its life (the names of those who participated in interviews, members of the Advisory Board, and a description of the process used to carry out interviews are included at the end of the book).

Special thanks are extended to the following people:

• Diana Hayman, Program Officer for the Fund for the Improvement of Postsecondary Education, for her inspiration, understanding guidance, and steadfast belief in the importance of postsecondary opportunities for learning disabled students and other nontraditional learners.

• Rhona Hartman, Director, HEATH Resource Center, the National Clearinghouse on Postsecondary Education for Handicapped Individuals; Linda Donnels, Assistant Dean for Educational Services, The George Washington University; and William Scales, Director, Disabled Student Services, University of Maryland, College Park, for their invaluable help in planning, providing information and ideas, reading drafts of manuscripts, and giving expert advice.

• Lynn O'Brien, Director, Specific Diagnostic Studies, Inc.; Pamela Leconte, Coordinator, Collaborative Vocational Education Program, The George Washington University; Faith Leonard, Director, Learning Services, Center of Psychological and Learning Services, The American University; Dr. Stephen Schulman, clinical psychologist; and Myrtle Snyder, founder of the HELDS (Higher Education and the Learning Disabled) Project, Central Washington University; for their kindness and generosity in sharing their inspiring insights.

• Jane Jarrow, Executive Director, and Sharon Bonney, past President, Association on Handicapped Student Service Programs in Postsecondary Education, for their advice and assistance in selecting campuses for interviews and in recruiting interviewers.

• Kathleen Kelley, Virginia Houston, Brenda Gaunt, and other members of the Closer Look staff, and Maxine Krulwich, HEATH Resource Center, for their research and guidance.

• Dale Brown, Program Manager, President's Committee for Employment of the Handicapped, for her breadth of knowledge and expertise as a writer and spokesperson for learning disabled adults.

• Richard C. Cooper, Ph.D., Director of Educational Services, Learning Disabilities Consultants; Gale Bell, Bachelor of Fine Arts, artist; Karen Franklin, M.A. in rehabilitation counseling, job developer, Multiple Sclerosis Society; Jo Ann Haseltine, Executive Director, Marin County Puzzle People; Charlotte Johnson, M.A., Ph.D. candidate, learning disabilities specialist; Bernard Kamenear, M.A. in education psychology, senior trade broker; Michael McMullen, B.A., graphics artist. All of these people are learning disabled adults whose individual successes symbolize the goals of this book.

• David Weidert for his help as special consultant; Laurie Dewhirst, of Sparkman and Bartholomew, for her creativity in composing the graphics for this book; Eileen Lavine, for her editorial review and assistance; and Jeremy Gaunt and Richard Cowan for contributing their talent and time on this manuscript.

• The Parent-to-Parent Program, Department of Special Education of The George Washington University, for establishing an internship that enabled Jeanne Talpers to contribute her talents to the writing of this book.

Suzanne Harmon, Deputy Director of Closer Look, deserves very warm and heartfelt thanks for contributing a wealth of knowledge and rare sensitivity to the needs of learning disabled people and their families. As Director of the Closer Look LD Hotline, Suzanne constantly made us aware of the urgent problems faced by learning disabled youth and adults. She conceived of and wrote the chapter, "Getting Ready: A Guide for Parents," carefully reviewed drafts of other chapters, and was a source of enlightenment and inspiration.

SECTION 504: A PREFACE

Section 504: No otherwise qualified handicapped individual ... shall, solely by reason of his handicap, be excluded from the participation in, be denied the benefits of, or be subjected to discrimination under any program or activity receiving federal financial assistance.

— Rehabilitation Act of 1973

Section 504 — a single paragraph in the Rehabilitation Act of 1973 — became a major catalyst for equal opportunity for all disabled people in our country. Regulations for Section 504, written in 1977, spelled out the mandate for equal opportunity in detail. They made clear how the law applied to programs and activities receiving federal funds, including education, employment, and social services.

Gradually, during the past decade, discriminatory barriers have begun to come down. Doors have opened. Thousands of disabled men and women have benefited, as institutions of all kinds have made headway in the pursuit of accessibility.

SECTION 504 AND POSTSECONDARY EDUCATION

Specific provisions of Section 504 related to postsecondary education prohibit discrimination against handicapped persons in recruitment, admission, and treatment after admission. According to the regulations, colleges and universities are required to make "reasonable adjustments" to permit handicapped students to fulfill academic requirements and to assure that disabled students are not effectively excluded from programs because of the absence of auxiliary aids.

WHO IS QUALIFIED?

A person qualified for postsecondary education under Section 504 is one "who meets the academic and technical standards requisite to admission or participation in the recipient's education program or activity."

A handicapped person is defined by the regulations as "any person who (i) has a physical or mental impairment which substantially limits one or more major life activities, (ii) has a record of such impairment or (iii) is regarded as having such an impairment." (Note: The definition of physical or mental impairment includes specific learning disabilities.)

PROVISIONS OF SECTION 504

Subpart E of the regulations describes ways of making postsecondary education accessible to disabled students. These include

• Modifications "as are necessary" to ensure that academic requirements are not discriminatory. Modifications may include changes in the length of time required for completion of degree requirements, substitution of specific courses required for the completion of degree requirements, and adaptation of the manner in which specific courses are conducted. (The regulations state that academic requirements that can be demonstrated as essential to a program of study or related to licensing are not considered discriminatory.)

• The requirement that exams given to evaluate a student's progress actually test the student's achievement, rather than reflect the student's impaired sensory, manual, or speaking skills.

• Auxiliary aids, including taped texts, interpreters for students with hearing impairments, readers for students with visual impairments, classroom equipment adapted for use by students with manual impairments, and other similar services.

CAMPUS RESPONSE

In response to the regulations for implementing Section 504, postsecondary institutions took steps to evaluate accessibility to campus programs and activities. Coordinators of services for handicapped students were designated on campuses that received federal funds, and a new breed of professional was born — the disabled student service provider.

Energetic, dedicated, and imaginative, these coordinators played a major role in bringing about change. They worked with administrators, faculty, disabled students, and others to translate the provisions of Section 504 into campus realities, including new support services, technological aids, and special accommodations. As programs and services took hold, the number of disabled students on campuses grew. The American Council on Education reports that from 1978 to 1985, the percentage of freshmen on postsecondary campuses who identified themselves as disabled rose from 2.7% to 7.7%.

BENEFITS TO LEARNING DISABLED STUDENTS

During the first few years after the issuance of Section 504 regulations, few learning disabled students attended postsecondary programs. Today, their number is rapidly increasing on college and university campuses, in vocational-technical programs and trade schools, and in adult education programs. Different causes account for this trend, including passage of the Education for All Handicapped Children Act of 1975 and the resulting improvement in identification and preparation of learning disabled children and youth. There is also a growing understanding of the educational needs of adult learning disabled students, and a new body of knowledge about how they learn.

Learning disabled students, the newcomers on campuses, are reaping the fruits of Section 504. They are the beneficiaries of accommodations that have been developed by the pioneers who came before them. Taped textbooks, extended time for testing, calculators, notetakers, tape recorders, and computers are all helping learning disabled students participate successfully on American campuses. In addition, implementation of Section 504 has set the stage for new programs, services, and classroom strategies that meet the unique needs of learning disabled students. Access for these nontraditional learners is expanding.

THE FUTURE

As with all laws, effective implementation of Section 504 has come about through changes in values and perceptions. As awareness of disabilities has deepened, the spirit of the law has been woven more deeply into the fabric of campus policies and procedures.

But there are still barriers to acceptance of people who learn in different ways. There are prejudices to be overcome through knowledge and shared experiences. Change is still needed if disabled students, including those who are learning disabled, are to participate fully in the mainstream of postsecondary education. The perspective of the past decade has shown that change can come — if there is mutual respect and understanding of human differences.

There is work ahead. Section 504 has challenged each of us to realize its vision of equity. In a real sense, it has written the preface to this book.

INTRODUCTION: FROM POTENTIAL TO REALITY

This book has been written to help learning disabled students achieve access to postsecondary campuses and to help campuses make accessibility a reality.

Underlying the purpose of the book is a growing demand for postsecondary education and training for what is the largest group of handicapped children and adults in the United States. In 1986, the U.S. Department of Education reported that 1,866,669 learning disabled students were enrolled in special education during the previous school year. This number does not include the many children and youths who are in school but have not been identified or served. It only hints at the millions of adults who grew up before public special educational services were available.

Most learning disabled adults have never been diagnosed or helped. Some have tried college, but could not make it; others have spent years in low-paying, dead-end jobs or have never found employment; others have given up and live isolated, dependent lives.

Whatever their stage of life, learning disabled people have the potential to be productive, self-sufficient members of society. Postsecondary programs can be the bridges to employment and independence. They can be the settings for devising new tools and nontraditional approaches that will benefit not only learning disabled students but all students. They can be the place where potential becomes reality.

BEHIND THE PAGES

Behind the pages of this book are hundreds of unwritten stories — stories of success, of failure, of creativity, of vision, and of hope. The stories are of learning disabled students who have found ways to cope with their disability; of college instructors and coordinators of services for disabled students who have committed themselves to creating programs for learning disabled students; of counselors who have often been the only persons to salvage learning disabled adults when repeated failure had almost destroyed them; and of parents whose determination and support made the difference in their children's lives. The stories are also about programs developed by colleges, vocational schools, prevocational projects, and independent living centers — all of which are reaching and serving people with learning disabilities.

We can quote statistics and talk in generalities, but nothing can replace the individual experiences of those who have struggled to succeed.

Mike is one of these stories. Mike flunked out of three universities but refused to give up. He believed that "somewhere in my head was intelligence. I just couldn't tap it."

After moving to the state of Washington and working in construction, Mike decided to try college once more. This time he was admitted into the HELDS (Higher Education for Learning Disabled Students) program at Central Washington University. The founder and director of this program, Myrtle Snyder, diagnosed Mike's learning disabilities — for the first time in his life. She helped Mike get what he needed — taped texts, tutors for his "atrocious" grammar and spelling, and permission to tape class lectures. Most of all, she saw Mike's talents in writing and drawing, and, in his words, "she made me believe in myself." Mike graduated with A's and B's and is now successfully employed as a graphic artist.

Others whose courage and perseverance overcame the difficulties caused by learning disabilities include people like

• Janet, who despite severe dyslexia, which was not diagnosed until she went to college, is now in medical school, where she is getting honors in clinical medicine.

• Robert, who dropped out of high school and drifted in and out of low-paying jobs for four years. Finally, with the assistance of a vocational rehabilitation counselor, he went to cosmetology school and became the assistant manager of a beauty shop.

• Tony, who spent five years completing a two-year associate arts degree at his local community college. Tony is now working as a dental lab technician.

• Louise, who works as an office clerk and wants to go to college. Louise finally got her high school diploma at the age of twenty-five. To prepare herself for a business course, she is getting special tutoring through her community adult basic education program.

Despite their natural intelligence, people like Janet, Robert, Tony, and Louise may be unable to decipher printed words, construct simple paragraphs, or do mathematical calculations. They may forget spoken instructions or strain to write or say words that get stuck in their memories. And despite excellent hearing, they may consistently misinterpret what is said because of failure to hear certain letters or sounds correctly.

With the right combination of support, understanding, skill-building, and compensatory strategies, these learning disabled adults can develop their aptitudes and talents to the fullest and can lead productive lives.

ORGANIZATION OF THE BOOK

The first two chapters of this book define and explain learning disabilities and describe the diagnostic processes used to determine the specific disabilities. The chapters that follow discuss postsecondary options; how to select an appropriate one; and how to achieve campus access through academic advising, accommodations, study skills, and personal adjustment. The last chapter of the book gives suggestions for starting postsecondary programs for learning disabled students.

TERMINOLOGY

This book is aimed at many audiences — learning disabled students and adults, their parents, and the professionals who work with them. Because terminology can be subjective, it will be helpful to clarify how some of the words most commonly found in the book are used.

• **Postsecondary** describes any formal educational or training program that follows the high school years.

• **Campus** means any setting in which these programs occur, including traditional four-year universities and colleges, two-year colleges, vocational and technical schools, adult education programs, and independent living centers.

• **Learning disabled** describes a person with normal or high intelligence who does not achieve at his or her expected level in academic, social, or daily living skills. These gaps in performance may arise from presumed neurological origins and are not the result of mental retardation, physical handicaps, emotional disturbance, or educational deprivation.

• **Accommodation** means services, teaching approaches, or compensatory strategies that can help learning disabled students overcome or cope with their difficulties and express their abilities.

• **Access** means a combination of attitudes, assistance, accommodations, classroom arrangements, and technological aids that make it possible for learning disabled students to succeed in an institution for which they are qualified.

3

SHARING SUGGESTIONS

Although most of the programs described in this book are located on college campuses, each chapter has applicability to other postsecondary settings. Tips for classroom teaching of learning disabled college students can be used in adult education classes or vocational training programs; study skills can be used by students in any setting or by teachers and tutors who are working with learning disabled students.

Diagnosis and evaluation can be used for high school and college students, as well as vocational rehabilitation and independent living center clients. Some of these diagnostic tests are being used in a few adult education programs.

Whether you are a learning disabled student or adult, a parent, a teacher, a counselor, or other professional working in one of many settings, you will find ideas and suggestions that are of value. Mutual understanding and sharing are the beginning of finding solutions.

THE STAKES ARE HIGH

The problems facing learning disabled adults in our society are complex; the stakes are high. The learning disabled person who fails to receive the help needed may never get a hold on life. The result may be endless dependency— on parents, on siblings, and on society. Alarming reports tell us of people with learning disabilities who have been broken by lack of understanding and opportunity, by rejection, and by failure. They are counted in mental illness and prison statistics.

The challenge of responding is not all on the doorstep of the postsecondary community. Many groups need to contribute to effective transitional services for learning disabled young people as they go from high school to adulthood. We need a pooling of thoughts and energies — a joining of educators and employers, mental health professionals, vocational rehabilitation workers, writers, researchers, parents, guidance counselors, and learning disabled adults themselves.

Each of us loses when potential is lost, when minds and talents and abilities go to waste. Our society needs the constructive energies of all of its citizens. The compassion and commitment we bring to understanding and helping learning disabled people will yield rich and varied fruits of human endeavor. The doors to higher education that are opened will give the learning disabled men and women in our midst the opportunity to fulfill the dream of an independent adulthood — a life of usefulness and joy that is their birthright.

1

LEARNING DISABILITIES: WHAT ARE THEY?

LEARNING DISABILITIES: WHAT ARE THEY?

"By recognizing individual differences, we foster individual gifts. By teaching to strengths, we help not only learning disabled students, but all students. By understanding learning disabilities, we learn more about ourselves."

Barbara Given, Associate Professor,
George Mason University (Virginia)

We all learn differently. We all gather and express information in our own special ways. Some of us learn more readily by reading or by seeing; some by listening. Some of us use our sense of touch to diagnose illness, to find the beauty in clay or wood, or to make machinery work smoothly. Some of us function efficiently and productively, with occasional lapses and mistakes; but some of us find academic or work tasks confusing and disabling.

A striking example of learning differences comes from the life of Albert Einstein. Despite his phenomenal gifts, Einstein had great difficulties with academic learning. He said of himself: "Writing is difficult, and I communicate this way (by speaking) very badly ... I very rarely think in words at all."

Einstein was unable to learn in traditional ways. His genius was rare, but his difficulties with school work were similar to the experiences of many learning disabled students. Like him, learning disabled people often acquire and express information in different ways. They

7

have many kinds of abilities, but these are often eclipsed by the differences that may stand out in the classroom and in interactions with peers.

Causes, Theories, and Concepts

What causes learning differences? Why are they strengths for some people and disabilities for others? Are they inherited? Did something go wrong during pregnancy or at birth? Are they a result of an injury, illness, or allergies? There is no *one* answer. The answers that do exist are complex and incomplete.

Not only are scientists seeking explanations for the origins of learning disabilities, but they are trying to analyze and decipher the cognitive process, how it works, and what disrupts it. The closer they come to understanding learning disabilities, the closer we will all come in our understanding of the learning process.

Theories about how the brain works, about the concept of intelligence, and about ways of measuring intelligence are being carefully evaluated for applicability to learning disabled people. Three recent contributions to understanding ways of learning are the right-brain/left-brain theory, the multiple intelligences concept, and Feuerstein's Instrumental Enrichment approach. The following brief descriptions are not in-depth analyses. References for further reading on these topics are listed at the end of the chapter.

Right-Brain/Left-Brain. According to recent scientific findings, the right and left hemispheres of the brain contribute different specialties to the thinking process. A fusing of left and right brain functions is essential to learning, but some people may be more dominant in one sphere than in the other.

It is thought that the left sphere specializes in "linear" thinking (verbal ability, logical sequencing of ideas, reasoning, interpretation of written and spoken language, and tasks related to phonics, reading, and dealing with facts) and the right sphere specializes in non-verbal, "holistic" thinking — seeing the whole rather than the parts. Other functions of the right sphere are intuition; imagination; visualization; and perception through motion, touch, color, and concrete experience.

These findings strongly suggest that our society has valued left-brain functions more highly than right-brain functions and that traditional classrooms have placed certain students at a disadvantage. "Left-brain" students are more likely to succeed in traditional classrooms, where they shine in verbal skills and abstract reasoning. "Right-brain" students, who are less verbal, may have difficulty with basic skills and are often seen in terms of their deficits, not in terms of their strengths, abilities, and creativity. Obvious questions arise. Are students who are right-brain dominant among those who have been labeled *learning disabled?* How can their particular strengths be valued and nourished?

Concept of Multiple Intelligences. Another contribution to the concept of differences in learning is the work of Dr. Howard Gardner, a neurologist on the staff of the Boston University School of Medicine. Dr. Gardner believes that we have limited our definition of intelligence by stressing linguistic and logical/mathematical intelligence in our

IQ measurements rather than giving equal weight to other areas of intelligence. Dr. Gardner proposes that we assess and teach competence in spatial, musical, and kinesthetic skills (such as those used in dancing, athletics, and surgery) as well as interpersonal or intrapersonal skills. He believes that all of these areas must be honored if we are to realize our potential as human beings.

Instrumental Enrichment. Psychologists and educators are becoming interested in the work of Reuven Feuerstein, an Israeli psychologist who has spent twenty-five years developing techniques for teaching low-functioning adolescents.

Feuerstein believes that intelligence is not predetermined or "fixed," nor can it be used to predict learning capacity. Rather, he believes that the mind is modifiable and that thinking can be improved through a process called instrumental enrichment. Through his research, Feuerstein has developed techniques to improve the ability to solve problems, perceive and analyze information, isolate main or relevant ideas, and organize thoughts. In some settings, teachers trained in his method are trying this approach with learning disabled students.

These and other new ideas are challenging traditional assumptions about intelligence, about teaching, and about human potential. As understanding grows, we become increasingly aware of the need to appreciate differences in the strengths and abilities that each person, including those diagnosed as learning disabled, brings to the act of learning.

DEFINING LEARNING DISABILITIES

Until recently, learning disabilities were thought to only affect school-age children who would be cured by the time they completed elementary school. It is now apparent that the condition persists into adult life, manifesting itself not only in academic settings but in the workplace and in social relationships.

This growth in the understanding of learning disabilities is reflected in the definition proposed in 1984 by the board of directors of the Association for Children and Adults with Learning Disabilities (ACLD).

Specific learning disabilities is a chronic condition of presumed neurological origin which selectively interferes with the development, integration, and/or demonstration of verbal and nonverbal abilities.

Specific learning disabilities exists as a distinct handicapping condition in the presence of average to superior intelligence, adequate sensory and motor systems, and adequate learning opportunities. The condition varies in its manifestations and in degree of severity.

Throughout life the condition can affect self-esteem, education, vocation, socialization, and daily living activities.

This definition stresses the lifelong impact of the disability as well as its intrusion into nonacademic aspects of living, especially in the areas of self-esteem, interpersonal relationships, and daily living skills needed for independence.

What is happening on college campuses illustrates the validity of this definition. Students whose learning disabilities did not disappear in their early school years are enrolling in colleges; many students who are having difficulty in college are finding out for the first time that they are learning disabled. Instructors are frustrated and dismayed by students whose classroom participation is superb, but whose exams are confused or limited in ideas; by students who seem well prepared and alert one day and unable to recall the same information the next day; or by students who are obviously smart but cannot do simple mathematical calculations or write an organized, neat essay.

WHAT IS IT LIKE TO BE LEARNING DISABLED?

To define a condition is one part of a problem; to understand and live with it is another. The combination of specific learning disabilities is very individualized. Symptoms differ in degree and form. Any assessment of a student's learning problems must seek out *specific* kinds of difficulties as well as specific learning styles. Any intervention must address those specific needs and the ways in which they can be accommodated. Intervention must also build on the student's strengths, abilities, interests, and aptitudes.

There is no typical profile of a learning disabled person. Some are poorly coordinated; others are outstanding athletes. Some are socially awkward and immature; others have excellent social skills. One highly intelligent student reads haltingly, reversing letters and leaving out parts of words or sentences. Another reads well but is barely able to construct a simple paragraph in writing and struggles to recall facts, proper names, or correct spelling. Another, adept at mechanics, has difficulty orienting his body in space and frequently drops equipment and bumps into machinery. His boss is afraid his clumsiness will cause an accident, and his job is in jeopardy.

No description can take the place of words written by learning disabled people about their own feelings. In *Steps to Independence for People with Learning Disabilities*, Dale Brown tells what it is like.

Many people with learning disabilities have ... difficulty right in their own homes. Some are unsure of where their bodies are in space. They do not have a secure sense of the floor beneath their feet ... It is extremely difficult for [them] to pick up the social customs many of their peers take for granted: small talk, entering a circle of people, introducing themselves to strangers. Learning disabled people are in culture shock in their own culture.

LEARNING PROCESSES: INPUT, INTEGRATION, AND OUTPUT

Perhaps a simple way to understand how learning takes place and what happens when the process is disrupted is to use computer terminology. To process information requires taking in or putting in information *(input)*, integrating it *(integration)*, and then expressing it *(output)*.

In the learning process, input is the way in which our senses (seeing, hearing, touching, smelling, or tasting) perceive or take in information. For a student, this can involve reading; listening to lectures, tapes, and discussions; and using hands-on experiences or observation.

Integration is how we convert that information into meaning. It involves sequencing (organizing what is seen or heard in logical order), remembering (storing information), and abstracting (seeing relationships of parts to the whole) or deriving meaning from a specific word or symbol.

Output is the way information is expressed through spoken or written words or body language, including gestures or facial expressions. In a school setting, output involves writing papers and exams; giving oral reports; participating in class discussion; and demonstrating proficiency in science labs, art, music, technology, and physical education.

Problems with perception and integration affect output. Difficulties seeing or hearing correctly, sequencing, and remembering can interfere with spelling, word recognition, oral speaking, organizing thoughts for a speech or exam, and mechanics of writing.

Again, personal descriptions make these concepts real.

An example of how writing is affected is this letter from nineteen-year-old Thomas Alva Edison, who was considered slow and had to be taught by his mother at home.

Dear Mother — Started the Store several weeks. I have growed considerably I don't liik much like a Boy now — Hows all the folk did you receive a Box of Books from Memphis that he promised to send them — languages. Your son Al.

Another young man described the act of phrasing words and ideas into oral language as similar to translating words and ideas into a foreign language.

Dale Brown summarizes the confusion that can occur when processing is disrupted.

Learning disabled adults receive inaccurate information through their senses and/or have trouble processing that information. Like static on the radio or a bad TV picture, the information becomes garbled as it travels from the eye, ear, or skin to the brain.

SPECIFIC LEARNING PROBLEMS

Following are descriptions of problems in specific learning processes. With common sense, ingenuity, creativity, and perseverance, ways can be found to accommodate or bypass many of the difficulties that occur.

Visual Perception Problems

People with visual perception problems (dyslexia) may have perfect eyesight but see letters incorrectly or in reverse order, or they may fail to perceive some letters, words, or even whole paragraphs. They frequently confuse letters that look alike, such as *b* or *d*, *g* or *q*. When reading, they may omit ends of words or jumble spaces between words. A passage may look like this:

No wisthe ti fo alpoobmen t com toth aib ofthe rcoutry. (Now is the time for all good men to come to the aid of their country.)

COMMOMLY USED TERMS

Dyslexia: Severe difficulty with reading.

Dyscalculia: Severe difficulty with mathematics.

Dysgraphia: Severe problems with handwriting.

FIGURE 1

Visual perception problems may also interfere with understanding social cues. This can result in misinterpretation of facial expressions that convey boredom, approval, anger, skepticism, or the end of a conversation or interview. The consequences can be painful.

Auditory Perception Problems

Auditory perception problems interfere with accurate interpretation of information received through the ears. Despite normal hearing, people may have difficulty differentiating between similar sounds (hear "crashed the car" for "washed the car" or "ninety minutes" for "nineteen minutes"). Or they may be acutely sensitive to background noises and be unable to screen out traffic, rustling of paper, whispers, or other sounds when listening to a lecture or a conversation or when trying to concentrate on an exam.

Auditory perception problems can make it hard to catch the implications of different tones of voice. Inappropriate reactions can occur when a questioning tone of voice is interpreted as an angry voice, or when a joke is taken as a serious comment.

Spatial Perception Problems

Spatial perception difficulties can produce inaccurate signals about where one's body is in space. This affects a person's ability to judge distances, differentiate between right and left, and follow directions. People with spatial problems frequently get lost, even in familiar territory.

Other Learning Problems

Memory. Memory problems plague many learning disabled students. For impressions received by the senses to be usable, they must be stored by the brain and retrieved when needed. Learning disabled students are more likely to have problems with short-term memory than with long-term memory. They dig and tug endlessly to find words, names, dates, and thoughts that seem lost inside their heads.

Sequencing. Problems with sequencing interfere with understanding the structure of a lecture or a reading passage or seeing the relationship of main ideas to subordinate ideas. Seeing the correct order of letters in a word, or numbers in a row or column, is also difficult. Students who have problems with sequencing information often have difficulty with outlining, choosing priorities, organizing notes, or keeping track of important materials or belongings.

Many people with learning disabilities find their own way of organizing. Their minds may work better when they are free to think nonsequentially or to follow the flow of their own thoughts and ideas. They may use original or insightful ways to arrive at conclusions. Others benefit greatly from learning how to structure tasks, how to outline assignments, and how to set up orderly systems for self-management.

Gross and Fine Motor Coordination. Motor problems can interfere with output. Poor coordination of large muscles (gross motor problems) can result in clumsiness — knocking things over and bumping into people and objects. Participation in many sports is often difficult. Poor coordination of small muscles (fine motor problems) can make writing very difficult. Messy, illegible papers are the bane of many students as well as those who must read them.

Visual motor/auditory motor. Visual motor coordination problems make it difficult for the hands or feet to obey commands from the eyes — to copy words from the blackboard, cut a pattern of a dress, type, or write legibly. Similarly, auditory motor problems interfere with following spoken directions or listening and taking notes at the same time.

FALLOUT

When learning disabilities are not identified or understood, the psychological toll is high. Some adults suffer great strain from efforts to hide their problems, fearful that they will be discovered as illiterate or be embarrassed, criticized, or hurt, as they were when they were children. Others lash out in anger at family, friends, and spouses, paying the world back for their misery. Some become violent. Others become depressed and withdrawn, leading lonely and limited lives. Others drive themselves mercilessly to prove they are worthy of respect.

Despite their intelligence and their often outstanding gifts, learning disabled people do not have a reservoir of success to replenish them after they have failed a task. The experience of repeated failure throughout their early school years can inhibit them from taking risks.

Yet many have succeeded. They have grown beyond their hurts and disappointments, they have overcome their problems, they have found help and support, and they have learned to appreciate and develop their strengths. They have discovered that their learning disability is only one part of their selves — a part that they have learned to manage. Their disability is no longer disabling.

THE FUTURE

In the past, efforts to help learning disabled people have emphasized remediation. For many, this approach has worked; for others, it has led to more frustration. This book concentrates on finding ways to accommodate the disability and views the disability as a condition to be understood and overcome. But the underlying theme is that everyone learns differently and that the task for educators and other professionals is to identify and develop each person's strengths in learning style and aptitude.

Dr. Mary Poplin, a well-known educator, beautifully summarizes this philosophy of differences in learning. In her farewell message as editor of the *Learning Disability Quarterly,* she speaks of the often overlooked creativity of learning disabled students. These students may be talented in music, poetry, dance, art, mechanics, computer programming, or athletics; but their abilities are usually forgotten or lost by "deficit-driven" approaches. Dr. Poplin challenges us to "reject our ... focus on disability, and courageously change our emphasis to abilities and talents."

Additional Reading About Learning Disabilities

An Uncommon Gift, by James S. Evans, Bridgebooks, The Westminster Press, 925 Chestnut Street, Philadelphia, Pennsylvania 19107. (189 pages, $10.95) 1983

"Feuerstein's Instrumental Enrichment; Teaching Intelligence to Adolescents," by Nicholas Hobbs, Educational Leadership, April 1980. (Reprints and information about Feuerstein's curriculum are available from Frances Link, Curriculum Development Associates, Inc., 1211 Connecticut Avenue, N.W., Washington, D.C. 20036.)

Journal of Rehabilitation: Rehabilitation of Adults with Learning Disabilities: Special Issue (April, May, June 1984). (Copies available from the National Rehabilitation Association, 633 South Washington Street, Alexandria, Virginia 22314, $7.50.)

"Language Disabilities in Men of Eminence," by Lloyd J. Thompson, M.D. (Reprint available from the Orton Dyslexia Society, 724 York Road, Baltimore, Maryland 21204.)

No Easy Answers, by Sally Smith. Bantam Books, New York, New York. (326 pages, $3.95) 1979

Reversals, A Personal Account of Victory Over Dyslexia, by Eileen Simpson. Washington Square Press, Pocket Books, 1230 Avenue of the Americas, New York, New York 10020. (263 pages, $2.95) 1979

Steps to Independence for People with Learning Disabilities, by Dale Brown. (Available through Goodwill of America, 9200 Wisconsin Avenue, Bethesda, Maryland 20814). (48 pages, free) 1980

"Summary Rationalizations, Apologies, and Farewell: What We Don't Know About the Learning Disabled," by Mary Poplin. Learning Disability Quarterly (Volume 7, Spring 1984). (For reprint, write to Council for Learning Disabilities, P.O. Box 40303, Overland Park, Kansas 66204.)

The Brain: A User's Manual, by the Diagram Group. Berkley Publishing Corporation, 200 Madison Avenue, New York, New York 10016. (511 pages, $4.95) 1983

The Misunderstood Child: A Guide for Parents of Learning Disabled Children, by Larry B. Silver, M.D. McGraw-Hill Book Company, Princeton Road, Hightstown, New Jersey 08520. (212 pages, $14.95) 1984

"The Remedial Thinker," by Paul Chance. Psychoiogy Today, October 1981. (Article on Feuerstein. Back copies available through Psychoiogy Today, 1200 17th Street, N.W., Washington, D.C. 20036, $3.00.)

"The Seven Frames of Mind," by Howard Gardner. Psychology Today, June 1984. (Back copies available through Psychology Today, 1200 17th Street, N.W., Washington, D.C. 20036, $3.00.)

The Tuned-In Turned-On Book about Learning Disabilities, by Marnell L. Hayes. Academic Therapy Publications, 20 Commercial Boulevard, Novato, California 94947. (63 pages, $2.50; cassette tape, $8.00) 1974

"Visually Mediated Thinking: A Report of the Case of Albert Einstein," by B. M. Patton. Journal of Learning Disabilities (Volume 6, 1973). (For copy, write to The Professional Press, Inc., 11 East Adams Street, Chicago, Illinois 60603, $3.50 per journal, $6.00, foreign.)

2

DIAGNOSIS: NOW WHAT?

DIAGNOSIS: NOW WHAT?

Diagnosis is not an end in itself. It is an information-gathering process to find out if learning disabilities are at the root of problems a person may be experiencing. Diagnosis also assesses a student's strengths and indicates how a student compensates for areas of difficulty. It is a way of discovering how a student learns.

When the diagnostic process is completed, it should be possible to get a helpful answer to the simple question: "Now what?" The answer should give down-to-earth guidance and recommendations for making choices. Are academic and career goals realistic? Is the student's current educational program too hard? In what ways? Where do specific problems lie? What aptitudes and abilities are apparent? How can these strengths be incorporated into the student's program? How can he or she compensate for areas of difficulty? Would counseling help to deal with problems of personal adjustment?

A complete diagnosis uses skilled observation, interviews, and formal and informal tests to assess a student's aptitudes, verbal and nonverbal strengths and weaknesses, and preferred learning style. Diagnosis becomes the tool for planning.

Diagnosis can take place at any time in a person's life. Although this chapter is about the uses of diagnosis in planning appropriate post-secondary education, the information can be used by diagnosticians in vocational rehabilitation, adult education, mental health, and other settings. Additional resources about tests and diagnostic procedures are listed at the end of the chapter.

DIAGNOSIS ON THE CAMPUS

Diagnosis plays a vital part in post-secondary planning for learning disabled students. In a sense, it is a "ticket" to appropriate services. Most campuses require that a student be diagnosed as learning disabled before plans or arrangements are made for course work accommodations. Results of tests indicating the presence of learning disabilities must be submitted for admission to special programs for learning disabled students. In addition, an institution looks at the results of diagnostic tests to determine if a student is qualified, has the potential for meeting academic or vocational standards, or needs support services.

Is a Student Learning Disabled?

The diagnostician looks for discrepancies of various kinds to determine if a student is learning disabled. Is there a discrepancy between potential and achievement? Is IQ high, but grades low? Is the student smart, even though classwork is poor? Is academic performance uneven? Can the student reason well, yet not remember words? Can the student understand a subject, but be unable to organize the answers for an exam? How does the student's educational level or social maturity compare with peers?

During the diagnostic process, the diagnostician also gathers evidence to determine whether physical disability, mental retardation, emotional disturbance, or visual or hearing impairments should be ruled out as primary causes of discrepancies.

CONTROVERSY ABOUT TESTING

Techniques of diagnosis are controversial. There is no universal agreement about how to assess potential, how to diagnose learning disabilities, what tests to use, or who should do the testing. In fact, only now are tests being developed specifically for the adult learning disabled population.

Intelligence tests are a particular focus of controversy. Testing for potential usually involves getting an IQ score. But an intelligence test is only a sample of behavior at a given time and reflects the test author's own definition of intelligence. An IQ score is not the last word about what a student can do. In many instances, tests measure how well a student is able to learn in a traditional classroom, not his or her innate intelligence. Many factors, such as anxiety, language problems, and limited experience can depress a score and give a false picture. And results can be distorted by underlying visual or auditory perceptual problems.

Learning disabled students, and other students as well, frequently have the potential for learning in unique ways not measured by IQ tests. A single test is not enough. Diagnostic assessment involves seeking information from a variety of sources and sifting the results of different tests, interviews, and observation.

THE DIAGNOSTIC PROCESS

On campus the diagnostic process starts when a distressed student seeks help. The student may turn to a disabled student service coordinator or a counselor or go directly to a diagnostic facility. (Suggestions for finding diagnostic services are listed in Figure 5 at the end of the chapter.) The first step, once the contact has been made, is screening.

Screening

Screening is a time to get a sense of possible causes for the student's distress. It is a time to probe gently for evidence of learning disabilities. It is a time to listen with sensitivity. What is the problem? When did it start? How has the student tried to deal with it? Gathering background information is an important part of screening and includes the following:

• *Educational history.* This includes finding out about learning problems during early grades, previous educational diagnoses, special education placement, and how well the student has learned to compensate for specific problem areas.

• *Family history.* In gathering information, the interviewer may look for signs of dyslexia or learning problems in other family members.

• *Medical history.* A thorough medical checkup should evaluate vision and hearing, injuries or illnesses, allergies, birth trauma, low birth weight, or related medical conditions, such as epilepsy.

• *Samples of academic work.* Screening often includes examining examples of work and giving informal tests. A student may be asked to decipher words or read a passage aloud to see if letters or words are reversed or misunderstood.

• *Samples of handwriting.* These samples can be particularly useful in detecting possible learning disabilities. Frequently, as Myrtle Snyder writes, the handwriting of a learning disabled person is not merely poor handwriting. Letters slant in different directions and are incompletely formed. There is inconsistent spacing between words and between letters in the same words. Capitals may appear in the middle of a sentence. Spelling errors are frequent and inventive, with different spellings of the same word in a single paragraph.

The screening stage itself may lead to helpful interventions. A student may decide to try the campus writing center or learning lab, to drop one heavy reading course, or to get tutoring. Change does not have to wait until all the results of a full-scale diagnosis are in. Some students may not actually require further diagnosis but can work out their problems on their own or with the assistance of an advisor.

Formal Assessment

If further diagnosis of learning disabilities appears warranted, screening is usually followed by formal assessment.

The WAIS-R. The WAIS-R (Wechsler Adult Intelligence Scale-Revised) is frequently the test used to measure potential and to diagnose learning disabilities. The purpose of the test is not to single out intellectual ability as the cornerstone of intelligence, but to evaluate different facets of intelligence. The test's author, David Wechsler, conceives of intelligence as "the overall capacity of an individual to understand and cope with the world around him."

The WAIS-R is divided into two parts: The Verbal section and the Performance section.

The Verbal section requires language skills and can provide specific information on verbal ability, capacity to think conceptually, and ability to exercise judgment.

The Performance section assesses nonverbal abilities and can yield information about visual memory, ability to think sequentially, orientation to time and space, understanding of the whole in relation to its parts, distractability, motor control, and motivation.

Each of the sections consists of a series of subtests that are scored separately to produce a Verbal IQ and a Performance IQ. The entire test provides a full-scale IQ.

Diagnosticians look closely at the scores of subtests for indications of strengths and weaknesses in verbal and nonverbal ways of thinking. Wide "scatter" on subtests or scores that show peaks and valleys of ability may indicate underlying processing problems. Interpretation of these discrepancies can suggest areas of aptitude as well as areas of functioning that need remediation or compensation. These results are meshed with input from other sources to draw a full diagnostic profile of learning strengths and weaknesses.

Woodcock Johnson Psychoeducational Battery. The Woodcock Johnson is increasingly used to diagnose strengths and weaknesses of learning disabled students and to get a picture of a student's aptitudes, achievements, and interests. This comprehensive test is divided into three parts.

Part 1 consists of twelve subtests for assessing cognitive ability and scholastic aptitude. This part can give information about memory, problem solving, visual-auditory strengths required for reading, comprehension, reasoning, verbal ability, visual-motor aptitude, and understanding of mathematical concepts.

Part 2 assesses academic achievement and skills in ten subtests that include recognizing letters, word attack, comprehending written material, math, writing from dictation, proofing, and general knowledge in science, social studies, and the humanities.

Part 3 is a test of interests in reading, mathematics, written language, physical activities, and social activities.

Academic Skills Tests. Additional tests may be selected to evaluate academic ability and to pinpoint specific areas that may require special help. Examples include the Peabody Picture Vocabulary Test (understanding of words, reading, and conversational level); Test of Adolescent Language (strengths and weaknesses in language and writing skills);

Wide Range Achievement Math, Spelling, or Reading Test; Gray Oral Reading Test; and The Stanford Test of Academic Skills. (Evaluation of vocational aptitudes is discussed in the chapter "Getting Ready: A Parent's Guide.")

In addition to one or more formal tests, diagnosticians frequently use their own informal tests of oral reading, reading comprehension, listening comprehension, writing, and study skills. These tests provide a more precise view of problems that need intensive instruction and/or compensatory strategies, such as omission of letters or words in reading, inability to recognize words and remember them, slow rate of reading, and problems with spelling, punctuation, and math skills.

Assessment of Perceptual Motor Skills. Perceptual motor skills may be tested to see if there are underlying processing problems that interfere with learning. These tests can also give clues to learning styles and can suggest accommodations to enable a learning disabled person to function in a regular classroom.

Examples of tests that may be used include Bender Visual Motor Gestalt Test (tests skills in copying nine geometric designs); the Malcomesius Specific Language Test (evaluates auditory discrimination, auditory and visual coordination, comprehension, and handwriting); Benton Visual Retention Test (evaluates short-term memory, eye-hand coordination, and visual perception); Wepman Test of Auditory Discrimination; and Willeford Central Auditory Battery (tests ability to screen out competing sounds).

Assessment of Social and Emotional Development. A student with social or emotional problems may or may not have underlying learning disabilities. This is one of many issues a diagnostician may need to investigate. Inappropriate or immature behavior, low

20

LEARNING STYLES

	CLUES	LEARNING TIPS
VISUAL	• Needs to see it to know it. • Strong sense of color. • May have artistic ability. • Difficulty with spoken directions. • Overreaction to sounds. • Trouble following lectures. • Misinterpretation of words.	• Use of graphics to reinforce learning — films, slides, illustrations, diagrams, doodles. • Color coding to organize notes and possessions. • Written directions. • Use of flow charts and diagrams for notetaking. • Visualizing spelling of words or facts to be memorized.
AUDITORY	• Prefers to get information by listening — needs to hear it to know it. • Difficulty following written directions. • Difficulty with reading. • Problems with writing. • Inability to read body language and facial expressions.	• Use of tapes for reading and for class and lecture notes. • Learning by interviewing or by participating in discussions. • Having test questions or directions read aloud or put on tape.
HAPTIC	• Prefers hands-on learning. • Can assemble parts without reading directions. • Difficulty sitting still. • Learns better when physical activity is involved. • May be very well coordinated and have athletic ability.	• Experiential learning (making models, doing lab work, and role playing). • Frequent breaks in study periods. • Tracing letters and words to learn spelling and remember facts. • Use of computer to reinforce learning through sense of touch. • Memorizing or drilling while walking or exercising. • Expressing abilities through dance, drama, or gymnastics.

FIGURE 2

self-esteem, anxiety about competition, and other symptoms may all have their origins in learning disabilities. Careful study of family, school, and medical histories and perceptive diagnostic interviewing are part of assessing emotional well-being. The diagnostician may also arrange for some formal testing, ask for additional professional consultation, or evaluate the results of some formal tests. Tests that may be used include the Minnesota Multiphasic Personality Inventory (provides scores on 26 phases of personality, including physical condition and moral and social attitudes) or the Rorshach Inkblot Test (a projective test in which the person describes shapes and pictures perceived within inkblots).

Learning Styles

Information gathered from the WAIS, Woodcock Johnson, perceptual motor tests, and observation can answer many questions about learning styles. However, no one knows better than students themselves what learning channel they prefer. For some students, the style of learning that works may be visual, for others it may be auditory. Others may be haptic learners and need to use their tactile senses to reinforce what is taught. Many learning disabled people use a combination of channels and learn best through multisensory teaching.

Checklists for Self-Assessment. The Learning Channel Preference Checklist in Figure 3, developed by Lynn O'Brien, can indicate the way a person prefers to learn. This is not a formal, timed test, nor is it a complete list of clues to learning channel preferences. It is a quick way to begin to check for the style of learning that makes a student "click." It can be used by a diagnostician or as a self-assessment tool.

After finishing the test, add up the scores. A score between 25 and 30 indicates a preference for a certain modality. However, Lynn O'Brien points out that there are no absolutes in dealing with learning preferences and that mood, subject matter, teaching approaches, and other variables can affect the way a person learns. It is also important to be aware of the second strongest channel as a learning style to build on.

A similar assessment tool, the Barsch Learning Style Inventory, was developed in 1980 by Jeffrey Barsch, and is available from Academic Therapy Publications, 20 Commercial Boulevard, Novato, California 94947.

WHO DOES THE DIAGNOSIS?

The more skilled and sensitive the diagnostician, the better the chance for a meaningful interpretation of diagnostic tests. The diagnostician may be a psychologist, an educational diagnostician, or a learning disabilities specialist; but most important, he or she should be experienced in working with learning disabled adolescents and adults. Many diagnosticians believe that accurate scoring of answers is not enough; it is equally important to note *how* a person arrives at an answer or solves a problem.

Observations by a discerning diagnostician give clues to underlying needs. How much strain is there in answering questions? Is there a residue of anxiety that goes back to the days when a student's papers were filled with red marks? Does there seem to be a need to develop more mature social skills? Picking up subtleties of behavior is part of the diagnostician's skill.

The diagnostician also sets the tone, assuring the student, by actions as well as words, that the diagnostic experience will be a positive one. Testing is stressful, and many students recoil from the idea of being labeled. Their fears are not easy to dispel. They need to know that the purpose is not to pin a label on them but to give them a key to self-understanding. They also need to know that they are partners in the process and that their questions and ideas will be treated with confidentiality and respect. Their full participation and understanding set the stage for self-advocacy.

REPORTING

Results of diagnosis should be explained as simply and clearly as possible. The student needs to know what the term *learning disabilities* means and how the condition is affecting his or her performance. The student should have

LEARNING CHANNEL PREFERENCE

Read each sentence carefully and think if it applies to you. On the line, write:

3 often applies   **2** sometimes applies   **1** never applies

Preferred Channel: VISUAL

_____ 1. I enjoy doodling and even my notes have lots of pictures, arrows, etc. in them.

_____ 2. I remember something better if I write it down.

_____ 3. I get lost or am late if someone _TELLS_ me how to get to a new place and I didn't write down the directions.

_____ 4. When trying to remember someone's telephone number, or something new like that, it helps me to get a picture of it in my head.

_____ 5. If I am taking a test, I can "see" the textbook page and where the answer is.

_____ 6. It helps me to LOOK at the person when listening. It keeps me focused.

_____ 7. I had speech therapy.

_____ 8. It's hard for me to understand what a person is saying when there are people talking or music playing.

_____ 9. It's hard for me to understand a joke when someone tells me.

_____ 10. It is better for me to get work done in a quiet place.

Visual Total _____

Preferred Channel: AUDITORY

_____ 1. My written work doesn't look neat to me. My papers have crossed-out words and erasures.

_____ 2. It helps to use my finger as a pointer when reading to keep my place.

_____ 3. Papers with very small print or blotchy dittos or poor copies are tough on me.

_____ 4. I understand how to do something if someone tells me rather than having to read the same thing to myself.

_____ 5. I remember things that I hear, rather than things that I see or read.

_____ 6. Writing is tiring. I press down too hard with my pen or pencil.

_____ 7. My eyes get tired fast, even though the eye doctor says my eyes are O.K.

_____ 8. When I read, I mix up words that look alike, such as "them" and "then," and "bad" and "dad".

_____ 9. It's hard for me to read other people's handwriting.

_____ 10. If I had the choice to learn new information via a lecture or a textbook, I would choose to hear it rather than read it.

Auditory Total _____

Preferred Channel: HAPTIC

_____ 1. I don't like to read directions; I'd rather just start doing.

_____ 2. I learn best when I am shown how to do something and I have the opportunity to do it.

_____ 3. Studying at a desk is not for me.

_____ 4. I tend to solve problems through a more trial-and-error approach, rather than from a step-by-step method.

_____ 5. Before I follow directions, it helps me to see someone else do it first.

_____ 6. I find myself needing frequent breaks while studying.

_____ 7. I am not skilled in giving verbal explanations or directions.

_____ 8. I do not become easily lost, even in strange surroundings.

_____ 9. I think better when I have the freedom to move around.

_____ 10. When I can't think of a specific word, I'll use my hands a lot and call something a "what-cha-ma-call-it" or a "thing-a-ma-jig."

Haptic Total _____

FIGURE 3

SAMPLE IEP

SHORT-TERM INSTRUCTIONAL OBJECTIVES

Student:_____   Long Term Goal:____To improve study habits____

Learning Disabilities Specialist:____P. Adelman____

Short-Term Objectives	Teaching Strategy/Materials	Measurement Procedures	Tutoring Hrs. Weekly	Date Instr. Begun	Date Objective Achieved
1. To keep assignments and due dates in assignment notebook	Assignment notebook	Spot check of notebook for entries list 95% of the time	15 minutes per week	9/14/82	12/82
2. To develop time line for task completion; prioritizing assignments	Teacher handouts/ checklist	Spot check of task completion 95% of the time	5 minutes per week	9/14/82	12/82
3. To learn the SQ4R techniques	Handout	Reading passage using SQ4R correctly with 90% accuracy	30 minutes per week	9/14/82	
4. To develop mnemonic devices for better recall	Student course material	Success on tests	10 minutes	9/14/82	

Form developed by Susan Vogel, founder of the Barat College Learning Opportunities Program.

FIGURE 4

the chance to ask questions. Above all, the student must know what his or her strengths are and how these strengths can be used.

Many people who have been diagnosed as learning disabled feel great relief. The years of frustration are finally explained by a physiological cause, and there are ways to compensate.

But although diagnosis can give a sense of new beginning, it can also be very hard news. It takes more than one explanation to assimilate the information. It is very helpful to have the opportunity for follow-up with a disabled student service counselor, an educational specialist, or a therapist. More questions may need to be asked, and help may be

needed in planning for the future. (Some ways to cope with reactions to finding out that one is learning disabled are discussed in the chapter, "Go the Road.")

USING THE RESULTS

On campuses that have special programs for learning disabled students, such as Barat (Illinois), Curry (Massachusetts), Marist (New York), College of the Ozarks (Arkansas), and the Achieve Program (Southern Illinois), students and learning disabilities specialists sit down together and draw up an individualized education program (referred to as an IEP), based on results of the diagnosis. The plan carefully outlines those academic areas that need strengthening, compensatory skills that should be taught, and types of accommodations that may be

WHERE TO GO FOR DIAGNOSIS

On many campuses, the office responsible for disabled student services will be able to identify diagnostic facilities — either on campus or in the community. Or, the student affairs office may be able to assist in finding diagnostic services. If not, check with the following sources of information:

State or local chapters of the Association for Children and Adults with Learning Disabilities (ACLD). Parents, professionals, or members of a youth or adult affiliate of ACLD might be able to recommend practitioners who have been helpful. To find the ACLD chapter closest to you, get in touch with the national office of ACLD, 4156 Library Road, Pittsburgh, Pennsylvania 15234. Telephone (415) 351-1212.

State or local vocational rehabilitation offices. These offices can arrange for evaluation services, including diagnosis of learning disabilities. (See chapter, "Other Options" for more information on locating and using vocational rehabilitation services.)

Agencies. Many public and private agencies that offer diagnostic services are listed in the yellow pages under "Education," "Schools," "Tutorial Services," or "Psychologists." Local private schools for learning disabled children may be aware of agencies that provide diagnostic services for learning disabled youth and adults.

Information and referral services. Check with city hall, the county administrator's office, public libraries, and state information offices for listings or directories.

Universities. Special education departments of universities may have diagnostic facilities or be able to make referrals to sources of diagnosis. Federally funded University Affiliated Programs (UAFs) may specialize in diagnosis of learning disabilities. For a directory (free of charge) write to American Association of University Affiliated Programs for the Developmentally Disabled, 8605 Cameron Street, Suite 406, Silver Spring, Maryland 20910.

Professional associations. You can get the names of private practitioners who have met professional standards in their fields by contacting state chapters of professional associations, such as the American Psychological Association or the Independent Educational Counselors Association. For a free directory of educational counselors, many of whom specialize in the field of learning disabilities write to The Independent Educational Counselors Association, Cove Road, P.O. Box 125, Forestdale, Massachusetts 02644.

Guidance counselors. Check with counselors at community colleges and local high schools for information about diagnostic practitioners who work primarily with adolescents and adults.

FIGURE 5

needed. A sample IEP shows how one Barat College student worked on the goal of improving his study habits (see Figure 4). At other schools, such as Miami-Dade and Central Washington, instructors work closely with students, varying individual teaching plans as progress is made.

Whether or not a formal plan is drawn up, a comprehensive diagnosis gives students and their advisors a basis for understanding and decision making. Disabled student service coordinators can be extremely helpful in taking first steps to implement the results of the diagnosis. If there is no person on campus to help, students will need to work out their own ways of using diagnostic information. This book describes many possible courses of action.

But, to repeat, no diagnosis is complete until the question, "Now what?" is answered in terms of possible solutions to specific problems.

Additional Reading About Diagnosis

Assessing the Learning Disabled: Selected Instruments (third edition), by August J. Mauser. Academic Therapy Publications, 20 Commercial Boulevard, Novato, California 94947. (287 pages, $17.50) 1981

Assessment in Special and Remedial Education (second edition), by John Salvia and James E. Ysseldyke. Houghton Mifflin Company, Two Park Street, Boston, Massachusetts 02108. (500 pages, $26.95 + $1.00 for instructor's manual) 1979

"Higher Education for Learning Disabled Students," by Mike Lopez and Myrtle Clyde Snyder. NASPA Journal (Volume 20, Number 4, Spring 1983). (For reprints, write to National Association of Student Personnel Administrators, Inc., Central Office, 160 Rightmire Hall, 1060 Carmack Road, Columbus, Ohio 43210, $7.50 per journal.)

Identification and Assessment of Learning Disabled Students at the California Community Colleges: Final Report of the Consortium for the Study of Learning Disabilities in the California Community Colleges, by Laurel Best and Donald Deshler, October 18, 1983. (For copies, write to Cypress College, 9200 Valley View, Cypress, California 90630.)

Journal of Rehabilitation: Rehabilitation of Adults with Learning Disabilities: Special issue (April, May, June 1984). (Copies available from the National Rehabilitation Association, 633 South Washington Street, Alexandria, Virginia 22314, $7.50 per journal.)

"Learning Disabled College Students: Identification, Assessment, and Outcome," by Susan A. Vogel. Understanding Learning Disabilities: International and Multidisciplinary Views (edited by Drake D. Duane and C. K. Leong). Plenum Press, New York. ($42.50, $51.00 outside U.S. and Canada) 1985

"Learning Disabilities and the College Student: Identification and Diagnosis," by Jonathan Cohen. Adolescent Psychiatry: Developmental and Clinical Studies (Volume 11, pp. 177-198); edited by Max Sugar. University of Chicago Press. (239 pages, $22.00) 1983

"WAIS Score Patterns for Learning Disabled Young Adults," by Barbara K. Cordoni, James P. O'Donnel, Nerella V. Ramaniha, Karen Rosenshein, and Jerry Kurta. Journal of Learning Disabilities (Volume 14, Number 7, August-September 1981). (For requests for reprints, write to Barbara Cordoni, Department of Special Education, Southern Illinois University, Carbondale, Illinois 62901.)

"The Learning Disabled University Student: Signs and Initial Screening," by Jonathan Cohen. NASPA Journal, (Volume 21, Number 3, Winter 1984). (For copy of journal, write to, National Association of Student Personnel Administrators, Inc., Central Office, 160 Rightmire Hall, 1060 Carmack Road, Columbus, Ohio 43210, $7.50 per journal.)

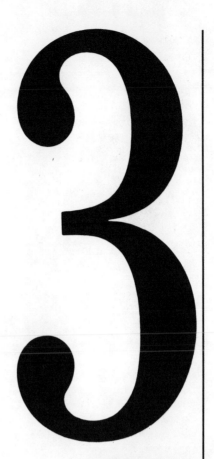

3

MAKING
CHOICES

MAKING CHOICES: OVERVIEW

"I needed a year of remedial classes so I could handle reading, English, and math better."

"I was too immature and angry to handle college the first time. I had to bottom out before I could figure out what my problems were and how to handle them."

"I fell in love with the college I went to. It was an art school, and for the first time I could concentrate on what I was good at."

"I took time off in the Marine Corps before I tackled college."

"High school was enough for me...I said to myself, 'There's a world out there and you can make it. You don't need college to make it.'"

"I had no idea what we would do when my son finished high school. How would he ever get trained for a job? Would he just sit at home and watch TV?"

What's ahead for learning disabled students after high school? As these words spoken by learning disabled adults and parents reveal, there are no simple answers. For some, colleges or technical schools are valid possibilities. For others, going to work or getting into a job-training or apprenticeship program are realistic choices. Others need extra time to set their goals.

Making decisions about postsecondary education is not limited to students graduating from high school. Many learning disabled adults now in the working world are anxious to return to school. Some may have dropped out in their teens. Others never knew they had learning disabilities and settled for jobs below their potential. They may want to learn to use a computer, to read music, to become a social worker, a practical nurse, or a carpenter.

Many learning disabled young people need a period of transition following high school before they are ready for a formal postsecondary education program. They may need time to mature, to develop socially, to learn skills of independent living. They may need counseling to overcome self-defeating attitudes. They may need job experience to gain self-confidence and help clarify career goals. Extra time and well-planned activities can lay the groundwork for success.

An open mind and a flexible attitude are essential in planning the future. Decisions need not be considered permanent. A learning disabled student may choose one route at one stage and another at a later time. The motivation that comes from achievement, self-awareness, and support from others can lead to the acceptance of new challenges or the willingness to take risks.

GETTING READY

How to begin? Taking stock is a good way to start. Students, parents, and guidance counselors can all be part of this process. The theme of the chapter, "Getting Ready: A Guide for Parents," is about taking stock of the student or adult before making specific plans. The chapter can be used as a guide on how and what to evaluate in each individual. Many questions need to be answered about potential, ability, interests, goals, talents, and independent living skills. Many ideas have to be thought out about ways in which the student learns and what accommodations might be needed so that the choice can be realistic.

OPTIONS

The next step in making choices is to know what some of those choices are. Other chapters in this section include information about levels of support services, types of colleges and technical schools, and additional options, such as job-training and adult education programs, independent living centers, and vocational rehabilitation services.

MAKING THE SELECTION

Campus options are expanding each year. This makes the task of narrowing choices and selecting schools more intricate and time consuming. But the reward of making a good match is worth it. The chapter, "Matchmaking: Selection and Admission," describes how to zero in on the right choice.

The more knowledgeable parents, students, and advisors are about the student as well as about the options, the better the chance for a successful choice.

GETTING READY: A GUIDE FOR PARENTS

Even before children are born, parents have fantasies. Will their children be bright, healthy, talented, and popular? Will their children achieve educationally and professionally? Will they be happy? Darker fantasies also lurk. What if their child is disabled or like a cousin who "never made it"? Whatever the fantasies, they can shape parents' expectations and fears, and they can become the driving force behind decisions about the child's future.

Many parents' dreams do come true. Their children grow up with minimal difficulties. For others, the dreams disappear and are replaced with anxiety about each day and with apprehension for the future.

The Early Years

For parents whose children are learning disabled, the early years of diagnoses and special education are often cycles of hopes, promises, and disillusionment. Appointments for diagnostic tests, Individual Education Programs (IEPs), and annual reviews are official acknowledgment of their child's disabilities. But these formalities can never record the daily hurt and sadness as well as the courage of living with a child who is irritable or withdrawn, who has no friends, who feels separated from peers, or who believes that he or she is defective. During these years, parents not only must battle to salvage their child's self-esteem, but must also become monitors of the school system —

31

ready to respond as advocates for their child if goals are not being met.

No wonder that by the time their learning disabled youngster is an adolescent and almost finished with high school, many parents are often worn out and defeated. They see their child as disabled and the future as dismal. To try and make plans for postsecondary education or training can become a major obstacle.

The End of High School

Yet this juncture — the end of high school, the beginning of adulthood — is when many parents must again gear up. It is a time of renewed hope, yet also a time to reevaluate expectations and plan new goals by considering different paths. It is a time for parents to help their son or daughter understand not only personal strengths and weaknesses but how to take responsibility for making decisions.

Before mapping out a postsecondary plan, parents need to be aware of how unspoken expectations might affect the planning and might add to the burden already carried by a learning disabled teenager. Children want to make parents proud; they want to live up to family expectations. By pushing for unrealistic goals, a child can be set up for failure. The more open-minded parents are, the more wisely they can evaluate an appropriate postsecondary program. Parents should also trust the special knowledge and understanding that they have of their child. Report cards and evaluations do not always tell the whole story.

For parents who were never told that their child was learning disabled or who might have suspected that something was wrong, it is not too late. Whether a child is still in high school or has been out of school for many years, the guidelines in this chapter and the suggestions in this book may be of help in making choices for a more satisfying future.

TAKING STOCK

Although this chapter is directed to you, the parents, the points and suggestions can be used as guidelines for counselors and students.

How do you begin to help your son or daughter make postsecondary plans? Will it be college or a technical school? Will it be a job? Will it be a transitional living program? Will your son or daughter be able to live away from home? Or are you confused and uncertain about what to do?

No matter what the direction — or lack of direction — this is a time to take stock of your son or daughter. Preferably, this can be done with the help of a guidance counselor, a teacher or teachers who know your child, or a qualified private educational consultant, if one is available and the cost is not prohibitive. This process should include an academic or vocational assessment.

Through stocktaking, you can identify interests, possible goals, and academic levels. You can also find out how to compensate for deficits and how to maximize potential strengths.

Include Your Son or Daughter

In figuring out directions and goals, sit down with your teenager and together try to identify major interests or talents. What does your son or daughter like to do outside of school? Does he or she enjoy sports, music, computers, sewing, photography, or mechanics?

Your teenager's selection of hobbies probably reflects activities that are enjoyable and that provide a sense of achievement and success. They could even be indicators for a career. By encouraging these interests, a child who has long struggled with low self-esteem and failure can begin to see that school problems are not the total definition of self.

Whatever interests or talents are apparent, they should be encouraged through related courses or school clubs. If, for example, your teenager is fascinated with cooking or with fixing engines, there may be courses in the school that would develop those skills further.

If your child has enjoyed working on a computer, see if there is a computer user club in the school or community. Check with a store where home computers are sold and consider buying a model you can afford. This expense or any extracurricular expense could be considered part of your child's total education for living.

Encourage a sampling of different interest areas until one clicks. No matter which hobby or interest your child develops, it is not so much the particular interest that counts at any one moment (this can change from year to year), but the overall trend. By weighing all of these factors and balancing them with academic and vocational strengths and weaknesses, you may begin to see some themes and get ideas for making post-secondary plans.

Team up with Your School Guidance Counselor

Another important resource is your teenager's school guidance counselor. Guidance counselors can give you information about characteristics of various campuses, including admission and academic requirements. But to help you make realistic choices, they need information about your son or daughter's specific problems, needs, and strengths. This is a good time to share any knowledge that you have about special programs.

An excellent reference for school guidance counselors and parents is Charles Mangrum and Stephen Strichart's article, "How Can Learning Disabled High School Students Prepare for College," in *News Digest*. (For a free copy, write to the National Information Center for Handicapped Children and Youth, P.O. Box 1492, Washington, D.C. 20013.)

ASSESSMENTS AND EVALUATIONS

Stocktaking can start in one of several ways. (The order in this chapter is arbitrary.) Arranging for a vocational and/or academic assessment can be one starting place. Whether you are considering college, a vocational school, or a job, these assessments might be very useful. Thinking about previous job experiences might provide further clues for an academic or vocational direction.

Academic Assessment

The best time to get an academic assessment is in the early high school years. If your son or daughter has been in special education programs, this has been done periodically. If not, or if it has been two years since the last evaluation, try and arrange to have an assessment by the beginning of the junior year. This gives you time to weigh options, to figure out what remediation may be needed, and to determine what compensating strategies may work.

Some skills, such as spelling, might never be improved (unless a computer program is used). Therefore, resource room time might better be spent on improving reading, math, or writing skills. Give priority to skills you think should be emphasized. It is important to keep track of the progress through a formal evaluation process, which usually precedes the writing of the IEP in the spring, and to monitor that progress throughout the school year.

You will also be better prepared to start the postsecondary selection process if you know how the student compares with peers in reading comprehension, word recognition, word attack skills, grammar concepts, vocabulary, spelling, math, handwriting, notetaking, and study skills. A realistic picture of the academic situation will reduce the anxiety involved in making the right choice.

After the evaluation has been completed, ask the special education teacher and the evaluator to meet with you and the school guidance counselor before you look into possible postsecondary programs. The evaluation information can also be of help when you talk with college admission counselors and disabled student services coordinators on campuses that you and your son or daughter are considering. Be sure to keep recent copies of diagnostic tests done while in high school. Schools do not automatically maintain these records.

Vocational Assessment

A vocational assessment can be very useful at this time. It can help to clarify career goals — whether a student plans to go on to college or to a postsecondary vocational education program. This part of stocktaking includes a review of your son or daughter's work experiences (work-study programs, summer, holiday, or part-time jobs, or volunteer placements), interests, and hobbies. As in any evaluation, the more input you can get from your son or daughter and from teachers and counselors, the more realistic you can be in helping develop postsecondary plans.

Ideally, you should be able to request a formal vocational evaluation through your school system, preferably in the ninth or tenth grade. In reality, vocational evaluations for learning disabled students do not exist in many school systems, although this picture is slowly changing for the better.

In some school systems, vocational rehabilitation services and schools have worked out cooperative agreements. Vocational rehabilitation counselors can be involved in transitional planning, and in some cases they might be able to arrange for a vocational evaluation before the end of high school.

What Is a Vocational Assessment? A thorough vocational evaluation can take several days or weeks and is administered by specially trained vocational educators. Standarized tests measure aptitudes, interests, and achievements. Work samples, work tryouts, and, in some cases, vocational course tryouts that replicate actual working conditions are used to assess characteristics needed to do specific types of jobs. Hands-on experiences are particularly appropriate for students with learning disabilities. By having this assessment early in high school, there is more opportunity for planning an appropriate curriculum and work-study programs. However, this type of vocational evaluation is useful whenever a person is considering a career choice.

After the evaluation, you should go over the results with all of the professionals involved in planning your child's curriculum. Make known any observations you think are relevant, including interests, hobbies, and extracurricular activities. If you and the school decide on a vocational education placement, be sure to inquire about any special support that may be needed by your child.

Note. Opportunities for learning disabled students in regular vocational classes are expanding. New legislation — the Carl Perkins Vocational Act of 1984 — requires public school systems to provide appropriate services and to adapt vocational curricula, instruction, and facilities for handicapped students who need special services in order to succeed in mainstream vocational programs. The law applies to secondary, postsecondary, and adult education.

WORK EXPERIENCES

Working is a way to sample and screen career fields. Perhaps your teenager didn't like flipping hamburgers at the local restaurant, or did enjoy selling clothes or helping people select hardware or plants. Maybe that summer volunteer job in the hospital made your son or daughter feel useful and needed. Each job experience, no matter how unskilled, can teach people about their likes and dislikes, about settings in which they feel comfortable or uncomfortable, and about chances for learning and advancement.

Working can also provide an opportunity to mature. By working with adults, teenagers can emulate the good work habits and interpersonal and professional skills that are the key to successful employment. Self-expression is also easier in settings where adults are accepting and eager to help a youngster without being as judgmental as a teen's peers.

Encourage and help your teen to find employment during the summer or on weekends during the school year. Contact the school's main office or career center to see if local businesses are looking for part-time help. Also check your county or mayor's employment office for part-time or summer job openings. Ask self-employed friends or neighbors who might know of a position. Many jobs are filled from the inside by "word of mouth."

WORK-STUDY PROGRAMS

A work-study program during the last two years of high school can sometimes break a cycle of boredom and failure, provide career awareness and motivation for postsecondary education, and build self-esteem by giving financial rewards for employment. Perhaps the most valuable by-product is the discovery of something positive in oneself.

A work-study program usually involves going to school in the morning for the required courses (and resource room help with homework) and going to work in the afternoon. Although these jobs are low paying and hard work, they can expose your son or daughter to the real world. For some students, this can be a rude awakening; for others, it can be a welcome relief and a boost to their morale; and for others, it may be a motivator to seek advanced training.

Be sure that work-study programs do not interfere with successful completion of basic courses required to graduate or get into a college. Meet with your son or daughter's guidance counselor, special education teacher, and any other relevant school official to establish the goals of this plan. Review progress at least once a year.

INDEPENDENT LIVING AND SOCIAL SKILLS

An accurate assessment of a young person's strengths and needs should include awareness of personal habits, social skills, and responsibility for knowing when, how, and where to get necessary help. At college, no one is going to fill your son or daughter's leisure time if he or she does not know how to make and keep friends. No one is going to get your child out of bed for class or make sure that daily living supports such as food and clean clothes are provided. No one is going to give reminders of exams and papers that are due.

There are many daily living skills that most people take for granted, including time and money management, hygiene, housekeeping chores, or transportation. But often these are the very skills that learning disabled people lack. Living at home is safe and comfortable. Parents are there to help or to anticipate what might be needed. When this support system is no longer available on a daily basis, will your son or daughter be able to manage? Many will; others will with some support; and others will, eventually, if they have more time at home or are taught appropriate life skills.

The checklist in Figure 6 may make it easier for you to assess your child's daily living and social skills. Remember that this is not a formal test. There are no scores. It is another way to take stock and to choose a postsecondary option that makes sense.

Use the checklist as one way of assessing your son or daughter's ability to live away from home. If you decide that going away from home after high school might be too much of a strain or might be a setup for failure, don't think of this decision as giving up the "last chance" for personal success. As we noted earlier, many learning disabled young people need a few more years than their peers to grow up. Living at home while learning some of these daily living and social skills, working at a full- or part-time job, and maturing a bit more might be the best option this year.

COPING STRATEGIES

Finally, in taking stock of your son or daughter, the most important and probably the most overlooked characteristic is the ability to cope. Look carefully at your son or daughter. Think about how he or she has handled frustrations. You might find that what seemed odd or peculiar was, in fact, an innovative way to deal with a specific problem.

Have you or the teacher encouraged your child to learn coping skills? Many learning disabled students do not know how to compensate and lose out when they get to college. How does your teenager adapt to academic and social deficits? Does your poor speller ask for help from friends and siblings? Has your poor reader met with peers to discuss an assignment? Has he or she asked you to get the book on tape or used published outlines (such as *Cliff* or *Monarch* notes)? How can your easily frustrated or visually distractible son or daughter simplify the environment or daily life or find ways to bypass tasks that cannot be mastered, (such as driving or cooking)?

Daily Living/Social Skills Inventory

DAILY LIVING SKILLS

_____ Getting to work or school on time and being prepared for the day

_____ Telling time

_____ Getting up without other's intervention

_____ Allowing time for personal hygiene, dressing, breakfast

_____ Remembering to take keys, books, and money for the day

Cooking and Nutrition

_____ Balanced diet

_____ Planning meals

_____ Preparing meals

_____ Using appliances

_____ Dining etiquette

_____ Shopping for food

Basic Hygiene/Personal Care

_____ Bathing/showering regularly

_____ Washing hair

_____ Shaving

_____ Brushing teeth

_____ Bathroom etiquette

_____ Wearing clean clothes

Clothing Care

_____ Keeping bureaus/closets organized

_____ Doing laundry

_____ Simple mending/hemming

_____ Taking clothes to dry cleaner

Taking Care of Health Needs

_____ Knowing simple first aid

_____ Knowing when, where, and how to get help if sick or injured

Housekeeping Skills

_____ Washing dishes

_____ Vacuuming, dusting, sweeping

_____ Cleaning bathroom

_____ Cleaning and picking-up after himself or herself

Money Management

_____ Understanding coins and bills

_____ Budgeting/saving/spending

_____ Using a checking/savings account

_____ Balancing a checkbook

Shopping

_____ Food shopping/using a list

_____ Shopping for bargains

_____ Ordering food in a restaurant

Transportation

_____ Getting information about rates/schedules

_____ Paying fares

_____ Making connections

_____ Responsibility for car maintenance

SOCIAL SKILLS

_____ Making eye contact

_____ Understanding body language and facial expressions

_____ Starting/ending conversations

_____ Responding appropriately in conversations

_____ Listening attentively

_____ Controlling egocentric remarks (talking only about yourself)

_____ Using a helping relationship

_____ Solving interpersonal problems

_____ Delaying gratification when necessary

_____ Being sensitive to the needs/feelings of others

_____ Sizing up social situations

_____ Accepting criticism/supervision

_____ Controlling voice volume

_____ Planning a social activity with others

FIGURE 6

37

Throughout this book are stories and tips from learning disabled adults on how they coped with academic and social problems.

SELECTING APPROPRIATE POSTSECONDARY OPTIONS

The beginning of this chapter focused on helping you take stock of your son or daughter's academic skills, extracurricular interests, career goals, vocational abilities, and daily living and social skills. It included suggestions and tools for gathering information that will help you make decisions and choices concerning a postsecondary program for your son or daughter. The next part of this chapter describes a method for helping you assess postsecondary choices by using the information you have gathered.

A MODEL FOR MAKING A DECISION

Following is an example of how one family went through the process of helping their son, Stephen, select a postsecondary option.

Stephen is an eighteen-year-old, learning disabled student. He and his parents looked at his academic background, the supports he might need in a postsecondary setting, his physical and mental health, his daily living and social skills, his ability to live independently and be self-reliant, and his interests, goals, and wishes. This is what they found.

Academic Assessment

Stephen's SAT scores are low (320 verbal/360 math). His grade average is C. He gets help with homework in the resource room one hour per day. Stephen reads on grade level, and his comprehension is high. However, his word-attack and spelling skills are poor (5th grade). His math achievement is also low (8th grade). Handwriting is slow and of poor quality, and he has difficulty organizing his thoughts sequentially to write an essay.

Supports Needed for Postsecondary Education

Stephen has the mental ability to do better work in most areas. His major problem is in writing essays and reports. He will need the most assistance in learning how to organize his thoughts to develop a coherent outline on which to base his essays. He will also need help in building his vocabulary and writing descriptive prose.

Stephen understands basic math concepts but would benefit from an algebra/high school math refresher course if he wishes to take higher level math courses.

Because of Stephen's poor handwriting, he would benefit from notetaker services or taping lectures. He should use a typewriter for written assignments. A personal computer or word processor and a printer would ease the laborious effort Stephen makes in preparing acceptable work. Stephen also needs extra time for exams because of his poor writing ability. Oral exams might be another way to solve this problem. Stephen is quick to understand but has short-term memory problems. He could use assistance in developing memory tricks, such as repetitive reviews or use of acronyms.

Physical and Mental Health

Stephen is in good health. He needs at least eight hours of sleep every night because without proper rest, he tends to get hyperactive and emotional. He is a sensitive boy who covers up his feelings of low self-worth by using his sense of humor and sarcasm to attract friends and admirers. He rarely gets truly depressed, but his mood swings are frequent — usually a tip-off that things are not going well in school.

Daily Living and Social Skills

Stephen has adequate daily living skills. He can be sloppy and disorganized but no more so than any other adolescent. His social skills are his strength. He is an attractive boy with good manners.

Independent Living/Self-Reliance

Stephen likes to make his own decisions and wants to be in charge of his life. He gets up on time for jobs and school without parental intervention, but he is generally late for deadlines on bills or papers or for social engagements. Stephen is immature and lacks self-discipline. Also because his education has partly been out of the mainstream, his cultural maturity has been delayed.

Interests, Goals, and Wishes

Stephen wants to be a real estate salesman. He is following the career footsteps of his father (real estate accountant), but he knows he cannot sit at a desk all day and work on figures. He wants to major in business.

After making this evaluation, Stephen and his family listed all of the possible choices. They drew up a chart to note the positives and negatives of each option. (See Figure 7.)

Together, Stephen and his parents decided that the two-year community college was the best option for him. He felt exhilarated about going to college, especially after his long struggle to build language and math skills. His parents saw this option as the first step in the long-range goal of continuing to increase basic skills while mastering the courses required to acquire the Associate of Arts degree. As much as they wanted him to go away to school like his peers, they knew that this option might lead to failure, given his lack of basic skills and maturity. But they also knew that with a little more time to mature and consolidate his academic achievements, he could transfer to a four-year college.

This is the way one family arrived at a decision that was appropriate for them. Whether your son or daughter is considering working after high school, attending a postsecondary school, or getting into a job-training program, the process of assessing the total person and listing all possible options is a valuable way to break through the confusion and fear that hit parents when they realize that their child is getting ready to go out in the adult world.

ASSESSMENT OF POSTSECONDARY OPTIONS

	EXPECTED POSITIVES	EXPECTED NEGATIVES

LOCAL TWO-YEAR COLLEGE	• Personal attention from staff and faculty
	• LD support available
	  – Language lab
	  – Tutors
	  – Notetakers
	  – Textbooks on tape available if needed
	  – Formal LD program
	• Many "getting ready" courses: How to study and organize
	• Time to adjust to demands of being self-reliant, leading to maturity
	• LD counselor on campus
	• Open admissions
	• Live at home — more study/quiet time
	• Help from Dad with accounting course
	• No SATs needed
	• Can transfer in two years with AA degree
	• Low cost for parents
	• Likes the school — familiar territory
		• Feels peers see community college as extension of high school
		• Feels uncomfortable about living at home while friends go away
		• Slower development of independence

STATE FOUR-YEAR COLLEGE (away from home)	• More prestigious vis-a-vis peers • Environment requires quick adaptations to independent life	• Campus too large and confusing (25,000 students) • SATs required • No special LD services • Noisy dorms very distracting • Poor counseling for LD students • More pressure to succeed at a faster pace
MILITARY SERVICE	• Time to mature • Nonacademic environment • Vocational skill development • Development of self-discipline/personal organization	• Cloistered environment of sameness • Nonacademic environment • Individual abilities may not be recognized • Enlistment period too long • Difficulty with writing and spelling may hamper success
FULL-TIME EMPLOYMENT	• Time to mature • Increased responsibility • Develop realistic view of working life • Develop career interest/job sampling	• Lose academic connections (may not return) • Learn to like having money more than further education • Get stuck in one job strand because it's easy • Get into debt for consumer goods — treadmill
TWO-YEAR VOCATIONAL EDUCATIONAL PROGRAM (Hotel Management School)	• "Hands on" learning — more on-the-job training than book learning • School is away from home in a city environment	• No support or tutoring for LD students • Heavy responsibility for managing academic life and independent living • Unsure — scared

FIGURE 7

SUPPORT—
HOW MUCH
IS ENOUGH?

As learning disabled students begin to sort out options — especially educational ones — they should determine what kinds of support they need, and how much.

Levels of support vary greatly from school to school. Because each school fashions and implements its own services and because there are no accrediting devices for learning disabilities programs, levels of service should be compared and measured before making a selection. These levels can be thought of as *minimal, moderate, or intensive* — and are not related to size or type of school.

Some learning disabled students will need minimal support, some will need services for a limited time, and some will need extensive help. Careful investigation of services can be the key to a successful match between a learning disabled student and a school. Reading between the lines of pamphlets and brochures, asking questions through letters and telephone calls, visiting campuses, and talking with students who have gone to specific schools can be productive ways of getting accurate information about support services. (For a fuller discussion about selection and admission and questions to ask, see chapter, "Matchmaking: Selection and Admission.")

The following pages briefly describe the levels of services and types of programs that accept learning disabled students. When considering schools, students can use these descriptions as a way to balance their needs with the services available. They should try and determine whether the assistance will enable them to adjust to the mainstream of postsecondary life.

MINIMAL SUPPORT: THE STUDENT ADAPTS

Campuses offering minimal support include colleges and technical schools where learning disabled students are accepted but do not receive specialized services. Bright and well-motivated learning disabled students have succeeded in such settings, but it is important to bear these facts in mind:

• Academic support services are those that are available to *all* students. These services may include tutoring and/or remedial or developmental classes in reading or math, writing labs, and study skill courses. However, basic remedial or developmental classes are not always appropriate for learning disabled students.

• No specific office or faculty member is designated to advise learning disabled students on use of appropriate campus resources, to discuss possible course work accommodations, or to interpret needs of learning disabled students to faculty members or tutors.

• Students on these campuses must be their own advocates. They must use their ingenuity to compensate for their difficulties. They should become familiar with provisions of Section 504. If they need accommodations, such as permission to tape lectures, they must be able to tell instructors *why,* in simple, clear terms.

Students who have done well on such campuses are usually confident of their abilities or talents and are able to cope with their disabilities. Often, they have had the advantage of excellent preparation in high school and strong family support. Relying solely on their gifts and

perseverance, some have succeeded at the most prestigious colleges in the country and have gone on to graduate school and successful careers.

MODERATE SUPPORT: THE CAMPUS HELPS THE STUDENT TO ADJUST

A growing number of campuses throughout the country recognize their responsibility toward learning disabled students who are qualified to attend the institution. Learning disabled students are admitted as part of the regular student body and are enrolled in mainstream courses. These campuses have a range of services that are available to help disabled students compensate for specific difficulties, such as writing, spelling, notetaking, and reading. For many learning disabled students, this level of support may be exactly what they need to succeed. Accommodations, advocacy, and referral can be obtained through disabled student services offices or other departments.

Coordination

Services and accommodations are usually coordinated by the staff of the disabled student services office or the handicapped student services office. (These offices have different names on different campuses. Check with the dean of students or the admissions office for the correct title.) Some campuses may coordinate services through the dean of students, the student affairs office, the counseling center, the English department, the psychology department, or the campus learning center.

In this book, DSS (disabled students services) is used to describe any campus office that works with handicapped students.

Advocacy

Disabled student services coordinators act as advocates for all disabled students on campus. They provide information to faculty about the disability and intervene if there is resistance to making accommodations.

Students who are having difficulty are expected to take the initiative in seeking help from the DSS office. Faculty members may refer students to the appropriate person, but the student must make the contact. Once the contact is made, coordinators meet with students individually on an as-needed basis to discuss problems, identify courses of action, and assist in obtaining needed course work accommodations. Students are expected to take major responsibility for follow up, explaining their needs to instructors and arranging for tutors, readers, and other services.

Referral

Students who need help with academic or study skills are usually referred to regular campus support programs (developmental or remedial courses, learning labs, etc.). If more specialized teaching is needed, DSS coordinators may work with the basic course instructors or refer students to private educational services in the community.

The University of Maryland is an example of a moderate-level support program. William Scales, who directs disabled student services at Maryland, says, "the learning disabled student holds the key to success. Students must come to this environment prepared to access services and staff, to identify their needs, and to be assertive."

According to Dr. Scales, learning disabled students who do best at the University of Maryland are often those who have had adequate training in handling their disability. Frequently, these students have attended a two-year college, a specialized learning disabilities college program, or a college preparatory school.

Fees

There is no charge for disabled student services or for work involved in arranging for accommodations that make campus life more accessible to learning disabled students. Services for personal use and study, such as tutors or readers, may have a fee.

INTENSIVE SUPPORT: PROGRAM IS ADAPTED TO STUDENT

A small but steadily increasing number of campuses have special programs for learning disabled students. The goal of these programs is to help students recognize and use their strengths, to manage their disabilities, and to participate and succeed in the academic mainstream.

Structure of Programs

Programs provide a period of intensive support to prepare students to function independently in regular classes. In addition to taking regular courses, students get special instruction several times a week to improve academic and study skills and to develop strategies to compensate for specific learning problems.

Most of these programs are separate entities within a two- or four-year college. They exist under different auspices within the institution's structure: The Program for Advancement of Learning (PAL) at Curry College (Massachusetts) is in the Office of the Academic Dean, the Achieve Progam at Southern

43

Illinois University is in the Office of Student Affairs, and the Learning Opportunities Program at Barat College (Illinois) is autonomous. One institution, Landmark College (Vermont), is entirely set up to meet the needs of high potential students with a learning disability.

Selection of Students

Students at these and similar programs are enrolled as part of the regular student body and must meet academic or performance standards of the institution. Learning disabled applicants are usually selected through a special admissions process, often called *cooperative admissions,* which means that they must be accepted by both the institution and the program. (See also the chapter, "Matchmaking: Selection and Admission.")

Most of these special programs have waiting lists, and students are advised to apply well in advance. In some cases, students already enrolled in the regular school may be referred to the support programs.

Program Components

No two programs are exactly alike. Common elements include

• a program staff trained to work with learning disabled students.

• a thorough assessment of individual learning styles and needs and individualized planning based on those styles and needs.

• courses, small group instruction, and/or tutorial sessions that are designed to prepare students for the mainstream curriculum. These courses include study skills, learning and compensatory strategies, and basic academics. All courses and sessions are taught by learning disability specialists.

• ongoing communication between the program staff and the institution's faculty to increase understanding of learning disabled students.

• liaison with regular academic support programs, such as writing labs and developmental classes, to assure follow up of individual needs.

• counseling and student support groups to assist with personal adjustment and to help strengthen interpersonal skills.

Fees

Private institutions usually charge a fee, in addition to tuition. The fee covers costs of special instruction and other services provided by the support program. Publicly funded two- or four-year colleges do not charge extra fees for support services.

REMINDERS

Whether campuses provide minimal, moderate, or intensive services, remember that

• students must be qualified to attend the institution and must have the potential to do the work,

• services vary greatly on different campuses,

• learning disabled students must meet the same academic standards in their course work as other students.

THE COLLEGE OPTION

College offers potential benefits for all students, including those with learning disabilities. For some, a two-year or four-year college or university program may lead to a career-entry job; for others, a college degree may lead to advanced graduate or professional training. Stretching one's horizons intellectually and socially can lead to personal growth. Experiences both in and out of classes can help to set a career course. For nearly all students, college provides exposure to new ideas and new friends and can have a lasting, lifelong effect.

In considering the college option, students with learning disabilities should not only review the levels of services, as previously described, but should know the goals and objectives of each institution and the advantages each offers to learning disabled students. (For additional help in narrowing choices, see the chapter, "Matchmaking: Selection and Admission.")

Two-year colleges

Public community or junior colleges differ from private junior colleges, but all of them offer students an opportunity to test the academic waters. For many students, this is a chance to prepare for further education, to learn an occupational skill, or to change careers; for others, it is a way to enhance personal development. Students who complete these two-year programs earn an AA (Associate of Arts) degree, and credits can be transferred to a four-year college or university. For courses of study in specific occupations (e.g., bookkeeping, child care, or graphics production), a certificate is usually awarded. (These courses frequently take less than two years to complete.)

Public Community and Junior Colleges

Publicly funded community or junior colleges exist in or near almost every city of the United States. These institutions are committed to serving the educational and training needs of the local communities. Open admission policies make it possible for anyone over 18 years of age to attend even if they do not have a high school diploma. However, most community colleges do require that students taking courses for credit pass a high school equivalency test (GED). Preparation for the GED is usually given on campus.

Community colleges offer liberal arts subjects as well as training in specific occupations, such as hotel management, auto mechanics, marketing, computer programming, or dental assisting. Most also have remedial or developmental courses for upgrading basic academic skills.

Community colleges are becoming increasingly responsive to the needs of learning disabled students, and many are developing excellent support services. To find out what services are available, contact the disabled student services (DSS) office.

Advantages for learning disabled students attending community colleges:

• The choice of living at home while making the transition to college.

• No admissions requirements, such as college entrance exams, grade point average, class rank.

• An opportunity to try out college by taking one or two courses.

• A chance to build a better academic record that can be transferred to a four-year college or university for which the student is qualified. A student transferring to a four-year college is not usually required to take entrance examinations, although other entrance requirements must be met.

• An opportunity to learn an occupation, to work on academic skills, or to learn ways to accommodate learning problems.

• The chance to return to school to upgrade academic and job skills and to work toward improved employment opportunities or a career change.

Private Junior Colleges

Of the approximately 200 private junior colleges in the country, most are small, residential schools that prepare students for transfer to a four-year liberal arts institution. Some offer occupational training. Upon completion of the two-year program, an AA degree is awarded. Entrance examinations are usually required, although in many cases, other criteria, such as work experience and extracurricular activities are considered.

Advantages for learning disabled students:

• An opportunity to live away from home in an intimate, supportive environment.

• Small classes in which instructors can provide individualized attention.

• Opportunities to work on improving reading, writing, and math skills.

• A chance to train for a new career after being in the working world.

FOUR-YEAR COLLEGES AND UNIVERSITIES

Four-year colleges and undergraduate university programs, including four-year technical schools, vary in tradition, size, admissions criteria, academic standards, course offerings, student population, location, and cost. All grant a BS or BA degree upon completion of four years of study with a concentration in a major subject.

In most college or undergraduate university programs, students are expected to sample a variety of courses during the first two years and select their major in the last two years. Requirements for graduation differ, although most colleges require a certain number of credits in English and foreign languages.

A number of colleges are specialized, such as the Massachusetts Institute of Technology, the Juilliard School of Music, and the Rhode Island School of Design. Students are expected to be proficient in their fields but must also take courses in other fields.

Tuition varies greatly. State-supported institutions tend to be less costly. Some financial aid is usually available.

Advantages for learning disabled students:

• An extensive selection of majors. There are over 400 majors offered in American colleges and universities. With appropriate accommodations and services, learning disabled students who have the potential to do college-level work can find many subject areas that are of interest.

• Several sources of help, such as counseling services, peer tutoring, learning labs, math centers. Some departments of education, special education, psychology, or English, particularly at universities, offer diagnostic and special tutorial services.

• Opportunities to develop talents (e.g., music, art, dance) either by majoring in that field or by attending a specialized four-year college.

• Availability of DSS offices on many campuses.

GRADUATE AND PROFESSIONAL SCHOOLS

Opportunities for learning disabled students in graduate and professional schools are opening up, and new and innovative support services are being developed.

At Ohio State University, the Office of Disability Services is working with the colleges of dentistry, medicine, and law to tape textbooks and make provisions for accommodations in testing situations.

A pioneering program for learning disabled students is under way at the New York University College of Dentistry. The program grew out of awareness that many bright, potentially good dentists were lost to the profession because of learning disabilities and that with appropriate accommodations, these people could fulfill all professional requirements and have productive careers.

Graduate students are entitled to the same types of accommodations and services that are becoming more available in undergraduate schools. Graduate students who think they have a learning disability can take advantage of campus diagnostic, tutorial, and other support services. If there is a DSS office on campus, this is a logical place to go for assistance. Graduate students, as well as other students, should familiarize themselves with Section 504.

FINANCIAL AID

College tuition varies greatly, with state-supported institutions tending to be less costly. There are no specific scholarships for learning disabled students, and they must go through the traditional channels of applying for grants, loans, scholarships, and work-study programs. Students who are vocational rehabilitation clients should check with their counselor to see whether tuition and/or accommodations are covered.

Any applications for funding should be obtained no later than the beginning of the high school senior year. These applications and information about funding sources are available in high school counselors' offices.

When applying to schools, remember to request information about financial aid or check the general college directories regarding financial aid policies of individual schools. These directories explain eligibility for each school's financial aid program and give application deadlines.

Information Sources

Financial aid programs are either public or private, and there are some excellent pamphlets, booklets, and organizations that have up-to-date material about these programs.

The HEATH Resource Center, the National Clearinghouse for Handicapped Individuals, has a fact sheet on financial aid and a list of state agencies responsible for postsecondary education. These state agencies are knowledgeable about financial aid as well as grant and loan programs for state residents. To get these fact sheets, write to the HEATH Resource Center, One Dupont Circle, N.W., Washington, D.C. 20036 or call the toll-free information number 800-54 HEATH.

The Federal Student Aid Programs, U.S. Department of Education, publishes an excellent, clearly written booklet, *The Student Guide — Five Federal Financial Aid Programs* (updated annually). This guide describes and gives the application process for five major federally supported student aid programs:

• Pell Grants

• Supplemental Educational Opportunity Grants (SEOG)

• National Direct Student Loans (NDSL)

• Guaranteed Student Loans (GSL)

• PLUS loans

• College work-study programs.

To get this booklet, check with your high school guidance department or career center or write to Federal Student Aid Programs, U.S. Department of Education, P.O. Box 84, Washington, D.C. 20044 or call (301) 984-4070.

A new organization, National College Services, provides information and advice about financial aid, tuition plan options, scholarship searches, and other special funding sources. For a brochure, fee schedule, and any free booklets, such as *The College Financial Aid Emergency Kit,* write to National College Services, 16220 South Frederick Road, Gaithersburg, Maryland 20877, Attention, Herm Davis, President.

Another new resource, *Mortgaged Futures: How to Graduate from School Without Going Broke* (available from Hope Press; P.O. Box 40611; Washington, D.C. 20016-0611; $9.95), is a well-written, factual book on the many ways to finance a college education.

COLLEGE PREPARATORY PROGRAMS

Some learning disabled students who have graduated from high school are capable of college-level work but still have needs in certain academic areas. For them, college preparatory programs for learning disabled students can help improve reading, math, writing, or study skills. Following are examples of specific programs; others can be found by looking in directories listed in the chapter "Matchmaking: Selection and Admission."

• **The Hilltop Preparatory School** in Rosemont, Pennsylvania, offers a transitional college program. Students work on areas of academic weakness while taking a number of college credit courses at nearby schools.

• **The Landmark School** in Prides Crossing, Massachusetts, a private residential school for learning disabled students, offers a one-year college preparatory course. The program provides intensive, individualized instruction in language arts, math, and study skills. Students also learn ways to cope with the challenge of organizing the demands of college life. The school offers a similar college preparatory program during a seven-week summer session.

• **Specific Diagnostic Studies, Inc.** in Rockville, Maryland, is a private diagnostic and tutorial program in which students get individualized tutorial or small-group teaching in areas that need strengthening. Some students receive help while attending college; others are helped to prepare for college and to take college admission tests.

IN CONCLUSION

Learning disabled students can succeed in all types of colleges and universities, including the most prestigious. But it is very important to be realistic about the level of support needed and to know in advance if that support is available.

THE VOCATIONAL EDUCATION OPTION

Postsecondary vocational education can hold the key to an independent and productive life. It can provide professional training that leads to a marketable skill and a job future. It can fulfill the ultimate goal of education by preparing a student to participate in society as a self-sufficient adult.

In the past, few learning disabled students have taken advantage of the opportunities offered by vocational education. Some have been deterred by lack of adequate support services. Others have been unable to get accurate information about available programs, or have been advised that vocational education was inappropriate for them, or have been poorly prepared in high school for postsecondary vocational education in the mainstream.

Some learning disabled students have been tracked into unskilled occupations, with little or no effort to determine their capabilities. Those who have enrolled in mainstream vocational programs have usually had to find ways to compensate for their difficulties on their own. As a result of these and other factors, only a small percentage of learning disabled students have succeeded in gaining access to the regular vocational education system.

But now the scene is changing. New legislation and committed vocational educators and advocacy groups are expanding vocational education opportunities for all disabled people, including those with learning disabilities. A major victory for parents, educators, and disabled people was passage in 1984 of the Carl Perkins Vocational Education Act. This act calls for sufficient appropriate support services to foster successful participation of disabled students in regular vocational programs on secondary and postsecondary levels.

Passage of this act underscores the excitement that is building up as vocational educators of special needs students are reaching out to one another, sharing ideas and materials, and creating resource centers that are accessible to all professionals working with disabled people.

This chapter describes what vocational education is, how individuals can make career and school choices, and where and how changes in vocational education for disabled people are occurring.

SCOPE OF VOCATIONAL EDUCATION

Vocational education is defined as education geared for employment that requires specialized education but not a baccalaureate (BA) degree. Vocational education programs are taught in both public and private institutions. Public programs include technical institutes, community colleges, and area vocational technical centers. Private (proprietary) programs include trade, technical, and business schools.

These programs teach skills in hundreds of occupational areas including agriculture, health, business, trade, industry, and marketing. Figure 8 gives an idea of the scope of vocational education.

WHAT DOES VOCATIONAL EDUCATION TEACH?

Vocational education is available in hundreds of fields. Following is a list of broad occupational areas that are taught at different schools throughout the country, with a few examples of specific occupations in each area.

Occupational Area	Examples
Agriculture /Agribusiness	Agricultural production, processing, inspection, and marketing; forestry; ornamental horticulture.
Marketing and Distribution	Selling and advertising, finance and credit, general merchandising, hotel and lodging, insurance, real estate, food services.
Health	Dental, radiology, nursing, rehabilitation, medical laboratory technology.
Business and Office	Accounting and computing, general clerical occupations, secretarial, personnel.
Trade and Industry	Masonry, carpentry, welding, electrical work, air conditioning, metal work, automotive services, small engine repair, upholstering.
Occupational Home Economics	Food management, cosmetology, fashion, clothing development, child care. (This area includes courses to help students improve the quality of their own lives.)

FIGURE 8

DETERMINING A CAREER DIRECTION

Knowing the variety of occupational possibilities and the settings in which they are taught are part of decision making. Another vital part is determining individual interests, abilities, and goals.

Tim, a bright, learning disabled student, became adept at using his personal computer while in high school. After graduation, he attended a public postsecondary technical school and received training as a computer technician. He is now employed by a large local retailer as a trainee in its purchasing/inventory control department. This is not the end of the line for Tim. It is a successful beginning that will lead to additional learning and advancement opportunities.

Tim chose his occupational training carefully. He understood his strengths and weaknesses. He knew that his auditory perceptual problems would not interfere with his ability to work on a computer. He also knew that he was capable of doing the English and math required by the course of study he chose. Requirements for vocational programs vary, and, students need to be ready to meet those requirements.

Many people, like Tim, make occupational choices on their own, especially if there is no opportunity for a formal evaluation. Others gather information about specific jobs, and find out what specific tasks are required.

Job Analysis

Analyzing the tasks involved in specific jobs can also help in making choices. Job analysis includes finding out what tools are needed, what performance standards are required, and what interests are involved. It is important to know the job's physical demands, how many hours would be spent sitting, standing, or walking, and what the job environment is like. Answers can make the difference in success in a training program and on the job.

The Job Analysis Exchange at the University of Wisconsin-Stout provides detailed analyses for more than 200 jobs. Although it is primarily used by professionals who train disabled people for employment, the information is available to anyone who wants specifics about certain jobs. *The Job Analysis Exchange Catalog* can be ordered free of charge by writing to Material Development Center, University of Wisconsin-Stout, Menomonie, Wisconsin 54751.

Vocational Evaluation

Vocational evaluation by qualified professionals is an essential part of making appropriate occupational choices for special needs students. The Perkins Act requires school systems to assess the interests, abilities, and needs of disabled students in vocational education. Therefore, parents should request that schools provide a thorough vocational evaluation for their sons and daughters before graduation. (See chapter, "Getting Ready: A Guide for Parents.")

A word of caution. Before selecting a private vocational evaluation agency or practitioner, be sure to check on qualifications and reputation, reasonableness of costs, ratio of students to evaluators, variety of occupational fields that will be sampled, and how the sampling will be done. Evaluees should receive a comprehensive, written report of all findings and specific recommendations.

The evaluation process can help a student answer questions about occupational goals. It can also spark new interests, or eliminate an unrealistic career choice. It can make clear what a student can or cannot do.

SELECTING A VOCATIONAL EDUCATION PROGRAM

Once a student has chosen an occupational area, the next step is to locate an appropriate school and check on its quality. Questions need to be answered about the time involved in completing course work, what degree or certificate is offered, experience of instructors, ability to accommodate disabled students, and job placement opportunities. For other questions to ask when investigating a school, see chapter, "Matchmaking: Selection and Admission."

Locating Programs

Each community has a different array of vocational education programs. They are not always easy to locate, and frequently students are unaware of what their community offers.

Note. Passage of the Perkins Vocational Education Act in 1984 should make it easier to get information from local school systems. The act requires schools to make information about vocational education programs available to students and their parents.

Following are some suggestions for finding appropriate programs:

• Check with the state and local chapters of the Association for Children and Adults with Learning Disabilities.

• Call the state office of the specialist for vocational education for handicapped students. Each state has a specialist who is usually located within the division of vocational education in the state department of education. One way to locate the address is to request your state's agency list from the HEATH Resource Center, the National Clearinghouse on Postsecondary Education for Handicapped Individuals, One Dupont Circle, N.W., Washington, D.C. 20036.

• Write to the National Association for Trade and Technical Schools, 2251 Wisconsin Avenue, N.W., Washington, D.C. 20007. Their handbook lists accredited trade and technical schools throughout the country.

• Write to the Association of Independent Colleges and Schools, One Dupont Circle, N.W., Washington, D.C. 20036, for its free directory of 630 accredited private business schools and colleges.

• Read the list of directories in Figure 13, in the chapter, "Matchmaking: Selection and Admission." Check to see if these books are in your public library or school.

Length of Time Required To Complete Course Work

Length of time for completing course work in a vocational education program varies, depending on the requirements of the occupational area and the level of skill to be attained. Training to be a practical nurse's aide may take ten weeks; to be a geriatric medical assistant, two years. Training to be a broadcast technician can take from ten weeks to two years. To become a veterinarian assistant can take from twenty-eight weeks to eighteen months.

Degrees and Certificates Earned

Vocational education students earn either a degree or certificate. After a full two-year course of technical training in an occupational area (such as computer programming, dental assisting, plumbing, air conditioning), a student usually receives an Associate of Applied Science (AAS) or an Associate of Applied Arts (AAA) degree. A student who completes the occupational skill training leading to a specific area of employment receives a certificate.

53

QUESTIONS TO ASK ABOUT VOCATIONAL EDUCATION PROGRAMS

Q What are the minimal academic skills required for entrance into the program? Can any accommodations be made for teaching students at a lower reading or math level (such as texts in simpler language)?

Q Must all students proceed at the same pace?

Q Is there a coordinator of services for the handicapped in the program or a vocational support team? Does the staff have an understanding of learning disabilities?

Q What basic knowledge of tools is needed for participation in the program?

Q What safety rules must be followed for entrance into the program?

Q Does training occur in places that closely resemble actual job sites? Is on-the-job training part of the curriculum?

Q Do instructors have recent job experience in their fields?

Q Will job opportunities be available after training? Will someone at the school help with finding employment?

Q If a student wants to transfer credits to a professional training school or a four-year college or technical institute, is there someone at the school who will help?

FIGURE 9

Certificate programs have the same requirements for mastery of occupational skills as degree programs, but they do not require the same amount of academic study and usually take one year or less. Possession of a certificate is recognized as an advantage by employers and enhances job possibilities. The certificate can also be used with apprenticeship programs or to obtain more advanced or specialized training.

In some cases, students in occupational programs of one year or less are awarded a diploma to signify completion of training.

If a license is required in a particular field (such as plumbing, nursing, or electrical engineering), the student must do additional work after receiving a degree or certificate.

Other Questions

Other questions that need to be asked in evaluating a vocational education program are noted in Figure 9.

TYPES OF VOCATIONAL PROGRAMS

Vocational education programs are either public or private. The settings range from community colleges to single-specialty schools. Following are descriptions of each type of school, divided into public and private categories.

Public Vocational Education Programs

State laws that govern public vocational education create different patterns of service in different parts of the country. One state may deliver postsecondary vocational education through its community college system, another through technical institutes. State requirements for licenses to practice certain trades or professions also differ, as do requirements for completing certain courses of study. Despite this diversity, the service system described in the next few paragraphs can help to identify the public vocational education services in a community.

Community and Junior Colleges. At two-year community and junior colleges, occupational training can be combined with liberal arts. (For further description, see chapter, "The College Option.")

Two-Year Technical Institutes. Two-year technical institutes, also known as technical colleges, are publicly funded institutions that offer degree programs in skills required to enter and advance in specific occupational fields. Columbus Technical Institute (Ohio), for example, gives training in thirty-five technologies, including business management, insurance, law enforcement, animal health, automotive maintenance, aviation maintenance, graphic communications, and social services.

In general, academic courses are related to occupational areas. Math, technical writing, physics, and chemistry may be required for certain courses of study but not for others. Courses such as communications, English composition, or algebra may be required for all courses of study. Students should check catalogs carefully for requirements and electives.

Advantages for learning disabled students in public two-year technical institutes:

• No admissions requirements other than age (eighteen years or over) and graduation from high school or GED, with some exceptions. Entrance exams may be required for certain technical courses of study, such as nursing and engineering.

• Availability of disabled student services on many campuses. In addition, a vocational support team may be available to help students master specific tasks or skills that present difficulties.

• An opportunity to get intensive and highly specialized training in an occupational area.

• Preparation for transfer to four-year college or professional school.

• Enhanced opportunities for job placement. Programs are usually geared to employment opportunities in the community.

Area Vocational Centers or Area Vocational-Technical Centers. Area vocational centers exist in many states. In some states, vocational centers serve high school students; in other states, they also serve postsecondary students. These centers usually offer training in a wide range of occupational areas. Time required to complete course work depends on the requirements of specific occupational areas. Although these are not degree-giving institutions, they award certificates after completion of a course of study.

Advantages to learning disabled students attending area vocational centers:

• No admissions requirement. High school graduation may or may not be required, depending on the course of study.

• Less emphasis on academic skills. The academic part of programs relates to the skills needed in jobs in a particular occupational area.

• The opportunity to obtain occupational skills needed in today's job market and to earn a certificate that will be an asset in gaining employment.

Single-Specialty Public Vocational and Technical Schools. In a few areas of the country, publicly supported schools offer training in single-specialty skills. Depending on the area, schools may specialize in such fields as aviation, truck driving, barbering, or cosmetology.

PRIVATE (PROPRIETARY) SCHOOLS

Private (proprietary) schools are trade, technical, or business schools that offer training in a variety of occupational skills. They are, for the most part, small, single-purpose schools that specialize in practical training in fields generally requiring two years or less to gain skills needed for employment.

Experience with Learning Disabilities

An increasing number of these schools are becoming aware of issues related to students with learning disabilities. Vocational rehabilitation agencies are opening up opportunities by placing learning disabled clients in proprietary schools and working with administrators and instructors to arrange appropriate accommodations. A school that is a "vendor" for vocational rehabilitation may have gained experience with learning disabilities and may be a good choice for other learning disabled students seeking occupational training.

Before applying to a proprietary school, it is important to find out whether instructors have had experience working with learning disabled students and whether accommodations can be made. An inevitable question before enrollment is whether to disclose the existence of a learning disability. Many vocational educators advise students to be honest about their limitations during admissions interviews and to explain their strengths and specific needs very clearly. It can be helpful for students to provide simple, printed information about learning disabilities.

It is also important for students to look into a school's reputation, whether it is accredited, and how much help it gives to students in finding jobs. In short, is it worth the investment?

Advantages to learning disabled students in proprietary schools:

• An opportunity to be prepared for a specific job in a wide span of areas such as inhalation therapy, cosmetology, real estate, golf course operation, offset printing, word processing, and other secretarial and office work.

• No admissions requirement at most schools other than the wish to learn. Many programs require a high school diploma or GED, but others prepare students for GEDs as part of the program. Some schools may test for aptitude or specific level of reading, writing, or manual dexterity before enrolling students.

NEW HORIZONS

As mentioned earlier in the chapter, opportunities for disabled students in vocational education are growing. Educators, parents, and disabled adults are advocating nationally and locally for appropriate vocational education programs that can prepare people for independence.

Vocational educators are examining traditional vocational education curricula and showing how vocational instruction can be adapted to include learners with special problems. They are analyzing the details of tasks within occupations to identify specific accommodations for disabled students.

Through the efforts of these educational advocates, outstanding new resources and approaches are being developed and are available to parents and instructors who want to bring about change in the vocational classroom. Resources include information, technical assistance, instructional materials, and suggestions for adapting equipment and developing teaching alternatives. Innovative ideas are being disseminated and exchanged through vocational support teams, national networks, special centers, and state departments of education.

Vocational Support Teams

One of the most innovative and promising new developments is the emergence of vocational support teams for disabled students in vocational education programs. These vocational support teams (or resource units) may be located in publicly funded technical institutes, in community colleges, or vocational centers.

Team staff members provide instructional assistance and teach tasks or skills that may be difficult because of a specific disability. They may, for instance, help a student learn to use a micrometer, interpret blueprints, or convert fractions to decimals, or they may simplify a vocational text, or add graphics to clarify materials. Team members also give instructors ideas for working successfully with individual students and help find job sites for work experience and placement.

States in the forefront of developing support teams include California, Colorado, Georgia, Kentucky, Maryland, Missouri, and Wisconsin. State specialists in vocational education for the handicapped can give specific information about the availability of support programs in each state.

The 916 Vocational Center in Minnesota. An exemplary support program at the 916 Vocational Center in White Bear Lake, Minnesota, provides special help to disabled students enrolled in the center. Eight Supplemental Resource Instructors (SRIs) on the staff have been trained in both vocational instruction and special education. If a student is having trouble, a resource instructor assesses the problem and provides appropriate help, whether it is in reading, math, vocabulary building, social skills training, or counseling. The resource instructor may also recommend alternative teaching approaches, such as use of audiovisual materials, or other accommodations.

National Networks

National Association of Vocational Education Special Needs Personnel (NAVESNP)

Contact Vice President, Special Needs Division, American Vocational Association, 2020 14th Street, Arlington, Virginia 22201, (703) 522-6121.

NAVESNP is a national association of vocational education professionals concerned with education of handicapped, disadvantaged, and other special needs students.

An affiliate of the American Vocational Association, Special Needs Division, the organization is a major stimulus for new activities and exchange of information. Many NAVESNP members are coordinators of special needs in vocational education in state departments of education. Founded in 1974, the organization publishes *The Journal for Vocational Special Needs Education* as well as a national newsletter. (Both are published three times a year.) There are five regional units of NAVESNP, and each of these units publishes a newsletter. There are also thirty-five affiliated state associations. For names and addresses of regional and state associations, call or write The American Vocational Association, Special Needs Division.

National Network for Curriculum Coordination in Vocational Technical Education
National Center for Research in Vocational Education
1960 Kenny Road
Columbus, Ohio 43210
Toll-free number (800) 848-4815.

The Network is composed of six regional Curriculum Coordination Centers, which distribute vocational instructional materials in every state. Each center serves secondary and postsecondary vocational educators in school systems within its region. The centers stimulate innovative curriculum development, make materials available on a loan basis, and can be accessed by computer, free of charge.

Regional centers are located in the northeast, east central, midwest, northwest, southeast, and western regions.

Each state has a liaison representative to its regional center. To locate a state's liaison representative, contact the state's division of vocational education, usually located in the department of education.

Special Centers
Materials Development Center
Stout Vocational Rehabilitation Institute
University of Wisconsin-Stout
Menomonie, Wisconsin 54751.
(715) 232-1342.

The center develops and disseminates information for vocational rehabilitation and training of disabled students. Materials include information on vocational evaluation, work adjustment, job placement, and independent living. The center maintains the Job Analysis Exchange, mentioned earlier, which publishes task analyses pamphlets for specific job categories. A free catalog gives job titles, job descriptions, and code numbers for ordering appropriate pamphlets. (Cost for each pamphlet is $.50.)

Missouri LINC,
University of Missouri-Columbia
609 Maryland Avenue
Columbia, Missouri 65211
Toll-free line for Missouri residents, (800) 392-0533.
Telephone number for out-of-state residents, (314) 882-2733.
(Call during school year.)

LINC provides instructional materials and technical assistance for vocational education of handicapped students in the public school systems. The center disseminates a newsletter five times a year, which reviews activities, programs, and resources. It also publishes informational packets on instructional resources and maintains a toll-free line for Missouri residents. Materials are free within Missouri and available at cost to nonresidents.

The Minnesota Curriculum Services Center
3554 White Bear Avenue
White Bear Lake, Minnesota 55110
Toll-free line for in-state residents,
(800) 652-9024.
Out-of-state residents, (612) 770-3943.

The center provides individualized competency-based learning guides for tasks within fifty-five occupational courses of study. Instructional materials used by the 916 Vocational Institute are available if specially requested. Materials are free in-state and available on a cost-recovery basis out-of-state. Write for free catalog, *The Gallery 1985.*

Vocational Studies Center
University of Wisconsin-Madison
321 Educational Science Building
1025 West Johnson Street
Madison, Wisconsin, 53706
(608) 263-3415.

The Vocational Studies Center is a research and development center in the School of Education at the University of Wisconsin-Madison. It serves the state and the nation with information on vocational education and career development. A division on Projects for the Handicapped, headed by Lloyd Tindall, offers services to help handicapped youth and adults gain access to vocational education and employment.

Activities of this special division include in-service training for Wisconsin secondary and postsecondary teachers and for university instructors of graduate students; dissemination of publications and films; and sponsorship of conferences and workshops on job training for audiences throughout the country.

For free catalogs, *Help for Special Needs Teachers* and *Instructional Materials Catalog,* write to the center's publication unit.

National Center for Research in Vocational Education
1960 Kenny Road
Columbus, Ohio 43210
Toll-free line for in-state residents
(800) 848-4815, for out-of-state residents, (614) 486-3655.

The center provides a wide range of materials on curriculum development, technical education, career planning, and preparation for employment. It operates an electronic newsletter, *Advocnet,* which includes a "Special Needs Exchange" for disabled, disadvantaged, and limited-English-speaking students. For more information on using the exchange, call one of the center's toll-free lines.

THE VOCATIONAL INSTRUCTOR'S CONTRIBUTION

No matter how many centers, resources, and networks are available, the bottom line is what happens in the classroom. Many of the vocational educators interviewed for this book told of their willingness to work with students on an individual basis. These educators stressed that vocational classroom instructors frequently take extra time with a student who is having difficulty. Task analysis is used to break down the steps of a specific task and to show the student how to do each step. If one part of a task is difficult, such as measurement or safety rules, the vocational instructor focuses on this part. Whether or not a student is identified as learning disabled, these instructors have a practical approach that works with many learning disabled students.

In other words, these educators view their classrooms as productive, supportive environments, providing the individualized teaching needed by learning disabled students. They see themselves as "naturals" in educating learning disabled students for success.

IN CONCLUSION

Vocational education can be a rewarding option for many capable learning disabled students. By combining textbook and classroom learning with hands-on experience, students have the chance to translate their knowledge and skills into real-life accomplishment.

Additional Reading About Vocational Education

A Guide to Job Analysis, Employment and Training Administration, U.S. Department of Labor. (Order from the Materials Development Center, Stout Vocational Rehabilitation Institute, University of Wisconsin-Stout, Menomonie, Wisconsin 54751.) (488 pages, $12.00) 1982

Dictionary of Occupational Titles (fourth edition), Department of Labor: Employment and Training Administration. Superintendent of Documents, U.S. Government Printing Office, Washington, D.C. 20402. (1400 pages, $23.00) 1977. Supplement to fourth edition also available. (50 pages, $4.50) 1982

Education for Employment: A Guide to Postsecondary Vocational Education for Students with Disabilities, by Maxine Krulwich and Nancy Stout. HEATH Resource Center, One Dupont Circle, N.W., Washington, D.C. 20036. Free

Handbook of Special Vocational Needs Education, by Gary D. Meers. Aspen Systems Corporation, 1600 Research Boulevard, Rockville, Maryland 20850. (334 pages, $32.00 prepaid) 1980

Occupational Outlook Handbook, by U.S. Department of Labor. Superintendent of Documents, U.S. Government Printing Office, Washington, D.C. 20402. (393 pages, $8.50) 1985

The Journal for Vocational Special Needs Education: Postsecondary Vocational Special Needs: Special issue (Winter 1985, Volume 7, Number 2). (Copies available from Division of Vocational Education, 629 Aderhodl Hall, University of Georgia, Athens, Georgia 30602, $6.50 per copy.)

Vocational Support Service Teams in Maryland, by Maryland Vocational Curriculum Research and Development Center. Department of Industrial, Technological, and Occupational Center, University of Maryland, J.M. Patterson Building, College Park, Maryland 20742. (235 pages, free for Maryland residents, $5.00 out of state) 1984

Vocational (Work) Evaluation, by Walter A. Pruitt. Walt Pruitt Associates, Route 7, Box 324, Menomonie, Wisconsin 54751. (265 pages, $10.00, plus handling fee) 1977

Vocational Evaluation and Assessment in School Settings, by Paul M. McCray. The Research and Training Center, Stout Vocational Rehabilitation Institute, University of Wisconsin-Stout, Menominie, Wisconsin 54751. (138 pages, $11.50) 1982

Vocational Skills Assessment for Disabled Students, by Preston Chipps. Educational Resources Center, Chaffey College, 5885 Haven Avenue, Alta Loma, California 91701. (218 pages, $16.15) 1981. (Copies can be ordered from ERIC Document Reproduction Service, 3900 Wheeler Avenue, Alexandria, Virginia 22304, (800)-227-3742. Use ED # 205702 when ordering.)

OTHER OPTIONS

Although the focus of this book is on postsecondary educational opportunities, many learning disabled students need other options to prepare themselves for employment and independence. Options described in this chapter include apprenticeship and job training programs, military service, academic skill-building and independent living programs, and adult education and vocational rehabilitation services.

Although these options may not be available, appropriate, or accessible for all learning disabled people, they should be considered as possible alternatives. One option may help a learning disabled person in transition between high school and further education; one may help a learning disabled youth or adult take those first steps to steady, full-time employment; or another may help an adult who left high school many years ago, but is now looking for ways to achieve greater independence and self-fulfillment.

Since many of these programs are in short supply, persistence and imagination may be required to track them down. Ideas for finding community resources are described at the end of this chapter.

Work

Working after high school at a minimum wage, entry-level job is a way of learning. Work can help to motivate a student who needs a break from the long struggle with school. Money and co-worker acceptance can lift self-esteem and lead to discovery of a specific career or vocational interest.

For students leaving high school who need to develop self-reliance and daily living skills, the answer may be to spend a year or more working while living at home, taking responsibility for household chores, and paying a nominal amount for room and board. Even minimum wages can give a young adult experience in managing money to pay for transportation, recreation, and other personal expenses. Catching the right bus or train, driving and taking responsibilities for car maintenance, getting to work on time, and mingling with co-workers can improve adjustment and interpersonal skills.

To get information about entry-level job opportunities, contact school guidance counselors; check want ads in newspapers and on public bulletin boards; or get in touch with state-operated employment services, which offer free employment counseling and referral to public and private employers.

Private employment agencies can be another resource. These agencies frequently require that a contract be signed committing a job-seeker to pay a commission — usually all or part of the first month's wages. Before signing, it is important to check the wording of all contracts to determine the amount of money services will cost and what services are provided. Check with others who have used these services to see if the investment is worthwhile.

District offices of vocational rehabilitation can assist eligible learning disabled youth and adults with job-training and placement. This national service is described later in the chapter.

Apprenticeship

Apprenticeship programs exist in over 700 "apprenticeable" occupations, such as graphic arts, electrical, and plumbing careers. The demand for skilled labor has increased the number of apprenticeship programs in many settings, especially in universities and local and state governments.

In an apprenticeship program, a student is hired at entry level to learn a trade or craft from an experienced supervisor. A learning disabled student who has the aptitude for a specific field and can meet the other eligibility criteria for specific apprenticeship programs may find apprenticeships a viable option.

An Example

The Department of Physical Plant, at the University of Maryland, College Park, has developed a highly successful apprenticeship program. Apprentices learn the skills of one of several trades, including air conditioning and refrigeration, plumbing, carpentry, steamfitting, temperature control, and automotive mechanics. In addition to holding a 40-hour week paid job in the trade they are learning, apprentices in this program participate in at least 144 hours of classroom and lab study each year. The program takes four years, after which students receive a nationally recognized certificate in their field.

State departments of labor can provide information about apprenticeship programs. For names and addresses of regional and state apprenticeship offices, write for *The National Apprenticeship Program,* Bureau of Apprenticeship and Training, Employment and Training Administration, U.S. Department of Labor, 601 D Street, N.W., Washington, D.C. 20213.

THE JOB TRAINING PARTNERSHIP ACT (JTPA)

The Job Training Partnership Act (JTPA) establishes employment training opportunities for out-of-work youth and adults in every state. Funded by the federal government, the JTPA program is run locally by Private Industry Councils (PICs), which include representatives of local businesses, education agencies, and state and local governments.

No special funds are set aside for serving handicapped people, but the law requires that disabled applicants over the age of twenty-one be considered a "family of one" for determining income eligibility. States have the option of designating handicapped youth between the ages of sixteen and twenty-one as a "family of one," and the governors of more than thirty states have done so. A learning disabled young person in these states is eligible for JTPA services even if the family's income exceeds upper eligibility limits.

A Success Story

A severely learning disabled young woman recently completed five months of job training under a JTPA program in Illinois. The young woman was unable to handle the community college program because of severe academic deficits. She sought help from the vocational rehabilitation agency, which recommended her for the JTPA program. In the course of training, she learned food preparation skills, received remedial instruction in English and math in classes at a junior college, and benefited from an individualized program to improve social and other personal adjustment skills. She is now employed in a full-time job preparing food in an industrial cafeteria.

Influencing Local Policies

Training opportunities for learning disabled people have expanded in communities where concerned parents and educators have organized to evaluate and influence the plans and policies of their local Private Industry Council. To find out who is on the local council, when and where it meets, and what training programs are available, get in touch with the office of the mayor or county executive, the state employment service office, or the Governor's Committee on Employment of the Handicapped in your state. If these offices do not have the information, write or call the National Association of Private Industry Councils, 810 18th Street, N.W., Suite 702, Washington, D.C. 20006, (202) 223-5640. The staff can give names and addresses of local private industry councils.

New Ideas

New ideas for creating training opportunities for youth and adults are being developed.

The Vocational Studies Center, at the University of Wisconsin-Madison, has just published a major handbook on JTPA and handicapped youth and adults. It also is sponsoring regional conferences on JTPA programs for handicapped students. To obtain information about these and related projects, write to Lloyd Tindall, The Vocational Studies Center, 964 Educational Sciences Building, 1025 West Johnson Street, University of Wisconsin-Madison, Madison, Wisconsin, 53706, (608) 263-3415.

The President's Committee on Employment of the Handicapped also has material on JTPA programs. Write to Paul Hippolitus, Director of Youth Services, President's Committee for Employment of the Handicapped, 1111 20th Street, N.W., Washington, D.C. 20210.

MILITARY SERVICE

Some learning disabled adults can benefit from the highly structured, repetitive, and physically active regime of military life — if training does not stress skill areas that are impossible to do because of the specific area of learning disability.

To weigh the pros and cons of enlistment as a postsecondary option, talk to any service branch recruiter about military life in general and the flexibility in choosing specific training options. Military service can lead to immediate postmilitary employment or additional education at the college level. Tuition benefits can be an enticing residual of military service.

However, it is important to know that uniformed personnel branches of the military are not covered by Section 504. No particular accommodations are made for learning disabled men and women, unless they are civilian employees.

Tests Required

Before enlisting in any branch of the armed forces a person is required to take the Armed Services Vocational Aptitude Battery (ASVAB). This series of tests measures a person's reading, spelling, math, general, and mechanical knowledge and usually screens out individuals who cannot perform adequately in the basic skill areas. One way to prepare for this exam is to get a workbook called *Practice for the Armed Forces Test*

(new revised edition) by E. P. Steinberg, Areo Publishing Company, New York, New York. If a learning disabled person passes the ASVAB test, placement in an appropriate training program is not necessarily assured.

Military training includes classroom work as well as field experience. Physical demands are strenuous. Before seriously considering the military as an option, be sure to know what barriers to success exist.

ACADEMIC SKILL BUILDING

Hundreds of learning disabled adults are working below potential because of severe problems with reading or writing and other academic skills. They want to get ahead, find a better job, or go back to school. Many have the ability to do college-level work. What can they do?

The Lab School

Tutorial programs or classes for upgrading academic skills of learning disabled adults are very much needed, but only exist in a few communities. A unique private night school, started by Sally Smith, founder and director of the Lab School of Washington, D.C., is one of the rare programs and is a model of what can be developed by imaginative professionals.

The program meets two evenings a week for twelve weeks and offers reading, math, study skills, GED preparation, writing, spelling, typing, word processing, all types of communication (through drama and informal seminars), and applied math (through woodworking). The students, all of whom work during the day, range in age from eighteen to forty-two, and must score average or above on IQ tests. Teaching is highly individualized, based on results of assessment of strengths and weaknesses.

"We are a school between schools," says Janet Schrock, director of the night school. She believes that setting up a program of this type should be done by teachers who have a masters degree, have had experience with learning disabled adult students, and can instruct through the diagnostic-prescriptive method. For more details, write to Lab School of Washington, 4759 Reservoir Road, N.W., Washington, D.C. 20007.

INDEPENDENT LIVING PROGRAMS

New programs are getting started to meet the needs of severely learning disabled adults who may not qualify for college but have the motivation and potential to hold jobs and live independently. Unfortunately, the demand for programs for this population exceeds the supply. But exciting models do exist. The programs described in this section are examples of different approaches to teaching work, social, recreational, and daily living skills.

Threshold

The Threshold program at Leslie College in Boston, Massachusetts, offers a combination of vocational education and life skill training to learning disabled students who function in the 75–90 IQ range. (It is based on the program of the Para-Educator Center for Young Adults at New York University.) Students, most of whom live in dormitories while they attend the program, concentrate on one of two vocational tracks: early childhood care or adult human services. The curriculum includes supervised on-the-job placement and classroom work related to populations the students are working with. In addition, students take courses on sexuality, medical care, apartment living, consumer skills, and money management, including handling checking accounts and making a budget.

Other aspects of the program include

• development of independent living skills. Each student spends three weeks in an apartment on campus and is responsible for making meals, cleaning, and shopping.

• discussion and practice of social skills, with emphasis on picking up conversational cues and body language, successful interviewing, and maintaining jobs.

• participation in group therapy once a week for ten weeks. Students talk about problems of growing up and feelings about being learning disabled.

• opportunities to learn how to act, dance, paint, do photography, and participate in sports.

Students receive a certificate upon completion. They spend a postgraduate year in their own apartments, with supervision and guidance from the Threshold staff. The thirty-six students enrolled in the program are eligible for student loans and vocational rehabilitation assistance to cover the cost of tuition and board.

For more information about the Threshold Program, write to Threshold, Leslie College, 29 Everett Street, Cambridge, Massachusetts 02238.

INDEPENDENT LIVING CENTERS FOR LEARNING DISABLED ADULTS

Chapel Haven
1040 Whalley Avenue
New Haven, Connecticut 06503
(203) 397-1714

JESPE
65 Academy Street
South Orange, New Jersey 07079
(201) 762-6906

R and D Independent Living Center
P.O. Box 15112
Phoenix, Arizona 85060
(602) 956-8334

STILE/MACLD Apartment Residence
501 Park Avenue
Asbury Park, New Jersey 07712
(201) 774-4737

TRYA Hostel
14 Elk Street
Hempstead, New York 11550
(516) 481-3833

The Springboard, Inc.
Box 1342
West Concord, Massachusetts 01742
(617) 369-1352
(Nonresidential as of now)

An excellent publication on independent living centers is *Independent Living and Learning Disabled Adults,* by Dale Brown, President's Committee on Employment for the Handicapped, Washington, D.C. 20210. (15 pages, free) 1982

FIGURE 10

The R & D Residential Independent Living Center

The R & D Independent Living Center in Phoenix, Arizona, is one of a handful of innovative residential centers in the country that are demonstrating their great value for severely learning disabled adults. These residential programs teach vocational, daily living, and social skills to prepare adults for employment and independent living.

The few excellent independent living centers that have been developed are often the result of parental concern and effort. The R & D Center is the product of the imagination and hard work of former ACLD president Dorothy Crawford and her son, Rob Crawford, who worked with the vocational rehabilitation office in Phoenix to set up the program.

Program participants live in a group home or an apartment and have responsibility for all household tasks. A structured daily schedule teaches appropriate social behavior, grooming, hygiene, nutrition, and stress management through group meetings, role play, and video feedback. Students learn how to apply for jobs, budget money realistically, and manage time.

Emotional development and self-esteem are fostered through all aspects of the program. The staff, all of whom are learning disabled adults, and vocational rehabilitation counselors work on job development and provide back-up to new job holders and employers during an adjustment period.

Some participating learning disabled adults go on to community colleges and universities. When program graduates move into their own living quarters and live independently, the center is still a place to come for meetings, support, companionship, and advice.

For more information write to: Independent Living Center, P.O. Box 15112, Phoenix, Arizona 85060.

LEAP (Life Experience Activities Program)

LEAP is a nonresidential, transitional program in Silver Spring, Maryland, which prepares young adults to make the transition from school to work. Students range in age from eighteen to thirty, and they spend an average of nine to twelve months in the program.

The program has three main components: job readiness, support for obtaining placement in competitive employment, and job maintenance. The emphasis is on teaching appropriate job behaviors and attitudes, communication skills, functional academics, and interview preparation. An on-the-job training component provides experience in the real work world. Trainees receive support in going through interviews and in managing relationships with employers and co-workers.

Much time is spent working on social and life skills and travel training. A therapeutic component provides group counseling to help with personal problems. Additional components include vocational, psychological, and academic assessment, a computer skills training program, and a social/recreational program. The program has led to successful job placement for the majority of young adults enrolled.

In most cases, fees for the program are covered by vocational rehabilitation. For more information, write to LEAP, 8719 Colesville Road, Suite 305, Silver Spring, Maryland 20910.

TWO SYSTEMS: ADULT EDUCATION AND VOCATIONAL REHABILITATION

Two systems — adult education and vocational rehabilitation — are potential sources of needed postsecondary services. The quality and extensiveness of services vary from region to region. Much depends on the sensitivity and commitment of individuals providing services in different localities.

ADULT EDUCATION

Adult education includes a range of useful learning experiences for people no longer in high school. Courses are designed for adults who wish to obtain a high school diploma, who need educational skills to function more effectively in society, or who simply seek personal enrichment.

The range of possible courses in adult education includes remedial reading and math; general education, such as speed-reading and American history; job skills; hobbies; and parenting, interpersonal communication, and other skills of adult living. Courses are given through county boards of education (at learning centers and in high schools), continuing education departments of colleges, and private programs and schools.

ADULT BASIC EDUCATION

An important part of the adult education system — the Adult Basic Education (ABE) program — provides basic education to people whose learning deficiencies, limited English language proficiency, or physical or mental disabilities have hindered their employability and their ability to meet adult responsibilities. Funds for the ABE program are appropriated by the federal government to the states and counties, and priority is given to people at the lowest literacy level.

ADULT EDUCATION FOR LEARNING DISABLED PEOPLE

Adult education, especially the ABE program, has great potential for people with learning disabilities. Although in reality most states and counties do not have the staff or resources to identify or work extensively with learning disabled adults, many adult education teachers are becoming more interested in meeting the needs of this group.

The London Procedure. One promising development that can help adult basic educators identify and work with learning disabled students is a forty-five-minute battery of tests called the London Procedure (named after a city in Ohio where the tests were piloted). The creator of this procedure is Laura Weisel, a learning disabilities specialist

67

who for many years has taught and worked with learning disabled children and adults.

Ms. Weisel is convinced that many adults who attend adult basic education programs are learning disabled and were never identified or helped when they were children. She thinks these adults can be identified and counseled about their learning problems and can benefit from remedial and compensatory methods designed to meet their individual needs.

The procedure includes a screening test to examine visual and auditory functions, and a diagnostic test to determine coding and decoding abilities and ways of processing information. These tests are given to students in adult basic education classes who have average or above average intelligence but function at or below the eighth-grade level.

Through in-service seminars, Ms. Weisel has taught adult educators throughout the country how to administer and interpret the tests and how to involve the students in the planning. Only educators trained by Ms. Weisel can use these materials. She believes that her approach can work if top-level administrators commit funds and specially trained teachers to this program.

Laura Weisel can be contacted by writing to her at The Administrative Training Section, Office of Education and Training, Ohio Department of Mental Health, 30 East Broad Street, Room 1340, Columbus, Ohio 43215 or by calling her at (614) 466-7347.

ABLE (Alternatives for a Better Learning Experience). Parents and educatiors in local communities are beginning to develop adult education programs for learning disabled adults who lack academic, work, social, or job skills. ABLE is a model program developed by The ACLD in Norwalk, Connecticut, and the Connecticut Department of Special Education. It was founded in 1982 for learning disabled adults who were no longer receiving services from the public school system.

According to Pat Giannini, who built the ABLE program, students have one of three goals: to prepare for other post-secondary schooling (college or vocational), to work toward the GED credential, or to keep up with practical skills of everyday life. Students come from miles around to take part in the program, which includes career guidance, reading, writing, math, personal money management, participation in emotional support groups, and learning compensatory strategies for overcoming deficits. After years of discouragement, learning disabled adults, ranging in age from seventeen to fifty-four, are gaining the coping skills and confidence they need to move forward. For details, write to Pat Giannini at the Office of Adult Education, 105 Main Street, Norwalk, Connecticut 06854.

Additional Resources For Adult Education

Local boards of education are good sources of information about ABE programs. Each state has an adult education department that can provide information about instruction for adults. State agency lists, available free from the HEATH Resource Center, the National Clearinghouse on Postsecondary Education for Handicapped Individuals, include addresses of Adult Education Departments. (Address One Dupont Circle, Washington, D.C. 20036).

A professional organization concerned with adult education issues is the American Association for Adult and Continuing Education (AAACE). The AAACE publishes several periodicals and holds meetings and conferences on adult education problems. (Address is 1201 16th Street, N.W., Washington, D.C. 20036.)

Getting a High School Diploma

Learning disabled adults who did not complete high school and want to earn a diploma or the equivalent of a diploma can look into three possibilities: the General Education Development Test, more popularly called the GED; adult high school programs; or, in some states, the External Diploma Program.

• **GED.** The GED is a timed test that covers reading and writing skills, social studies, science, and mathematics. The GED is recognized by most employers and many colleges.

Preparatory courses and pretests are usually available through adult education programs. Books, such as the *Baron* series, can be obtained in bookstores or libraries. GED tests can be taken with accommodations, such as extended time, in a separate room, or with a reader. To make these arrangements, contact local or state boards of education.

• **Adult High School Programs.** Adult high school programs are another way to complete high school. Classes are usually small and are held during the day or evening.

• **External Diploma Program.** The External Diploma Program is primarily designed for older adults who never finished high school and who now wish to earn a diploma. Adopted by thirteen states (although not in each county), this is a flexible, self-paced way for adults to complete high school by demonstrating current competency in basic skills and life experiences.

Before being accepted by the program, each person is screened for level of reading, writing, and math. If skill standards are met, the adult is accepted into the program and works on other areas of competency. In some states, instruction is offered; in others, students work on their own, with guidance from advisors. These programs are noncompetitive, students get immediate feedback, and they always have the opportunity to rectify mistakes.

These programs were not set up with learning disabled adults in mind, but they have potential for learning disabled students who meet the screening criteria. Should a person not pass the screening test, the director of the local or state program may know of community resources, such as tutors or basic skills classes.

For information about any of these programs, contact the adult education department in the county or city public school system.

Literacy Groups

Adult education includes a network of literacy groups in communities across the country. These groups are staffed by trained volunteers who give one-on-one tutoring to students no matter what their level of literacy. People who are totally illiterate are accepted for teaching by Laubach Library International, as well as other groups. Teaching methods are highly structured and individualized.

Although their approaches are not necessarily geared toward learning disabilities, many literacy tutors are trying to pick up the existence of a learning disability and adapt teaching to special needs. Before starting a tutorial program, it is important to know if the tutor's methods are appropriate or flexible.

To find out about a local literacy organization, call the toll-free number of the Coalition for Literacy Hotline (800) 228-8813.

VOCATIONAL REHABILITATION

Vocational rehabilitation — a nationwide employment training program funded jointly by federal and state governments — can be a link to educational and other services needed to prepare disabled persons for employment and independence.

Depending on the employment goal, these services can include vocational evaluation; job training; prevocational, academic, social, or daily living skills training; adult education courses; trade or technical schools; and a wide range of other public or private services. If college is a way to achieve an employment goal, services may, in some instances, include financial assistance for tuition or cover costs of needed equipment, such as 4-track tape cassettes.

Services are available to disabled people, starting in high school. In some school systems, vocational rehabilitation counselors are participating in IEPs by helping parents and educators make transitional plans.

Learning Disabilities and Vocational Rehabilitation

Learning disabilities have only recently been recognized by the vocational rehabilitation system. Some counselors are trained to evaluate and develop plans for learning disabled clients; others are finding out about learning disabilities for the first time. Because the mandate to cover this disability is new and because appropriate community resources are not always available, services are inconsistent.

When making the initial contact, a learning disabled person should ask if there is a counselor on the staff who is trained in working with people who are learning disabled or if the area has a learning disability specialist. When meeting with a vocational rehabilitation counselor, clients should bring along documentation, such as recent school records and test results. They should also share articles and pamphlets that explain learning disabilities. Whatever placement is suggested, it is important to make sure that it is appropriate.

If clients disagree with the counselor's recommendation, and the problem cannot be resolved, state Client Assistance Projects (CAPs) have been set up in every state to provide ombudsmen for clients who are dissatisfied. The addresses and phone numbers of the nearest CAP are available from the vocational rehabilitation office.

Eligibility

The presence of a disability does not in itself assure acceptance in the vocational rehabilitation program. The disability must be considered severe enough to prevent employment commensurate with a person's abilities. There must also be a reasonable expectation that rehabilitation will result in employment.

To find out if you (or your son or daughter) are eligible, make an appointment for an interview with a counselor at the nearest vocational rehabilitation office. The counselor will arrange for an evaluation, free of charge, to determine if a learning disability exists, the nature and extent of the learning disability, and whether the learning disabled person meets other eligibility criteria.

Individualized Planning

If accepted, the client works with the counselor on an Individualized Work Rehabilitation Plan (IWRP). The plan is based on the interests, abilities, and aspirations of the individual; the results of evaluation; and the availability of resources. Input from others, such as parents, teachers, and other professionals who know the person well is important in drawing up a meaningful plan of action.

How to Find the Vocational Rehabilitation Office

Vocational rehabilitation offices are located in or near every city. However, they are known by different names in different states. If you can't find your local office in the phone book under state government listings, try the city, county, or state information service, the library, the school system, or the nearest chapter of the Association for

Children and Adults with Learning Disabilities. Or write to the HEATH Resource Center for its state agency listing.

TIPS FOR FINDING OTHER OPTIONS

There is no single system in place that is responsible for providing the combination of daily living skills, academic skills, and prevocational and vocational skills needed by many learning disabled adults. Your district school system may know where some of these services exist.

Parents are in the forefront of the effort to develop services and are often the best sources of information. One way to reach experienced and knowledgable parents is through state or local chapters of the Association for Children and Adults with Learning Disabilities (ACLD). To locate the nearest chapter, write to the ACLD national office, 4156 Library Road, Pittsburgh, Pennsylvania 15234.

Parent Training and Information Centers, organized and run by parents, are another source of help. About sixty-five centers throughout the country have received federal funds to assist them in carrying out their activities. For information about local or regional centers, contact the Division of Personnel Preparation, Office of Special Education and Rehabilitative Services (OSERS), Washington, D.C. 20202, or the Federation for Children with Special Needs, 312 Stuart Street, Boston Massachusetts 02116.

Other local parent groups have founded coalitions to provide help to parents in need of services for their handicapped sons and daughters. Coalitions in six states (Oregon, Colorado, Virginia, West Virginia, Ohio, and Illinois) are developing direction services, using a case-management approach to solving problems. For more information, write to the National Services Assistance Project, 867 High Street, Worthington, Ohio 43085, (614) 431-1911.

Here are some additional strategies that can help to locate hard-to-find resources:

■ Make a list of community groups that might provide services you are looking for or that can tell you where to turn. Include organizations and agencies such as the public school system, libraries, youth agencies, church groups, Y's, local recreation departments, civic groups (Kiwanis, women's clubs), U.S. Department of Agriculture extension services, mental health associations, and community colleges and adult and continuing education programs.

■ Check the yellow pages of the telephone directory for tutorial programs or listings of private schools for learning disabled students. Staff members may have information about opportunities beyond high school.

■ Call mayor or county administrator offices. They frequently give information about community services. Ask about directories of community programs that have been published recently.

■ Write to the HEATH Resource Center for its new directory of transition specialists in each state.

There are thousands of learning disabled youths and adults who need the postsecondary services that have been described in this chapter if they are to avoid a lifetime of illiteracy, unemployment, dependency, and personal unhappiness. Creating these options takes energy, time, and commitment. Parent and other advocacy groups are giving that assignment the highest priority.

Additional Reading About Other Options

Adult Education

Barron's GED Getting Ready for the High School Equivalency Exam: Beginner's Preparation in Reading and English, by Eugene J. Farley and Alice Farley. ($5.95) 1973

Barron's GED Getting Ready for the High School Equivalency Exam: Preparation in Math, by Edward Williams. ($6.95) 1976

Literacy Resources: An Annotated Check List for Tutors and Librarians. (Available from the Enoch Pratt Free Library Literacy Resource Center, 400 Cathedral Street, Baltimore, Maryland.)

Postsecondary Education Institutions and the Adult Learner: A Self-Study Assessment and Planning Guide. Commission of Higher Education and the Adult Learner, 10598 Marble Faun Court, Columbia, Maryland 21044 ($15.00, $2.25 postage and handling charge) 1984

Vocational Rehabilitation

Journal of Rehabilitation: Rehabilitation of Adults with Learning Disabilities: Special issue (April, May, June 1984). (Copies available from the National Rehabilitation Association, 633 South Washington Street, Alexandria, Virginia 22314, $7.50 per copy.)

Rehabilitating the Learning Disabled Adult, by Dale Brown. President's Committee on Employment for the Handicapped, Washington, D.C. 20210. (15 pages, free) 1982

Specific Learning Disabilities, A Resource Manual for Vocational Rehabilitation. (Available from the Allegheny County ACLD, 4900 Girard Road, Pittsburgh, Pennsylvania 15227.) (48 pages, $12.00) 1983

Supervising Adults with Learning Disabilities, by Dale Brown. President's Committee on Employment for the Handicapped, Washington, D.C. 20210. (7 pages, free) 1985

Vocational Rehabilitation Services — A Student Consumer's Guide HEATH Resource Center, One Dupont Circle, Suite 670, Washington, D.C. 20036. (Free)

What Do You Do After High School?, by Regina and Gil Skyer. Skyer Consultations, Inc., P.O. Box 121, Rockaway Park, New York 11694. (357 pages, $29.95) 1982, with 1984 update

MATCHMAKING: SELECTION AND ADMISSION

This chapter is addressed directly to the student who is concerned about getting into a postsecondary school.

You have examined postsecondary options, including college, vocational education, job training, work, or military service. You have evaluated your abilities, disabilities, needs, and goals; and you have decided to try a formal postsecondary program.

Now the task is to find a college or vocational education program that fits your needs. The search process can be an exciting one. It can be an opportunity to learn about many types of schools: What they offer, what they require, and what they have that appeals to you. You might discover majors and careers that you had never thought about; you might discover colleges or vocational programs that you never knew existed; and you might discover schools you thought would never admit a learning disabled person but are now accessible.

FIRST STEPS

To narrow the choice is not easy. But there are steps to take that can help in this selection and matching process. Gathering information through directories and catalogs, talking with your high school guidance counselors, and interviewing college faculty members who work with disabled students are all part of the process. Understanding the various admission policies, including issues of disclosure and entrance exams, is another part of the procedure. In this chapter, we describe some of these steps, discuss some of the resources, and provide references of directories, organizations, and publications that can be used in your personal search.

Before going into detail about the selection process, we encourage you to develop a list of questions that reflect what you are looking for in a college or vocational school. These questions can be divided into two categories: *questions to ask yourself* (Figure 11) and *questions to ask of the schools you are considering* (Figure 12). Keep your questions in mind when you read directories and catalogs, and think about them when you talk with admissions officers, disabled student service coordinators, or other people who are knowledgeable about the schools you are investigating.

SOURCES OF INFORMATION

Information can be collected from many sources. Directories, literature about specific colleges or vocational schools, organizations, college fairs, and high school and private guidance counselors can all be valuable resources. Campus visits and interviews can also be useful.

Questions to Ask Yourself

Q What size school are you looking for? Do you want to be in an urban or rural environment? Do you want to be on a large or small campus?

Q Do you want to live at home? Do you need time to be with your family while you are trying out the academic world?

Q Do your SAT and ACT scores, grade point average, courses, and class rank match the requirements of the schools you are considering? If not, do you have talents, interests, motivation, and ways of compensating for your learning problems that might be taken into consideration by an admissions officer?

Q Are you comfortable explaining the different ways that you learn and how you have coped with these differences?

Q What kinds of support services do you need? (Review the chapter, "Support — How Much Is Enough?")

Q What is your financial situation? Do you have to work part time? Can you get assistance from vocational rehabilitation or can you get a loan?

FIGURE 11

Educational Directories

Directories are a good way to start the selection process. They describe the characteristics of the schools and list the entrance requirements, including exams and scores needed, grade point average, class rank, and, in some cases, level of selectivity. Some directories note services available for disabled students; others note colleges that have structured postsecondary programs for

Questions to Ask Schools

Q What is the school's attitude toward learning disabled students? Are faculty and administrators aware of the problems and needs of learning disabled students as well as their potential for success?

Q What are the admission requirements? SATs, ACTs, grade point average, class rank? Are there nonstandard ways to take entrance exams? Are letters of support, extracurricular activities, or personal essays considered?

Q Are there other ways to be admitted? Special admission policies, transfer, provisional admission?

Q What are levels of support services? If a school says that it has support services, what are the specific ways in which help is available, and how does a student get that help?

Q What accommodations are available (untimed tests, alternatives to taking written exams, access to taped texts, notetaker services, tutors, readers)?

Q Are waivers granted to disabled students who, because of their disabilities cannot pass certain courses, such as foreign languages or statistics?

Q Is there a disabled student service office on campus? If so, is there someone in that office who has a special understanding of learning disabilities?

Q If more intensive counseling is needed, is there a counseling service on campus?

Q If tutoring is available, who does it? Is there supervision? Are tutors trained to work with learning disabled students? What is the cost?

Q If this is a technical or vocational education school, does it have a coordinator of services for the handicapped or a vocational support team?

Q How available are faculty members to students?

Q How many credits must be taken for a student to be considered full time?

Q Are special study skills courses given for credit, and/or can they be counted as hours toward full-time status?

Q What are the experiences of other learning disabled students on that campus?

Q Is there a learning disabilities student self-help group?

FIGURE 12

learning disabled students. A few directories have extensive listings of majors and where they are offered. When using directories, be aware that information can be outdated or not based on firsthand knowledge and should be checked against other sources. (See Figure 13 for a list of directories.)

Organizations

Several national organizations can provide information about college, university, technical, and vocational education options for learning disabled students. These organizations include the HEATH (the National Clearinghouse on Postsecondary Education for Handicapped Individuals); the Association for Children and Adults with Learn-

GUIDES TO POSTSECONDARY PROGRAMS FOR LEARNING DISABLED STUDENTS

A Directory of Two- and Four-Year Michigan College Programs Serving Special Education Students. (Available from Southfield Education Center, 16299 Mount Vernon, Southfield, Michigan 48075, $2.50.)

A Guide to Colleges for Learning Disabled Students, edited by Mary Ann Liscio. Academic Press, Inc., 6277 Sea Harbor Drive, Orlando, Florida 32821. (490 pages, $24.95) 1984

BOSC Directory of Facilities for Learning Disabled People, edited by Irene Slovak. BOSC, Department F., Box 305, Congers, New York 10920. (200 pages, $28.00 plus $2.00 for postage and handling) 1985

California Community College Programs and Services for the Learning Disabled. (Available from Educational Services Center, 9200 Valley View, Cypress, California 90630, free.)

FCLD Guide for Parents of Children with Learning Disabilities, Federation of Children with Learning Disabilities, 99 Park Avenue, New York, New York 10016. (409 pages, $5.00) 1985

Lovejoy's College Guide for the Learning Disabled, by Charles Straughn II and Marvelle Colby. Simon and Schuster Publishers. (Available at local bookstores and libraries or write to Simon and Schuster, 1230 Avenue of Americas, New York, New York 10020.) (144 pages, $10.95 postage and handling included) 1985

Peterson's Guide to Colleges with Programs for Learning Disabled Students, by Charles T. Mangrum II and Stephen S. Strichart. (Available from Peterson's Guides, P.O. Box 2123, Princeton, New Jersey 68540.) (400 pages, $13.95).

The Directory for Exceptional Children (eleventh edition). Porter Sargent Publishers, Inc., 11 Beacon Street, Boston, Massachusetts 02108. (1428 pages, $40.00 plus $4.00 postage) 1985-1986 (For information about prep schools)

What Do You Do After High School?, by Regina and Gil Skyer. Skyer Consultation, Inc., P.O. Box 121, Rockaway Park, New York 11694. (357 pages, $29.95) 1982, with 1984 update

What's Available for the Learning Disabled College Student in Florida. (Available from the Clearinghouse/Information Center, Florida Department of Education, Knott Building, Tallahassee, Florida 32301.) (34 pages, free) 1984

GUIDES TO PROGRAMS FOR ALL STUDENTS

American Community, Technical, and Junior Colleges: A Guide (ninth edition), by Dale Parnell and Jack W. Peltason, editors. The American Council on Education/Macmillian Publishing Company, Front and Brown Streets, Riverside, New Jersey 08075. (1000 pages, $85.00) 1984

Directory of Educational Institutions. Association of Independent Colleges and Schools. One Dupont Circle, N.W., Suite 350, Washington, D.C. 20036. (Single copies, free) 1985

Handbook of Trade and Technical Careers and Training. National Association of Trade and Technical Schools, 2251 Wisconsin Avenue, N.W., Washington, D.C. 20007. (73 pages, free) 1985

Peterson's Annual Guide to Undergraduate Study, Four-Year Colleges. (Available in most bookstores or libraries or write to Peterson's Guides, P.O. Box 2123,

Princeton, New Jersey 08540.) (2175 pages, $12.95) 1985

Peterson's Annual Guide to Undergraduate Study, Two-Year Colleges. (Available in most libraries and bookstores or write to Peterson's Guides, P.O. Box 2123, Princeton, New Jersey 08540.) (2175 pages, $12.95) 1985

1984-85 Accredited Institutions of Postsecondary Education, edited by Sherry S. Harris. Published by the American Council on Education for the Council on Postsecondary Education, Washington, D.C. (Order from Macmillan Publishing Company, Inc., Front and Brown Streets, Riverside, New Jersey 08075.) (450 pages, $19.50)

For copies of these directories, check public and school libraries, school guidance counselor's offices, or bookstores.

FIGURE 13

ing Disabilities (ACLD); and the Association on Handicapped Student Service Programs in Postsecondary Education (AHSSPE); and the Orton Dyslexia Society. Addresses for these organizations are listed in the section, "Organizations That Can Help."

Counselors

High school guidance counselors are available to all students in helping them think about appropriate colleges and vocational education schools. Counselors have directories and catalogs, they arrange college nights and schedule sessions with college representatives. They will welcome participation in collecting information about schools with learning disabilities programs.

Private educational counselors might also be of help. To find such a service in or near your community, check the yellow pages ("Education," "Schools," "Counselors"), contact an ACLD chapter, or talk with your school guidance counselor. If you do locate a private counselor, make sure that he or she knows about programs for learning disabled students.

School Visits

A visit to a school — preferably during the junior year — is a good way to gather information that might be of interest. It is a time when you can talk with coordinators of disabled student services (DSS) or the coordinator of a learning disabilities program to determine what supports and accommodations are available. The DSS coordinator is the person who can answer questions about your specific needs and can advise you on whether to disclose your disability (see below). The coordinator can also indicate whether your chances for admission are realistic.

A visit can be a time to talk with other learning disabled students on campus to see what their experiences are. It can also give you a sense of the campus. Do students and faculty seem friendly and eager to talk about the school? Is the school isolated? Are the dorms crowded and noisy? Are there quiet places to study? Can you visualize yourself on that campus?

ADMISSIONS INTERVIEWS

An informal visit is a chance to decide whether you should apply to specific schools. An admissions interview usually occurs either before or after you make a formal application. Some schools require these interviews, others do not. Interviews can take place on the campus or in your community if the school has representatives — usually alumni — who can perform this function.

Importance of Interviews

For some learning disabled students, the interview can make the difference. If you do not meet the entrance requirements of the school you are interested in but you believe that your talents, determination, and methods of coping will enable you to "make it," then a strong, positive interview may outweigh the other criteria. Your commitment and your comfort in discussing how you work with your learning problems and what specific help you might need could be the turning point in convincing the admissions officer that you should be given a chance.

Interviews are an important part of admission to a special learning disabilities program. Students will be extensively interviewed, and at least one parent might be asked to participate. The interview will probably include a developmental history and an evaluation of assessment testing done either by the college or by qualified psychologists or special educators. These programs emphasize not only potential, but goals and motivation of the student.

Role Play. Many students report that practicing for an interview by role playing is a good way to prepare for the actual experience. Counselors, parents, and friends can be helpful in coaching you on how to dress, how to behave, and how to talk and listen.

Advance Planning. Appointments for interviews should be arranged in advance and can be made through the dean of admissions, the disabled student services office, a learning disabilities specialist, if there is one on campus, or the director or admissions counselor of a technical, trade, or business school.

By planning in advance, residential colleges might be able to arrange for a student to sleep in a dorm and attend some classes. Students applying to vocational educational schools or local community colleges might want to spend a day touring the school and asking questions of students and instructors.

To TELL OR NOT TO TELL: DISCLOSURE

Should a learning disabled student disclose the disability? Section 504 prohibits postsecondary institutions from making preadmission inquiries about any disability. Application forms *cannot* have questions about disabilities; admissions personnel are trained *not* to inquire about or indicate an obvious disability observed in an interview; and secondary schools *cannot* release this information unless authorized by the student.

However, many learning disabled students want and need to know what their prospects are for admission. A careful reading of recruitment materials and school catalogs can frequently provide some information about services and accommodations; but it is more effective to discuss needs, problems, and strengths with the disabled student services coordinator before applying.

The question of disclosure elicits responses on both sides of the issue. Some learning disabled students advise students who are applying to regular campus programs not to disclose their disability. Others urge students to discuss the disability but to be very specific about the problem and about the ways in which the problem can be accommodated. A comfortable, positive attitude can be the most effective approach.

Disclosure is essential for admission to special programs.

Private Vocational Schools

When applying to a private trade, technical, or business school, the same concerns about disclosure arise. As previously mentioned, many vocational educators think that students should discuss their disability when talking with an admissions officer.

However, much depends on what you sense when you visit or make inquiries. If you feel comfortable about your learning differences and if you can explain how you learn and what accommodations may be helpful, then the responsibility is on the school to be upfront about its ability to teach you.

If you feel uncomfortable about disclosure or asking the school about its attitudes toward accommodations, try and find out if the school has vocational rehabilitation clients, talk with other students or graduates, or ask more general — or hypothetical — questions.

On balance, considering that you are making a financial investment, make sure that you will be able to learn the skills that are being taught.

COLLEGE ENTRANCE EXAMS

Entrance exams are obstacles for many learning disabled students. College entrance exams were developed to predict a student's ability to do college-level work. The two most commonly used exams are the SAT (Scholastic Aptitude Test) and the ACT (American College Testing). A practice version of the SAT is the PSAT (Preliminary Scholastic Aptitude Test). Many high school students take the PSAT in the fall of their sophomore and junior years and the SAT in the spring of the junior year and the fall of the senior year. Colleges consider the best scores.

To relieve anxiety, some parents and teachers encourage learning disabled students to take these exams as frequently as possible. (This does not mean that you have to send all of these scores to colleges you are considering.) Preparation courses and software programs are other ways to practice.

Both the SAT and ACT exams can be taken under standard or nonstandard conditions. Nonstandard conditions include

- Extended time,

- Use of a cassette or a reader,

- Use of an aide to mark the answers,

- A large-type version.

Requests to take the exams under nonstandard conditions must be made well in advance of the exam date. Detailed information about the special testing can be obtained from the high school guidance office or the following testing servces:

- SAT-Admissions Testing Program (ATP) Services for Handicapped Students, Box CN 6200, Princeton, New Jersey 08541-6200, (609) 771-7600.

- PSAT-ATP Services for Handicapped Students, Box CN 6720, Princeton, New Jersey 08541-6720, (215) 750-8300.

- ACT Assessment, Test Administration, P.O. Box 168, Iowa City, Iowa 52243, (319) 337-1332.

Graduate Record Exams

Exams for admission to professional and graduate schools can also be given under nonstandard conditions. For information, contact the ATP Services.

ADMISSION POLICIES AND REQUIREMENTS

Each school has its own requirements for admission. Figure 14 is a summary of admissions requirements and procedures for different types of institutions. Note that in addition to regular admissions requirements, four-year colleges and technical schools may have special/provisional or cooperative admissions policies.

ACCREDITATION

In selecting a college, a university, a technical or vocational education school, questions may arise about accreditation. The answers are important because, in some fields, students must graduate from an accredited program in order to be licensed to practice. Accreditation can also be important if a student transfers credits to another school or applies to a graduate program.

Schools usually state in their literature that they are accredited. If there is any question, a parent or student should ask to see the certificate of accreditation or find out if the school is in the process of being accredited.

Accreditation means that an institution has been examined by and met the standards of a recognized accrediting body. Accrediting organizations are national or regional nongovernmental groups, such as the New England Association of Schools and Colleges and the National Association of Trade and Technical Schools.

In addition, specialized accrediting bodies evaluate particular programs within an institution in fields such as allied health, art and design, construction engineering, law, and medicine.

Both institution- and program-accrediting bodies are selected by the Council of Postsecondary Accreditation, a nongovernmental organization that reviews the quality and performance of accrediting groups on an ongoing basis.

Accredited Institutions of Postsecondary Education, published annually by the American Council on Education, gives information about all accredited institutions, professionally accredited programs, and candidates for accreditation in the United States. The book also includes a list of all national and regional accrediting bodies for postsecondary schools and programs and explains the accrediting process.

EXPERIENTIAL LEARNING

Many colleges and universities are offering adults a new opportunity to work toward a degree by giving them credit for life experiences. Each college has its own procedures and standards. *Earn College Credit for What You Know,* by Susan Simosko, is a practical, step-by-step book that describes how you can go through this process. It also lists over 500 colleges that have this program.

For further information about experiential learning programs, write to the Council for Adult and Experiential Learning (CAEL), 10840 Little Patuxent Parkway, Suite 203, Columbia, Maryland 21044.

SUMMARY

In selecting and applying to colleges or vocational educational schools, keep in mind that "the times they are a-changing." Many postsecondary institutions are becoming aware and sensitive to learning disabled students. Individual teachers, counselors, learning disabilities specialists, and coordinators of disabled student services are establishing and building support services and getting faculty cooperation. On many campuses, students themselves are becoming more active in advocating for support services.

New programs are surfacing in large and small colleges, community colleges, technical schools, and some vocational educational schools. The important point to remember is that you have options. The more curious, creative, and determined you are, the more rewarding your search for those options will be.

ADMISSION REQUIREMENTS AND PROCEDURES

COMMUNITY AND JUNIOR COLLEGES, PUBLIC, TWO YEAR
• Usually open admission
• 18 years or older
• Most require high school diploma or GED for credit courses. GED may be taken during freshman year.

JUNIOR COLLEGES, PRIVATE, TWO YEAR
• High school diploma or GED
• Usually require some type of entrance exams (SATs, ACTs)
• Usually request grade point average, and/or class rank
• Experience and personal qualities usually given consideration.

COLLEGES, UNIVERSITIES, AND TECHNICAL SCHOOLS, PUBLIC AND PRIVATE, FOUR YEAR

Regular Admission
• High school diploma or GED usually required
• Entrance exams (SATs or ACTs)
• Grade point average and/or class rank
• Interview may be required.

Special or Provisional Admission
• SATs or ACTs may be waived or lower scores may be accepted.
• Student's potential, goals, interests commitment, and demonstrated ways of coping with disability are given weight.
• Remedial or study skills classes may be required as basis for admission.

Cooperative Admission
(Special program for learning disabled students within college)
• Admission jointly decided by college and special program.
• Students *must* disclose disability.
• Usually open admission
• Some schools require high school diploma or GED.
• Some schools or programs require SATs, ACTs, or admissions tests to determine aptitude for the curriculum.

VOCATIONAL EDUCATION SCHOOLS, PUBLIC AND PRIVATE, TWO YEAR OR LESS
• Usually open admission
• Some schools require high school diploma or GED.
• Some schools or programs require SATs, ACTs, or admissions tests to determine aptitude for the curriculum.

FIGURE 14

81

Additional Reading About Selection and Admission

Academic Preparation for College: What Students Need to Know and Be Able to Do, by The College Board. (Available from College Board Publications, Department A35, Box 886, New York, New York 10101.) (45 pages)

College and the Learning Disabled Student, by Charles T. Mangrum, II and Stephen S. Strichart. Grune and Stratton, Inc., 111 Fifth Avenue, New York, New York 10003. (205 pages, $24.50) 1984

Earn College Credit for What You Know, by Susan Simosko. Acropolis Books, 2400 17th Street, N.W., Washington, D.C. ($8.95)

Guide to External Degree Programs in The United States (second edition), Eugene Sullivan, editor. The American Council on Education/Macmillan Publishing Company, Front and Brown Streets, Riverside, New Jersey 08075. (120 pages, $16.95) 1983

The National Guide to Educational Credit for Training Programs. The American Council on Education/Macmillan Publishing Company. Front and Brown Streets, Riverside, New Jersey 08075. (500 pages, $37.50) 1985

The 1984 Guide To The Evaluation of Educational Experiences in The Armed Services. The American Council on Education/Macmillan Publishing Company. Front and Brown Streets, Riverside, New Jersey 08075. (1,750 pages, sold in sets of 3 or individually, $50 per set) 1984

4

CHOOSING
COURSES

CHOOSING COURSES

During registration at an institution of higher education, all students go through an academic advisory process to select and sign up for courses needed to fulfill requirements for degrees, majors, or certificates. In each case, a faculty advisor gives the final approval.

Students with learning disabilities are no exception. However, on many campuses, they can get additional help and advice before finalizing their choices. This preregistration period is a time to gather as much information as possible about course requirements; instructors' attitudes and teaching techniques; reading load; and availability of resources, such as tutors, notetakers, or study skills classes.

Before registration, Susan would go to the campus bookstore to look over the required texts for courses she was considering. Because she was dyslexic, Susan would check to see if a book was too thick or the print too small. If she thought the book would be too difficult to read, she would then check the texts used in other sections of that course or reconsider her decision. Susan also listened to the student underground. If a student criticized a professor because he or she only lectured from the book, she knew that professor could be just right for *her* — because the lecture would reinforce the text.

Ultimately, Susan figured out what worked for her. She also knew when she needed extra help. However, it took a few semesters and familiarity with the campus before she could begin to work out her own solutions.

GETTING HELP WITH PLANNING

Some students, like Susan, can gather their own information before and during registration; others need careful and understanding guidance. The more thought that goes into planning at registration time, the less chance of experiencing overload during the semester.

Students who need extra help and have documentation of their learning disability or who suspect that they have a disability should contact the disabled student services (DSS) office or learning disability coordinator before finalizing their course selection. Many DSS staff members are knowledgeable about learning disabilities. They can give students tips about courses and instructors; they can help students decide on a full or partial course load; and they can also talk with faculty advisors about students' special needs.

FULL- OR PART-TIME COURSE LOAD?

Learning disabled students always need more time to study; more time to schedule tutors, readers, and study skills classes; and more time to listen to tapes of books and lectures. Many have jobs. Because of these extra pressures, some learning disabled students may not be able to take a full-time course load. Rather they choose to extend the time for completing their degree, or they finish within the regular time by taking summer school courses.

Before a student makes a decision about going to school on a full- or part-time basis, the following questions should be asked, and the answers weighed carefully.

Q How many credit hours must a student earn to maintain full-time status?

Q What is the usual time frame for earning a degree at the institution? How are exceptions made for disabled students?

Q What benefits would be lost if a student does not have enough credits for full-time status? Would financial aid be jeopardized? Would the student be charged by credit hours?

Q Can the DSS coordinator make special arrangements for disabled students to keep their financial aid, even though they are unable to attend full time?

Q Are credits given for study skills or remedial courses? At some schools, these courses earn credit toward full-time status, although not toward a degree. In other schools, these courses earn credits toward the degree.

Whatever the decision, it is important to remember that length of time taken to complete a degree does not detract from its value.

EXAMPLES OF COLLEGE ADVISORY SYSTEMS

Excellent advisory services for learning disabled students can be found on any campus — large or small, public or private. Following are examples of different types of advisory systems for learning disabled students.

Barat College

At Barat College (Illinois), learning disabled students have been carefully evaluated prior to admission to the college's Learning Opportunity Program. Because communication is excellent among faculty members, academic advisors on the program staff have current information on courses, instructors, methods of instruction, level of difficulty, and time needed to prepare for each course. At registration time, the advisor can mesh knowledge about each student with information about the college. The result is a manageable, individualized schedule. Barat advisors also encourage students to make a preliminary survey of courses during intersessions or summer breaks.

College of the Ozarks

At the College of the Ozarks (Arkansas), the Special Learning Center assigns each learning disabled student to a program coordinator. Prior to course selection, the coordinator discusses with the student the student's interests, hobbies, goals, skills, and problems. This information is then compared with the diagnostic evaluation to determine placement and scheduling. In the first year, students develop and strengthen basic skills; in the following years, students are increasingly integrated into the regular college program. An evaluation at the end of each semester determines the scheduling for the next semester.

Achieve Program, Southern Illinois University

Learning disabled students who are part of Southern Illinois University's Achieve Program go through regular registration. However, after they complete this process, they meet with an Achieve Program staff member who reviews their course selections and either approves or suggests changes. Good liaison with the regular faculty advisor makes this flexibility possible. The program's staff also determines what special courses, in addition to the regular college course, each student needs. Some of these classes, such as a special English composition and/or sociology course, library research, or interpersonal communications, are for credit; others, such as study skills and reading comprehension, are not.

Ohio State

Large universities also respond to learning disabled students' needs. Ohio State has developed services for the learning disabled student through the Office For Disability Services. A staff member recommends appropriate courses in reading, study skills, and personal assessment before learning disabled students meet their academic advisor. Depending on individual needs, the staff helps the student figure out a balanced course load. The staff can also have learning disabled students placed on a priority scheduling list so that they will be assured of placement in their selected courses.

LAUNCH, East State Texas University

The LAUNCH program at East State Texas University provides a comprehensive support system for learning disabled students. At registration, learning disabled students work with an academic advisor on the LAUNCH staff. This advisor knows the previously assessed strengths of the student, the many university options, and those professors who are successful in working with learning disabled students. Learning disabled students are urged to contact the LAUNCH program any time during the semester if they need help with problems.

Miami-Dade

Colleges with open admission policies are also responsive to learning disabled students. Although disclosure of a handicapping condition is not required, Miami-Dade Community College (Florida) makes every effort to have students identify themselves prior to registration. These students can then be advised by a learning disability specialist who works out programs and scheduling, including placement in bridge or transitional courses, if necessary.

TIPS FOR STUDENTS

Whether you are on your own during the registration process or get specific help, here are some tips and recommendations for planning a balanced and controllable schedule:

■ Become involved in the planning of your schedule. Understand your abilities and disabilities, your learning style, and your need for specific accommodations or special services. Explain these to your faculty advisor.

■ If you plan to request assistance in obtaining accommodations, bring any recent documentation of your learning disability.

■ If you do not have recent documentation or if you have never been evaluated but suspect that you might have a learning disability, you might inquire before registration whether diagnostic services are available to students through the DSS office or the learning disabilities coordinator.

■ Check to see if your school has an orientation program for learning disabled students during the summer or a few days before school starts. These programs can give you an opportunity to learn about special resources, talk with instructors about the course work, and obtain reading lists and assignments.

■ Find out about course requirements. Get as much information as you can about specific courses and instructors. Find out which instructors have more empathy for learning disabled students' needs. Ask other students. If you are working with a DSS coordinator or learning disabilities specialist, get their opinions about courses and instructors.

■ Check the required textbooks and readings before you sign up for a particular instructor or course section. If textbooks are easier to read in one section of a course, then this might be a deciding factor.

■ Find out what the drop/add dates are. Some students use this deadline to assess how they are doing in a course. It is preferable to drop a course than to fail it.

■ Balance your course load. Many learning disabled students and people who work with them advise taking no more than twelve hours per semester; some even recommend nine hours. Another recommendation is to take one difficult course, two moderately difficult courses, and one easy course each semester. If reading is your area of difficulty, don't take more than one heavy reading course per semester.

■ If you are short of credits and want to finish college within four years, consider taking courses in summer school or through an accredited correspondence school.

Summary

With academic advice, a student can evolve a schedule balanced in terms of time and level of difficulty. But no matter how excellent the advisory system, the chance of a successful college career is greater when the student is involved in planning and self-managing.

5

KEYS TO UNLOCKING ABILITY: ACCOMMODATIONS

OVERVIEW: ACCOMMODATIONS

"Having a brain that can't express itself is an incredible frustration."

These words, spoken by a learning disabled adult who struggled long and hard to overcome his disabilities, underlie all efforts to provide accommodations for learning disabled students. Accommodations are keys to unlocking potential. They make it possible for learning disabled students to use their innate abilities — in a college course, a vocational education school, or any other postsecondary program.

Accommodations can include alternative ways to fulfill course work, innovative classroom techniques, supervised tutorial assistance, or use of technology. To be of value, accommodations must be tailored to individual needs. The more complete the information about a student's specific strengths and weaknesses, the better the chance for selecting and customizing appropriate accommodations. The changes that are suggested have successfully been carried out in postsecondary programs throughout the country.

Two recent pamphlets are examples of how these changes have unlocked ability. Both pamphlets were written on college campuses, as a result of rare and sensitive communication between learning disabled students and the professionals who worked with them. One of these publications, *Dispelling the Myths,* is from Hunter College; the other, *College Students with Learning Disabilities,* is from DePaul University.

THE QUESTION OF EQUITY

Everyone — students, parents, counselors, and educators — must agree at the outset that it is reasonable, fair, and entirely proper to offer accommodations for students with disabilities, including those with learning disabilities. Educators use the term *equity* to mean that achievement of equal opportunity for certain groups may depend on providing special support or additional services. Support services do not give disabled students any advantage over others; they merely enable disabled students to overcome the disadvantages with which they would otherwise begin.

The process for learning, for receiving, and for demonstrating information — not changing course content or lowering academic standards — is the focus of accommodations for learning disabilities. Every campus representative and every learning disabled student interviewed for this book emphasized that course content should not be changed.

Despite a prevalent fear that the quality of education will be lowered by making accommodations, experience has shown that this does not happen. On the contrary, many of the techniques for helping learning disabled students use their abilities are also extremely helpful to other students. Instructors who have adapted their classroom approaches to teach learning disabled students repeatedly discovered that they had sharpened their teaching skills and that their students' overall performance had improved.

NO MAGIC ANSWERS

There are no magic or perfect answers. Learning disabled people must always be on the lookout for ways to work around their difficulties and solve their problems. Those who work with them — tutors, instructors, counselors, program coordinators — are their allies in the constant search for new ideas.

Additional Reading About Accommodations

College and the Learning Disabled Student, by Charles T. Mangrum, II and Stephen S. Strichard. Grune and Stratton, Inc., 111 Fifth Avenue, New York, New York 10003. (205 pages, $24.50) 1984

"College Programming for the Learning Disabled," by Barbara Cordoni. Journal of Learning Disabilities, November 1982. (For a reprint, write to Barbara Cordoni, Special Education Department, Southern Illinois University, Carbondale, Illinois 62901.)

College Students with Learning Disabilities: A Student's Perspective, by Carol Wren and Laura Segal. (For copies, write to Carol T. Wren, Director, Project Learning Strategies, DePaul University, 2323 Seminary, Chicago, Illinois 60614.) (10 pages, $1.00) 1985

Dispelling the Myths, College Students and Learning Disabilities, by Katherine Garnett and Sandra LaPorta. Hunter College, 695 Park Avenue, New York, New York 10021. (21 pages, $3.50) 1984

Hill Top Spectrum (quarterly newsletter), June M. White, editor. Hill Top Preparatory School. South Ithan Avenue and Clyde Road, Rosemont, Pennsylvania 19010. $16.00.

"Postsecondary Education for Learning Disabled Students: A Review of the Literature," by M. Lewis Putnam. Journal of College Student Personnel, January 1984

"Postsecondary Education, Where Do We Go from Here?" by Barbara Cordoni. Journal of Learning Disabilities, May 1982. (For a reprint, write to Barbara Cordoni, Special Education Department, Southern Illinois University, Carbondale, Illinois 62901.)

"Services for College Dyslexics," by Barbara Cordoni. Reading Disorders, Varieties and Treatment (R. Madatesha and P. Aaron, editors). Academic Press, 111 Fifth Avenue, New York, New York 10003. 1982

The College Student with a Learning Disability: A Handbook for College and University Admissions Officers, Faculty, and Administration, by Susan Vogel. Association for Children with Learning Disabilities, 4156 Library Road, Pittsburgh, Pennsylvania 15234. (12 pages, $3.00) 1985

ALTERNATIVE WAYS TO LEARN

George, a learning disabled student at Southern Illinois University, was allowed to submit a written assignment on tape. He received the first A of his life. The opportunity to do his course work in an alternative way gave him a large dose of self-confidence, and he went on to excel as a major in architectural technology. Once his self-esteem took hold, he was also able to work methodically on the basic mechanical skills that had overwhelmed him in the past.

The use of alternative ways to fulfill course requirements helps lay the groundwork for academic success. Successful accomplishment leads to motivation, which in turn can lead to further accomplishment. Students who have been filled with self-doubt can begin to shine.

Alternatives are modifications of traditional ways to do course work, to read print, to take notes and exams, and to write papers. They differ from approaches that remediate basic academic skills or teach study skills and learning strategies. (Study skills are discussed in Section 7, "A Bag of Tricks: Study Skills." Alternatives are ways to *bypass* obstacles caused by the learning disability. Study skills teach people to learn *how to learn.*

96

ALTERNATIVES TO PRINTED MATERIALS

Many learning disabled students find it helpful to listen to taped textbooks or to have material read aloud by readers. Tapes used in combination with reading can strengthen the visual input of print by adding the auditory input of the recorded voice.

Readers are helpful when an instructor gives an unscheduled assignment and there is insufficient time to tape it. These are usually assignments not included in the regular text, such as reprints, library readings, and handouts. Some learning disabled students also need to have exam questions read aloud to them.

Reader services are usually coordinated by disabled student service offices (DSS). On some campuses, readers are volunteers; on others, they are paid.

Recording for the Blind

The major source of taped texts is Recording for the Blind, Inc. (RFB), 20 Roszel Road, Princeton, New Jersey, 08540, (609) 452-0606.

A national, nonprofit organization, RFB provides recorded educational materials to visually, physically, and perceptually handicapped people. Recorded tapes are loaned free of charge to persons eligible for the service. The organization has a recorded library of 60,000 texts, and it tapes about 4,000 new books each year. Borrowers are permitted to keep tapes for up to one year and must submit written requests for an extension.

To obtain RFB texts, learning disabled persons must fill out an application form and give detailed diagnostic information indicating their organic dysfunction and their long-term need for taped, educational books. Forms must be signed by a doctor or learning disability specialist.

Tips for RFB borrowers, given by Mangrum and Strichart in *College and the Learning Disabled Student,* include the following:

• Try to get requests in before peak periods of January-February, June-July, and August-September.

• For new recordings of books not already in the RFB tape library, a special request is needed, plus two copies of the printed text. To save time, mail first class or parcel post, *not* Free Matter for the Blind.

• Recordings are mailed by installments. Allow four to six weeks for the first installment.

Talking Books

The Talking Book program is maintained by the National Library Service for the Blind and Physically Handicapped, The Library of Congress (NLS), 1291 Taylor Street, N.W., Washington, D.C. 20542, (202) 882-5500.

Through this program a wide range of publications, free of charge, is available on loan to eligible persons. The collection includes popular novels, classical literature, poetry, biography, and magazines. A doctor must certify that an individual wishing to use the service has a reading disability due to organic dysfunction.

Talking Books are distributed through a network of regional and subregional libraries. To get information about applying, check with a local library. Some of the local NLS libraries can arrange to have text materials taped by volunteers for individual borrowers.

The NLS also publishes a directory, *Volunteers Who Produce Books.* This directory lists, by state, the names and addresses of volunteer groups and individuals who tape materials. It is available through libraries affiliated with the NLS.

Playback Equipment

Tapes recorded by RFB and NLS cannot be played on standard 2-track cassette machines bought in stores. A special 4-track playback machine is required. The equipment is available on extended loan basis (for eligible borrowers) from regional branches of The Library of Congress or can be purchased from the Massachusetts Association for the Blind, 200 Ivy Street, Brookline, Massachusetts 02146, or the American Printing House for the Blind, 1839 Frankfort Avenue, Louisville, Kentucky 40206.

Campus Libraries

Some campuses are developing tape libraries that provide excellent resources for learning disabled students. The College of the Ozarks has a library of more than 14,000 taped texts available to the Special Learning Center. A number of DSS coordinators are currently looking into the possibility of exchanging tapes with other campuses to augment their own tape libraries.

ALTERNATIVES TO NOTETAKING

Some learning disabled students need alternative ways to take notes because they cannot hear correctly, or write legibly, or organize and remember while listening to a lecture. If problems are identified and documented, arrangements can be made to find alternative ways to take notes.

Notetakers

Getting the services of a notetaker usually requires that the student, the instructor, and, if necessary, the DSS coordinator talk over the problem.

Notetakers are usually volunteers, although they may be paid. In most cases, teachers will ask a classmate who is a good student and capable notetaker to share class notes. In some instances, two volunteer notetakers are used. This helps if one is absent.

Special Paper. Notetakers can use carbon sets, ordinary carbon paper, or other types of treated paper. A special noncarbon duplicating paper that can make two or three copies makes it easier for someone else to take notes. It can be ordered by the college bookstore or the DSS office from the National Institute for the Deaf, Rochester Institute for Technology Bookstore, Post Office Box 9887, Lomb Memorial Drive, Rochester, New York 14623.

Taped Lectures. Many learning disabled students tape lectures and then listen to them in a quiet, nondistracting atmosphere. It is essential to get the instructor's permission before taping a lecture. In some situations, it may be necessary to sign a formal statement that the material will only be used for study purposes.

Listening to a tape requires the same skills as listening to a lecture, except that it can be done in private, stopping the machine as needed.

Tips for taping class lectures:

■ Use a different tape for each class.

■ Label the tape with date, class, and lecturer.

■ Set counter at 0. When an important idea is stated, make a note of the number on the counter to listen to later. For class discussion, use the pause button and only tape the essentials.

■ Allow sufficient extra study time for listening to tapes.

■ Use rechargeable battery-operated tape recorders to eliminate the need for sitting next to electrical outlets. To avoid changing tapes during class, use 120-minute tapes.

■ Review tapes as soon as possible after a lecture. Some students have become adept at listening for main ideas on one tape, then repeating these ideas into a second tape. The second tape becomes their class notes.

At Barat, tapes are used as tools for learning notetaking skills. Honor students are paired with learning disabled students to go over taped notes, teach outlining, and integrate lecture notes with reading.

Voice Indexing. A new method for indexing tapes, developed for blind people, can be used by learning disabled students. Using this voice-indexing technique on special taping equipment, the student can record headings and subheadings for lectures and other taped materials. Students can then skim a taped text by listening to headings, much the way one skims a book by reading boldface subheadings, italics, marginal notes, and so forth. A system that a learning disabled student might use to index taped lectures is described in *Voice Indexing: A Programmed Text,* by Gerald Jahada at Florida State University. This guide is available in one cassette from Elpro Associates, P.O. Box 3634, Langley Park, Maryland 20787. For more information on voice indexing, write to Voice Indexing for the Blind, Inc., 9116 St. Andrews Place, College Park, Maryland 20740.

ALTERNATIVE WAYS TO TAKE EXAMS

The goal of all students in taking exams is to demonstrate mastery and understanding of course material, not of test-taking techniques. All disabled students should also have this opportunity without being penalized for their disability.

Because of one or more specific disabilities, learning disabled students are often unable to take exams in the traditional way. They may have trouble reading and/or understanding the questions; writing under pressure; organizing thoughts; or remembering mechanics of spelling, punctuation, and syntax. Even the slightest noise, like the scratching of pencils on paper, can be distracting to learning disabled students.

Possible Solutions

To compensate for these difficulties, some students need additional time to complete their exams. Others need to take tests in a separate, quiet room, with a proctor. Some need to listen to exam questions on tape or give their answers orally.

Learning disabled students on different campuses have worked with individual instructors on alternative ways to handle the problem of taking exams. One student was permitted to write papers instead of taking tests. Another outlined the test, then met with the professor to give oral answers. Others wrote tests in the classroom and, to compensate for handwriting disabilities, were permitted to type them or use a word processor in the DSS office.

Readers and Scribes

On many campuses, readers and scribes are available, usually through DSS, to read test questions aloud and/or write down dictated answers. Readers and scribes (also called clerks, secretaries, and exam writers) are oriented to needs of disabled students and trained to assure that no assistance is given in answering questions.

At Central Washington University, a cadre of readers is selected for good reading and speech skills. At the University of Maryland, readers and scribes are trained members of the Special Services staff. Where rapport between DSS and faculty is good, as it is at Maryland, readers or scribes can also administer exams. In some cases, college departments prefer to have their own proctors present as well.

Arranging Test-Taking Alternatives

Making arrangements for alternative test-taking procedures must be done in advance, preferably soon after a course begins. Readers and proctors need to be lined up and test-taking rooms or offices reserved. Learning disabled students are expected to take responsibility for informing the faculty and DSS officer or learning disability specialist that special test-taking services are needed. Students must usually bring a copy of the course syllabus to the DSS office to verify testing dates.

To assure faculty members of the security and integrity of the alternative exam process, campuses have developed forms that explain the special arrangements. An example, designed by the DSS office at Southern Illinois University, is reprinted in Figure 15.

What Colleges are Doing

Following are examples of test-taking alternatives offered at various colleges:

• At the College of the Ozarks (Arkansas), students are given the option of taking tests in the classroom or at the Special Learning Center. The form of testing depends on the student's needs:

Some have material read to them, some have tests taped, some dictate answers, some need more time, and some need clarification of questions.

• At Southwest State University (Minnesota), students have several choices. They can dictate exam answers onto a tape and then type them, dictate answers to a proctor, get help in proofreading answers for spelling and syntax errors, or use a typewriter. They can have extra time if needed.

• At Marist College (New York), faculty believe that oral exams are often better for a student who has trouble with written expression. The college encourages the use of true/false tests rather than multiple choice, allows sufficient time and extra exam books, and recommends that large print be used on tests, if needed.

• At Barat College (Illinois), students may have extended time, take tests in a separate room, listen to test questions on tape, or take tests orally. To compensate for memory deficits, students are permitted to use calculators in basic math exams and to use spelling dictionaries and handbooks of commonly misspelled words in other exams. Scratch paper is also made available for outlining and drafting.

ALTERNATIVES TO WRITTEN COMPOSITION

Written assignments can be difficult for many learning disabled adults. Despite their intelligence, they frequently have trouble putting ideas together, using correct grammar and spelling, and writing legibly. Alternatives that can help these students include dictating and editing services and use of word processors (see chapter, "Using Technology").

ACHIEVE PROGRAM PROCTORING FORM

Among other services, the Achieve Program at the SIU-C Clinical Center is responsible for proctoring course exams for its students with learning disabilities when it is necessary for the student to have extra time or other assistance to complete a test (e.g., someone to read aloud the questions and/or to write down the student's verbal response to test questions).

Following are the procedures that students and instructors are requested to use if test proctoring is necessary.

1. If test proctoring services are required, the *student* should personally talk with each instructor during the first week of classes to explain the need. Instructors are understanding of the need once they are aware of the student's situation. Instructors may call the Achieve office (453-2595) if there are questions about the needs or procedures.

2. The instructor is requested to mail or deliver such exams 2-3 days (or whenever the exam has been written) prior to the testing date. The exam can be sent by campus mail, hand delivered or picked up by an Achieve staff member. The student is encouraged to remind the instructor of the need to mail or deliver a test *before* the actual testing date. Achieve assumes the responsibility of securing the exams.

3. The *student* is responsible for contacting or calling Achieve *as far in advance as possible* in order to schedule the date and time of the test. This should usually be the same time the rest of the class is taking the exam. Students who feel they have a good reason (e.g., a class scheduled during the following hour) for taking the exam other than during the regularly scheduled time have to get the permission of the instructor before Achieve will approve. If the student should receive a schedule of test dates at the beginning of the semester, these dates can be scheduled then. All exams must be *pre-scheduled* with the Achieve office.

4. The student should call the Achieve office before coming in to take the exam to make sure it has been delivered to us. If the exam has not been delivered, the student should contact the instructor. The Achieve office logs all receipts of tests, time of tests, test proctor's names and receipt of the test when returned to the professor.

5. Once the student has begun the exam, he/she will not be allowed to leave and return to finish the exam at a later time. Exceptions to this can only be made if Achieve has received written permission from the instructor.

6. As a common procedure, Achieve will return the completed exam to the instructor via messenger. If the instructor prefers to have the exam delivered by campus mail or pick it up him/herself, the instructor should indicate this to Achieve at the time the test is delivered. In either case, a receipt must be signed by the instructor of his/her designee in the department, signifying that the test has been received. The receipt must then be returned to the Achieve office.

The test proctoring service is designed as an appropriate academic accommodation for the Achieve Program learning disabled student, and to benefit faculty. Through alternate test administration, if it is needed, the faculty member can evaluate the learning disabled student on the same basis as other students. The service is designed to assist the program's learning disabled student in demonstrating his/her skills or acquired knowledge rather than his/her disability.

For further information, contact the Achieve Program:

> SIU Clinical Center
> Pulliam 108 or 122
>
> Barbara Cordoni, Coordinator
> Sally DeDecker, Assistant
> Program Coordinator

FIGURE 15 Developed by Disabled Student Services Office, Southern Illinois University

Intensive teaching by sensitive instructors, specialists, and tutors also helps develop needed skills. Problems with writing and strategies for compensating are discussed in more detail in the chapter, "Writing."

Using Special Talents

Some students have been able to work with their instructors on substitutions for traditional research or writing assignments. They have drawn on their special talents to express the ideas called for in an assignment.

One student presented a beautiful photographic essay on rural life instead of a written report for a sociology course. Another student presented a fine oil painting to illustrate an oral report on dreams. An education student observed and reported orally on techniques of teaching in four different classrooms to fulfill a research assignment on teaching methodology. A student in a class on criminology spent many hours in court learning about the justice system and was given extended time to write an essay.

Both reading and writing difficulties were overcome through these nontraditional ways of doing assignments. Yet in each case, the objective of the course was met. Actually, more time may be spent in completing alternative assignments than in doing the work in a traditional way.

WAIVERS

As more learning disabled students are going to college, many faculty members are confronted with problems of granting waivers in areas that are particularly difficult for learning disabled students, such as foreign languages, statistics, and English composition. Philosophically, this issue touches the core of the academic world. The legal obligation to make college education accessible to all who are qualified, regardless of handicap, conflicts with the concern of administrators and faculty that changing requirements for degrees or majors or bypassing certain courses will dilute the meaning of a diploma. These are very difficult questions, and answers will be debated for a long time.

Grounds for Requesting Waivers

The question of equity is linked to acceptance of learning disabilities as a handicap, definition of the disability, and appropriate, convincing diagnoses. As with other disability groups, the question focuses on what a student can or cannot do because of the interference of a disability. A deaf student would not be expected to take a music appreciation course that depended on listening. The grounds for revising specific requirements for learning disabled students are similar.

Substitution of Courses

Learning disability specialists and DSS coordinators have looked at the purpose of including certain required courses in the curriculum, and some have recommended substitutions for those requirements. If the purpose of studying foreign languages is to experience a foreign culture, then courses in that country's history or literature might be appropriate substitutes. At George Washington University, a learning disabled history major with dyscalculia (inability to do math) was permitted to substitute a class in oral interviewing techniques for a statistics class. The rationale: The statistics class was required as a research tool, not as a math requirement.

Foreign Language Waivers

Because foreign languages create severe problems for many learning disabled students, the McBurney Learning Center at the University of Wisconsin surveyed seventy-three colleges and universities to see what solutions, if any, they had worked out. Of the fifty-nine institutions that responded, fifty-three required a foreign language for some majors. Of these, thirty-two permitted some form of modification, including dropping the requirement; substituting courses on literature, history, and culture for the language of the country; modifying the instructional approach by eliminating reading, writing, or oral/aural components; or providing taped texts and/or extensive tutoring.

No college is immune from the foreign language waiver problem. Kenneth Dinklage has written thoughtfully about this dilemma. He developed an evaluation method out of his work with Harvard students who were very bright yet could not pass the language requirements.

The criteria included by Dinklage were the student's score on the Carroll-Sapon Modern Language Aptitude Test; past school history; special difficulty in reading and spelling due to reversal problems; background of parents and siblings to see if there were familiar patterns of right-left confusion; and the student's inability to pass the course, despite tremendous effort. When all of these factors are added up, according to Dinklage, a decision can be made. The college can either give the student a waiver, or let the student fail and then use the reasons for the failure as evidence for the need for a waiver.

Examples of Strategies

Determination of eligibility for waivers or substitutions differs from college to college. Some colleges require evaluation by a specialist and allow students who are diagnosed as learning disabled to petition a dean or committee. Still others allow the student to petition for a waiver or other modification only after unsuccessfully trying the course.

Another strategy that has been used is retroactive withdrawal from a failed course. In some cases, colleges recommend that a student take a difficult course at another school, such as a community college, during the summer and transfer the credit.

Following are a few examples of how some campuses have resolved the waiver issue:

• The College of the Ozarks (Arkansas) offers a general studies degree in which the "hardcore" courses can be audited. The student gets a degree in general studies, with an emphasis on a major field of study (e.g., business). In addition, a course may be waived if a student has attempted several times to pass it.

• At Ohio State University, an advisory committee has been set up for learning disabled students who request curriculum modifications. The committee, which consists of a neurologist, a professor of educational theory and practice and a speech pathologist, makes recommendations following presentation of cases by the director of learning disabilities services. Results of diagnostic testing must document reasons for requests for waivers or substitutions. The academic unit involved participates in making a final decision based on the committee's recommendation.

• At the University of Arizona, the Dean of Fine Arts has developed a list of courses that are accepted as fulfilling the purpose of language in liberal arts. In order to arrange for substitution of those courses for sixteen units in foreign language, a student must verify the disability and take additional English credits.

• At The American University (Washington, D.C.), learning disability advisors try to have a student change the emphasis in a major, thus bypassing a requirement yet staying in the same field.

103

• At The George Washington University (Washington, D.C.), the disabled student services staff works with individual learning disabled students, as necessary, to petition for waivers or work out substitute courses within their college. Waivers have been granted in foreign languages and statistics.

• Professional, technical, or vocational schools are constrained from waiving or substituting certain courses because of state licensing requirements. At Columbus Technical Institute (Ohio), students must meet all licensing requirements for its technical programs; however, waivers or substitutions can be arranged for courses not required for licensing. The school grants waivers for its English composition course for deaf students (a specialized English course is given), and the same arrangement could be made for learning disabled students. At the present time, learning disabled students do all of their writing for English composition at the Handicapped Student Services office. Staff there proofread the writing and mark errors, with students making the corrections on their own.

A Different Way

Each of the alternative methods for fulfilling degree requirements, including waivers, has the same purpose. Each provides a learning opportunity for the student who cannot acquire or express knowledge in traditional formats. Each makes it possible for learning to take place — a different way.

Additional Reading About Waivers

"Inability to Learn A Foreign Language," by Kenneth Dinklage, Emotional Problems of the Student (edited by G. Blaine and C. MacArthur). Appleton-Century-Croft, 1971. (For reprints write to Kenneth T. Dinklage, Harvard University Health Services, 75 Mount Auburn Street, Cambridge, Massachusetts 02138. Enclose self-addressed, stamped, business-size envelope.)

"MY TUTORS DESERVE ROSES"

For many students with learning problems, a tutor is the person who brings out their best efforts. A tutor can patiently review and clarify a difficult assignment, help a student find the main ideas in a complex reading passage, organize notes for an exam, or check papers for spelling, grammar, and appearance. A tutor who is willing to take the time to understand how a student learns can play a pivotal role and may be the first person to help that student experience the thrill of successful accomplishment. One student expressed his gratitude by saying, "My tutors deserve roses and champagne. They are my mainstay."

It may be necessary for the tutor to prod and push. It may be necessary, as one tutor put it, to act as "the student's ego" until the student can go on alone. But the tutor is not there to do the student's work. Whatever the student's learning needs may be, the goal of tutoring is to make it possible for the student to work independently.

Schools vary greatly in how they orient, train, and assist tutors in working with students who have special problems. Without the backup of training or supervision, many tutors find it difficult and frustrating to work with students whose learning problems are severe. Without a pool of experienced tutors to choose from, students may waste time spinning their wheels. This chapter describes tutoring options, approaches to training of tutors, and some strategies for successful tutoring.

WHAT TUTORING SERVICES ARE AVAILABLE?

Most campuses offer some form of tutoring service. These services are usually given by peer tutors who are graduate students or upper-level students with superior academic records. Arrangements for a peer tutor can usually be made through an instructor or department head, or through the student affairs office. Peer tutors may be paid by the institution, through a work-study arrangement with the financial aid office, or by individual students.

Peer tutoring services work well for many students with learning difficulties. These students have found that they can explain their particular problems to their tutors. Together, they are able to develop practical strategies for doing the work.

If peer tutoring doesn't work out, or if such services are not available, a student has other options. A part-time instructor or retired professor may be willing and able to tutor in specific subject areas. Reading centers or graduate departments of special education may have instructors who can teach on an individual basis. High school special education teachers or remedial teachers in reading or math may be available to tutor after school hours. These professionals have experience and expertise that can make a difference in working with students who are having difficulties.

Professional Tutors

Professional tutors of learning disabled adolescents and adults offer a higher level of skill. These educational specialists are not always easy to find, although their ranks are growing. They often have advanced degrees in special education, with a specialty in learning disabilities.

A student looking for a professional tutor should check with local chapters of ACLD or the Orton Society, chapters of the Association of Educational Specialists (see Figure 5 in chapter, "Diagnosis: Now What?"), guidance counselors at public and private high schools, and special education departments of district school systems or universities. Private agencies that offer tutoring services may be listed in the yellow pages under "Education," "Schools," or "Tutoring." Be sure to check on the qualifications and records of private practitioners by asking for names of previous clients.

The Tutoring Network

Some communities are developing services to help match students with educational specialists who can meet their needs. One outstanding example is the Tutoring Network, formed in 1983, which refers students to educational therapists in the greater Boston area and in parts of Rhode Island, Vermont, New Hampshire, and western Massachusetts. The network screens and registers specialists, answers calls for information about other resources, and provides information about learning disabilities through conferences and a newsletter, *The Exchange.*

For more information, get in touch with the Tutoring Network, 88A Beach Street, Cohasset, Massachusetts 02025, (617) 383-6134.

SUPERVISION OF TUTORS

On some campuses, formal training programs prepare tutors to work effectively with learning disabled students. On others, orientation and preparation of tutors are loosely organized. Disabled student coordinators or other professionals may work informally with a network of tutors. Whether or not the approach to training tutors is tightly planned, ongoing supervision and communication are keys to success. The tutor needs to have access to a person (a learning disability program director, a disabled student service coordinator, a professor, a reading specialist, or a counselor) who can provide clear, accurate information about the student's strengths and weaknesses, can discuss ideas for teaching, and can help resolve problems that arise.

Regular communication provides a nerve center for tutoring services. The supervisor not only monitors progress but is often aware of subtleties that can affect the tutor-student relationship. The supervisor may know of events that could be disturbing to the student and may help the tutor cope with an overwhelmed or uncooperative student.

On one campus, the coordinator discovered that a student was balking at attending tutoring sessions because she "didn't want anyone to do my work for me." It was made clear to her that although tutoring was essential, she was considered a capable and responsible person. The tutor was there to help, not to take over. Once the air was cleared, the student was able to use tutoring sessions productively.

FORMAL TRAINING

A trained cadre of tutors is a great asset to a campus program for students with learning difficulties. Most training programs work with peer tutors and frequently seek students who are special education majors. Training programs include seminars, workshops, or minicourses on learning disabilities, conducted for tutors before each semester. These are followed by regular meetings or individual conferences between tutors and coordinators.

Initial workshops may cover information about good tutoring practices, possible effects of learning disabilities on a student's academic and social life, effective teaching and compensatory strategies, and alternative ways to fulfill course requirements. When tutors are assigned to specific students, information drawn from assessments of the student's strengths and weaknesses may also be shared, with the student's consent.

EXAMPLES OF TUTORING PROGRAMS

Achieve Program

At the Achieve Program at Southern Illinois University, peer tutors either are undergraduates in special education, specializing in learning disabilities, or are students who specialize in specific content areas. These peer tutors are supervised by a graduate student in a master's or doctoral program in learning disabilities. Tutors are required to attend training sessions at the beginning of each semester. The agenda includes confidentiality, characteristics of learning disabled students, and simulations of learning disabilities. Diagnostic summary sheets and information about the student's strongest learning modality are used to develop individualized teaching strategies.

Throughout the semester, tutors and students attend remedial sessions on paragraph and essay composition, reading comprehension, and notetaking and listening skills. They apply these skills to current assignments, papers, and exams.

Central Washington University

At Central Washington University, many of the students selected as peer tutors are learning disabled themselves. They have learned to deal successfully with their problems and can extend an extra measure of support and understanding. Initial one-day training of tutors stresses characteristics of learning disabled adults, compensatory techniques, multisensory teaching, and study skills. On-going contact with the coordinator to check on progress and problems is an essential part of the program.

107

Miami-Dade

At Miami-Dade Community College, paraprofessional tutors work on remediation and compensatory strategies with students in the learning disabilities program. Tutors are given intensive in-service training in techniques of teaching reading, writing, and math skills and in applying these skills to college-level courses. Dianne Rossman, the learning disabilities specialist, supervises daily tutoring and ongoing needs assessments and holds workshops throughout the year to sharpen tutors' skills.

University of Missouri

A special tutoring program conducted jointly by the University of Missouri at St. Louis and St. Louis Community College has trained special education graduate students to work with learning disabled adult students. Graduate students, who were previously trained only to work with children, have developed new skills in working with students enrolled in the community college. They meet with the program supervisor weekly, as a group, to discuss problems they are facing and to exchange possible solutions.

Project Success, University of Wisconsin-Oshkosh

Project Success, at the University of Wisconsin-Oshkosh, trains tutors to use the Orton Gillingham tri-modal, simultaneous, multisensory approach in teaching language skills to dyslexic students. This approach incorporates the senses of sight, hearing, and touch. Tutors are graduate and undergraduate students who work with each student for five hours every week. With a professor's permission, they also may assist students to reread exam questions that they have misread. In addition, the tutors help students with social skills, personal appearance, assertiveness, and efficient management of their time.

COMMITMENTS

Rapport and mutual respect between tutor and student underlie successful tutoring. A tutor's friendliness, ability to put the student at ease and to be relaxed and accepting all help to create a positive milieu for tutoring.

However, for tutoring to succeed, both the tutor and the student must make a commitment to the goals of tutoring. Before tutoring starts, decisions need to be made about time, place, and frequency of sessions. The choice of a site for tutoring must weigh convenience, atmosphere conducive to study, and other factors. Some tutoring programs draw up a simple contract signed by each participant, agreeing to basic responsibilities, including arriving promptly, contacting one another if it is necessary to cancel, and being prepared for each tutoring session.

The number of sessions each week varies. The LAUNCH Program at East Texas University, which has a highly structured tutoring program, requires freshmen students to be tutored for a full hour after every class hour. By the end of the second year, most students no longer need such intense tutoring, although it is available until they graduate. LAUNCH uses graduate students for this program.

STRUCTURE OF SESSIONS

Tutoring sessions have to be focused. The tutor needs a firm idea of what the course covers and what assignments are due. A copy of the syllabus, with a detailed course outline, is a must. Contact with instructors is important to determine areas in which students need help and to evaluate progress.

108

Tutors and students need to have a clear idea of what will be worked on at each session and what is expected to be completed by the next meeting. To conduct the session, tutors should know what was covered by the instructor in the last class or classes and what reading has been required. Time should be spent finding out how well the student already grasps the content and what help the student actually needs in organizing an effective study plan for learning required content.

Depending on the student's needs, sessions can include work on skills in listening, organizing notes, managing time and assignments, reading for main ideas, outlining and summarizing, devising memory techniques, and studying for and taking exams. The tutor may help a student learn compensatory strategies. For instance, if a student with auditory problems decides to tape lectures instead of taking notes, the tutor can give the student tips for listening to tapes for main and subordinate ideas.

HELP WITH SOCIAL SKILLS

Tutors can also help students whose social behavior interferes with satisfactory relationships. The tutor can model appropriate behavior, give tactful feedback, suggest alternatives to impulsive responses, and help a student anticipate and deal with difficult social situations. If tutors sense a need for more emotional support than they can give, they should discuss the problem with their supervisor or suggest sources of professional counseling.

One tutor of learning disabled students described himself as a "catalyst, stabilizer, and expediter — with a little bit of counselor added." He saw his greatest achievement as giving students a sense of their own competence and capacity to succeed.

TIPS FOR TUTORS

- Give your students your undivided and sincere attention at every session.

- Use the first meeting to set up a positive, friendly relationship.

- Set goals for each tutoring session.

- Be patient. Think of alternative ways to explain ideas and concepts. Break teaching into small units.

- Admit when you don't know all the answers.

- Use materials in simpler language — but don't use juvenile materials.

- Use a multisensory approach. Think of ways a student can visualize, hear, touch, and move around to learn a new idea or concept.

- Take breaks. Put a record on for ten minutes and relax. Go back to tutoring promptly.

- Be encouraging. When praise is due, give it; but don't give false praise.

- Keep logs of appointments. Keep track of progress.

- Emphasize the positive. Teach to success!

Note to students: Tutors work hard. A sincere "thank you" is worth a dozen roses.

USING TECHNOLOGY

"When that paper comes out of the word processor I feel really liberated. All that messy scratching is gone. I can get my thoughts out in an orderly way."

"The spelling check makes me spell like other people. You can't imagine the relief."

"When I turn on the tape recorder, I can really pay attention in class. I don't have to worry about taking notes."

Learning disabled students are finding that microcomputers, Kurzweil Reading Machines, and other technological devices are freeing them in ways they never thought possible. They now have tools to help them overcome problems with remembering, taking notes, handwriting, reading, spelling, and math skills.

COMPUTERS

The computer (also called the microcomputer, personal computer, or PC) is the exciting new kid on the block. Almost everyone's life is going to be affected in some way by this technology. Elementary school students are already becoming computer users; parents are buying PCs for home use; students are taking them to college or using the college computers; and many workplaces are computerized or are planning to make the change in the near future.

The value of computers in learning academic and occupational skills has been proven; the possibilities of computers for all disabled people, including those who are learning disabled, are impressive.

Although not much software has been developed for learning disabled students, the computer makes it possible to individualize and strengthen learning through consistent, immediate, and nonthreatening feedback. It expands writing capability, provides multisensory reinforcement through voice synthesizers, and increases memorization through drill in math and other subjects. It motivates by holding a student's interest through the use of color, motion, and sound.

Word Processors

Word processors are the big breakthrough for many learning disabled students. Word processing can be done on a word processor machine or on a computer that uses word processing software. With the use of word processors, students who were never able to hand in a neatly written, well-organized paper are now composing and editing their assignments and producing papers that they can be proud of.

By learning to use the word processor, students think more freely and do not freeze up. "It ties words to my fingers," is the way a dyslexic university professor described his reaction. Another learning disabled adult, who has a doctorate in counseling, says that with the word processor she can now write with ease and fluency for the first time in her life.

The word processor is like a notepad that never gets messy. Ideas can be gathered and organized throughout the writing process, and drafts can easily be made and changed. Erasing, crossing out, changing words or paragraphs, correcting spelling, grammar, or punctuation are simple procedures, not the exhausting process that can be so discouraging to many learning disabled people.

Programs

Most word processing programs have the capability of adding, moving, inserting, and deleting blocks of text; searching for and replacing words; formatting text; defining printing specifications; and underlining and boldfacing.

Some word processing programs have added features that are especially useful for learning disabled people. They include spelling checks, proofreading, or automatic hyphenating. If one word processor program does not have the added features (and most do not), they are available in other programs.

For people who have not learned how to type, there are very good software programs that can teach this skill. The better the typing skills, the more efficient the use of the computer. Some learning disabled students have found that they can handle the word processor keyboard, although they were never able to use a typewriter.

Portable Word Processors

Portable word processors can serve several functions. Because they are lightweight and can fit into briefcases, they can be used to take notes in class or the library. Some, like the Brother Word Processor, have built-in printers; others have compact printers that are easy to carry. The Sony Typecorder also has a built-in tape recorder.

These portable machines do not have monitors, but they do have small screens that display a line or more of print. Although they are not as versatile as a computer or a larger word processor, most portable machines can do editing functions such as deleting, inserting, and correcting spelling, grammar, and punctuation. Memory is built in, and the machines are compatible with other computers. The cost for these portable word processors is approximately $500.

Examples of Computer Usage

At LaGuardia Community College in New York (CUNY), students who take developmental English are required to write an essay of at least 300 words on an unannounced topic; they are allowed a maximum of eight major grammatical errors. Students who had failed this test three or more times were screened for learning disabilities. Some of these students were placed in an experimental ten-week writing program in which they were taught how to use a word processor and how to apply it to the content, phrasing, and organization of essays. Students learned to write and improve drafts, their writing styles became more vivid and interesting, and they experienced a sense of accomplishment after so many failures. Eighty percent passed the course — most with A's and B's.

Barbara Berkovich, director of the Individual Learning Program at the University of New England, requires all of the students in her program to learn how to use the Apple. If they cannot type, they self-teach with the Apple Writer program.

A learning disabled adult who has his own photography business reported that he had tried several computers in his organization. The breakthrough for him was the Apple Macintosh, which he thinks is the easiest computer to learn.

KURZWEIL READING MACHINE

Dyslexic students are beginning to benefit from a machine originally designed for blind or visually impaired people — the Kurzweil Reading Machine (KRM). This machine can scan and read aloud English text set in any one of 300 typefaces. It can also read five languages. The KRM is being used on some college campuses (usually in libraries or multimedia centers), as well as in public school systems and public libraries.

Although it takes time to learn how to operate the KRM, once students have mastered the technique, they can read any books that are not on tape. This enables students to do research or additional reading that has not been previously taped by one of the recording services. It is especially advantageous if students can get second copies of the material they are using in the KRM and follow along with the machine. This way they visually reinforce what they hear. The KRM is particularly useful for learning disabled students who have good listening and comprehension skills but are weak in decoding and spelling.

There are some drawbacks. It takes about fifteen hours to learn to use the machine, and this is hard for an already pressed student.

Because KRM use for learning disabled students is still in the early stages, information on its advantages and disadvantages is limited. But anyone who is interested can contact the local library or university, or write to Kurzweil Computer Products, Inc., 185 Albany Street, Cambridge, Massachusetts 07139.

PLAYBACK EQUIPMENT

Tape recorders are becoming standardized equipment for many learning disabled students who use them to listen to taped books, to take notes in class, or to dictate answers to questions, assignments, or papers. They can be purchased in many types of stores. In some cases, students who are vocational rehabilitation clients might arrange to get them through their counselors.

A recent innovative tape recorder now on the market is a unit called the Variable Speech Control tape recorder. This machine sells for approximately $100 and is now available through Radio Shack stores. It is a regular tape machine but has the capacity to play back any tape twice as fast without changing the voice pitch. This could be a major advantage for students who depend on taping lectures and then have to allow time to listen to them.

SOURCES OF INFORMATION

The growing enthusiasm over the use of computers and other assistive devices for disabled people is reflected in the development of resources that students, parents, teachers, and employers can use to check out appropriate technology. Following is a list of national organizations that provide information about computers and other machines and their adaptability for specific disabilities. They also answer questions about suitable software programs.

• The Center for Special Education Technology, funded by the U.S. Department of Education, is jointly sponsored by Council for Exceptional Children, JWK International, and LINC Resources. The center's toll-free number is 1-800-345-TECH (in Virginia it is 703-750-0500). Hours are 1 p.m. to 6 p.m. EST.

• SRI reviews software programs for handicapped children and youth. Its toll-free number is 1-800-327-5892 (9 a.m. to 5 p.m. EST).

• Closing the Gap evaluates software and hardware for handicapped users. It also publishes a newsletter. For information, write to Closing the Gap, P.O. Box 68, Henderson, Minnesota 56044.

• ABLEDATA has a computerized listing of commercially available products for all types of disabilities. The address is ABLEDATA, National Rehabilitation Information Center, The Catholic University of America, 4407 Eighth Street, N.E., Washington, D.C. 20017, (202) 635-5822.

TIPS TO STUDENTS

- As with any investment of time or money, it is important to determine what your needs are. Do you need a computer, or would a word processor be appropriate? Is there someone who can show you how to use the computer? Some computers take time to learn. Manuals are complicated. Screen colors vary; some are easier to read than others. Ask what colors are available.

- If you buy a tape recorder, do you have the time to listen to your lectures and have you learned how to take notes? If you think that a Kurzweil machine can help you, is there someone on your campus, such as a librarian, who can teach you how to use it?

- Once you establish need or possible need for a computer or other technological aid, then investigate your options. If you cannot have access to these machines through the DSS office, library, or media center, and if you decide to purchase one, then make the rounds of stores. Explain what you think you are interested in and what your particular problems are. Most salespeople are very willing to advise you.

- Talk with friends who use any of these technical devices, or check with local computer clubs (ask a dealer for information about clubs). Don't forget the hotlines mentioned earlier in the chapter. Time spent exploring will not be wasted.

- If you are eligible for DSS services, talk with the DSS coordinator or vocational rehabilitation counselor about trying out an aid. Find out if the cost can be covered by vocational rehabilitation. If the device you are interested in is not covered, you will have to decide whether to purchase your own or use equipment in libraries or multimedia centers.

- One final comment. Familiarity and comfort in using computers or other technical equipment gives you an additional job skill.

Additional Reading About Technology

Microcomputer Resource Book for Special Education, by Deloris Hagen. Reston Publishing Company, Inc. Reston, Virginia 22091. (207 pages, $15.95) 1984

Effective Microcomputer-Assisted Instruction for the Vocational Education of Special Needs Students, by Lloyd Tindall and John Gugerty. The Vocational Study Center, University of Wisconsin-Madison, Publications Unit, 265 Educational Sciences Building, 1025 West Johnson Street, Madison, Wisconsin 53706. (343 pages, $25.00) 1983

Computer Technology for the Handicapped: Proceedings from the 1984 Closing the Gap Conference, edited by Michael Gergen and Deloris Hagen. (For a copy, write to Closing the Gap, P.O. Box 68, Henderson, Minnesota 56044.)

THE ART OF COORDINATION

"I felt like a thousand pounds had been taken off my back. I finally had someone who was there for me."

This is how one student described the help he received from the coordinator of services for learning disabled students on his campus. Others have described coordinators as a lifeline — the first person to give them the support they needed to discover how to use their strengths.

For accommodations to work, coordination is essential. Key roles are played by coordinators of services for learning disabled students, administrators, and faculty members. Parents, diagnosticians, counselors, and tutors are also involved in identifying, planning, and following up on appropriate services. In the final analysis, the most important role is played by students themselves.

116

THE ROLE OF THE COORDINATOR

Coordinators of services for learning disabled students are pivotal to the success of accommodations. They must be able to work with each student, assess needs, and develop and implement appropriate plans. Coordinators act as liaison with faculty and administrators — raising awareness of learning disabilities, explaining accommodations, intervening on behalf of specific students, and winning institutional support for services. They respond to questions about campus services from prospective applicants and counsel with parents before and after admissions.

Where a special program for learning disabled students exists, coordinators also discuss admission of qualified applicants with admissions counselors. To do these many tasks, coordinators need a combination of tact, empathy, knowledge of learning disabilities, interpersonal skills, and administrative ability.

Who has the role of coordinator depends on the institution. On most postsecondary campuses, it is the disabled student services (DSS) director or a DSS staff member. It may be a learning disability specialist, the director of a separate program for learning disabled students, a counselor at a learning center, a faculty member, or an administrator.

We use the word *coordinator* to refer to the person on campus who is designated to work with learning disabled students in obtaining accommodations and dealing with related problems.

Relationship with Students

Students find their way to the coordinator's office by different routes. A faculty member or counselor may recommend that a student contact the DSS office; an admissions officer may refer the student to the coordinator during the admissions process; or a student may initiate the contact.

Frequently, learning disabled students knock on the coordinator's door only after a long period of feeling overwhelmed. They may be unable to admit defeat or be fearful of the stigma of being labeled *learning disabled*. Some may be adults who have returned to the campus and, for the first time, realize that they are learning disabled. They may be grieving about the knowledge that something is wrong with them, hoping for a cure, and fearful that somehow the disability will hurt their jobs or their marriages.

The coordinator must be able to see past the defensiveness and anger that may be present, acknowledge the pain, understand the fear of experiencing repeated failure and rejection, and perceive feelings of self-worthlessness. Starting with the first meeting, the coordinator must communicate respect for the student's worth and belief in the student's capacity to manage his or her life.

The Need to Gather Information

The coordinator's first task is to gather information. If the student has recently been diagnosed as learning disabled, the coordinator usually asks for the diagnostic report, including recent assessments of the student's academic skills, learning styles, and social and emotional needs. If no such documentation exists, and if the coordinator suspects that a learning disability is at the root of the student's problems, testing is usually recommended. The testing may be done by the coordinator's office, by campus testing services, or by an agency in the community. (More information on types of tests that may be given, and how they are used, is in the chapter, "Diagnosis: Now What?")

Even before the test results are in, it may be necessary to work with the student on crisis management. Immediate arrangements may have to be made to drop a course or to begin intensive counseling. At the HELDS Project, in Central Washington University, students in danger of failing were placed on "academic protection" by the director while the problem was investigated and solutions were sought. On most campuses, the coordinator has access to a network of support services that can offer temporary safety.

Planning

Once diagnostic results are in, the coordinator's job is to help the student understand the information in clear, nontechnical terms. At this point, students need to be reassured that having a learning disability is not the end of the world and that there are ways to cope with their problems.

This might also be the time to help a student reassess goals and choices. Does a student need more remedial work? Is the current program the right one? Is the level of support sufficient? If the decision is to continue in this setting, then plans must be made for needed support services and/or accommodations. These plans should be reviewed regularly.

Use of Resources

To implement plans, the coordinator must make use of resources on and off campus. These include academic support services (math labs, writing workshops, study skills seminars, developmental reading courses); courses in the regular curriculum that can strengthen a student's social skills and personal development (communications, assertiveness training, psychology and human development); and tutoring, counseling and self-help programs. Cost effectiveness requires that existing resources be fully used.

Often, coordinators themselves work intensively with students in building academic and social strengths. They may give individual assistance in teaching study skills strategies, counsel students on career goals and interpersonal problems, and supervise tutors. A coordinator may sit in on a lab or a class to help a student figure out how to get around a problem.

Obtaining Accommodations

To obtain course work accommodations, students must be able to explain their needs to instructors. The coordinator's sensitive leadership can help students learn to communicate information about their learning disabilities in a positive way and to discuss their needs with clarity and confidence.

Many coordinators set the stage for communication between students and instructors by writing letters to instructors — with the student's consent. Letters usually include general information about learning disabilities, explain the student's specific problem, and make clear that coordinators are available for further information. Frequently, students themselves bring the letters to instructors.

118

On some campuses, the coordinator and the student may meet jointly with an instructor. In that way, a student who is not ready to be a self-advocate can learn to negotiate and do it alone next time. Frequently, coordinators use role playing to prepare students for situations that inevitably produce tension and uncertainty.

One Coordinator's Approach

At Northern Virginia Community College (Annandale campus), Carol Sullivan, Special Service Team Counselor, has developed a successful system for encouraging student self-advocacy. She meets with the student to talk over problems and to review diagnostic reports and records.

Together, she and the student take a good look at the student's strengths — including such traits as strong motivation, ability to analyze problems, and a talent for fresh and original ideas. They then analyze the student's weaker areas, such as difficulties with short-term memory, spelling, punctuation, or notetaking. All of the strengths and weaknesses are listed on a worksheet, which is also used to make notes on accommodations that would equalize the student's chances of success.

With the worksheet as a guide, students fill out a Disability Data Sheet on their own, listing their strengths, their weaker areas, and accommodations that would be helpful. Carol Sullivan sees this data sheet as a way to break the ice. At meetings with each of their instructors, students present the data sheets and explain their needs. They also distribute a handout describing learning disabilities. (For a sample data sheet, see Figure 16.)

Students in the Northern Virginia program receive a page of tips for negotiating, reminding them that in asking for understanding, they must understand the needs of instructors, many of whom have never had a learning disabled student in their class. If an instructor needs more background information about learning disabilities, the counselor provides it. If an instructor is unwilling to make requested accommodations, students are asked to contact the counselor.

Relationship with Faculty

Many faculty members are unaware of learning disabilities or have misconceptions about the handicap. Some may believe the myth that learning disabled people are retarded and do not belong in a postsecondary program. They may express the feeling that accommodations are cheating—a way of getting away with doing less work.

On campuses throughout the country, coordinators are working to overcome misconceptions and are enlisting the cooperation of faculty members. They have developed excellent fact sheets and brochures for distribution to faculty, describing learning disabilities in clear, plain terms. In addition, coordinators hold workshops, in-service training, and informal meetings with faculty, at which they simulate learning disabilities, explain how learning disabled people learn, and discuss how various accommodations work.

Disability Data Sheet

NORTHERN VIRGINIA COMMUNITY COLLEGE — ANNANDALE CAMPUS

Date September 19, 1985

To: Instructor Professor Smith

From: Student John Doe

I have been identified as having the following disability/disabilities:

Learning Disabilities

My areas of strength include:

Motivation, verbal expression, good follow through on assignments,

good problem solving skills, abstract reasoning, practical judgment,

and auditory processing.

My weaker areas include:

Spelling, note-taking, grammar and punctuation, writing mechanics,

visual processing, visual memory, reading speed.

To equalize my chances of success in the classroom I would benefit from
the following accommodations:

use of tape recorder

additional time to complete tests

have tests read to me, if needed

Note to the Instructor
From: Carol Sullivan, Annandale Campus Special Services Team Counselor

This data sheet has been prepared through consultation with me. This information should be considered confidential. The accommodations as listed above are among those identified in Section 504 of the National Rehabilitation Act of 1973 which deals with non-discrimination of disabled students in postsecondary settings. You and the student may want to negotiate the options that will be best for both of you in meeting the accommodations. The Learning Lab (Ext. 3221) is an excellent resource for students taking tests untimed and/or having tests read. Please contact me (Ext. 3211) if you have any additional questions or concerns regarding this student. Thank you for your consideration of this student's special needs.

_____   _____
Carol Sullivan   Date

FIGURE 16

Building a Network

Gradually coordinators build a network of supportive faculty members, who, in turn, use the coordinators for help with learning disabled students in their classes. Ongoing dialogue creates an environment of trust and cooperation in which referrals can be made, problems resolved, and appropriate accommodations implemented. As faculty members get involved in working out accommodations for students in their own classrooms, myths disappear and empathic understanding of learning disabilities grows.

Relationship with Parents

Parents frequently need support when their son or daughter enters a postsecondary program. On some campuses, coordinators are available to counsel parents during this transition period.

At the University of Arizona, Eleanor Harner, the Director of SALT (Special Academic Learning Techniques), says, "Parents of learning disabled students hurt. They have been through so much to bring their child to this point. They are fearful that something will go wrong and, therefore, they stay close to be there to catch their child if he or she falls." She meets regularly with parents to discuss their son or daughter's progress and to help parents deal with the difficult process of letting go.

The Program for Learning Disabled College Students at Adelphi University (New York) sponsors groups for parents of students in the program. Parents learn about the program and are relieved of some of their anxiety through communication with the staff. The program also offers family counseling for parents, as well as for other members of the family, to help with changing relationships.

The Goal

The art of coordination requires that coordinators know how to work with many people to facilitate a student's success. However, the ultimate goal is to enable students to take responsibility for resolving their own problems, getting accommodations, and becoming active participants in their education.

THE ROLE OF THE STUDENT

"It is the student who has to bite the bullet and, ultimately, take responsibility for himself or herself. We (coordinators) can pave the way and give support. But the student has to decide what needs to be done — and pursue it."— Linda Donnels, George Washington University.

No matter how many accommodations or services are available on a campus, it is the learning disabled student's responsibility to obtain and use them.

Some learning disabled students have already taken the first steps. They know their academic strengths as well as their stumbling blocks and they know what accommodations to ask for. Other students must go through a crisis before they begin to understand and resolve their problems. For many who do not know why they are failing, the shame, the confusion, and the panic can be immobilizing. For others, the fear of disclosure or the lack of information about where to turn for help can also keep them from taking action.

There are solutions. But the search for them must start with the student assuming responsibility. This involves understanding one's problems, explaining them in a simple and clear way, and becoming a self-advocate. None of these are easy tasks, but for some, the most difficult one is self-advocacy.

121

Self-Advocacy

To be a self-advocate means being able to articulate needs and negotiate for assistance. It means being assertive in a diplomatic way. It means choosing words that accurately describe what accommodations are needed and why. It means expressing confidence in one's ability to do the work.

Some students find the task comfortable. Their instructors are easy to talk with and may already be sensitive to problems of learning disabled students. Other instructors simply need reassurance that students will fulfill the course requirements.

For many students, negotiation can be scary and unnerving, but it can be learned from DSS coordinators, counselors, or other students who have been through the mill. As discussed earlier, coordinators have developed instructional material and techniques to help students work out their individual situations. Form letters, checklists, documentation, role playing, and modeling are all in the coordinators' tool box.

What if there is no DSS Coordinator?

For students who do not have access to structured guidance and services on their campuses, learning self-advocacy is more difficult. But even in this situation, the more self-knowledge the student has, the better the possibility of explaining the disability; the more information about learning disabilities the student can bring to the instructor, the better the chance for starting a dialogue. (This book might help the instructor understand the students' problems.)

If students are willing to share the problem with other students, they might discover ways to work out some of their difficulties, such as forming study groups or finding students who are willing to tutor them or check their notes and papers for correct spelling.

Successful Negotiating

As in any negotiating, attitude is important. An angry, bitter student will be less likely to convince an instructor of the need for alternatives than will a self-assured, cooperative student. Successful negotiating depends on students' knowledge of their learning styles and their ability to assure instructors that granting accommodations does not mean granting special advantages. Determined, motivated students who are successful in negotiating will gain coping skills that can be used no matter when or where problems arise.

New Challenges

As learning disabled adults move through postsecondary education, their role is constantly challenged by new courses and new tasks. As one college graduate, David, put it, "We learning disabled people are always navigating new waters." David's undergraduate years were tightly scheduled to allow time to work with readers, to write and rewrite notes and outlines, to dictate to scribes, to manage a part-time job, and to keep up with other demands of college life. He is an example of the tremendously hard work most learning disabled people must do and the long hours of study they must invest to succeed. He and others like him become skilled in finding creative solutions to problems, in taking risks, and in testing their resolve. Their greatest accommodation is to keep trying, despite the odds . . . whatever the downs, to get up and try again.

122

6

HOW TO KEEP THE GLARE OFF THE CHALKBOARD

HOW TO KEEP THE GLARE OFF THE CHALKBOARD

The environment in which teaching takes place can make a difference in a learning disabled student's ability to participate and keep up with course work. Seemingly little things can prevent the student from picking up essential information, following the flow of a course, carrying out assignments, or even knowing what is expected.

The sun may glare on the chalkboard, making it hard for the student with visual perception problems to distinguish letters. Or the instructors may speak too softly or too rapidly, making it difficult for the student with an auditory perception problem to comprehend a point or catch the announcement of a quiz.

Learning disabled students, struggling hard to listen, take notes, and remember all at once, may be bombarded by unclear perceptions and fail to get the theme of a lecture. Tension mounts, intensifying the impact of the disability and the likelihood of mistakes.

This confusing scenario can be changed by the classroom instructor. A range of techniques can foster full participation not only by learning disabled students, but by other students as well. These techniques are not complex. They include course work organization, clear expression of ideas, selection of appropriate materials, and opportunities to demonstrate knowledge in alternative ways.

125

Most of these classroom techniques are tried-and-true approaches for effective teaching. But they have the power to create accessible classrooms in which expectations are clear; students' questions and problems are respected; and communication is informal, relaxed, and often mixed with humor.

CREATING FACULTY AWARENESS

The HELDS Project

One university's effort to create an accessible learning environment resulted in a campus-wide awareness program. At Central Washington University, the HELDS project, under the direction of Myrtle Snyder, sensitized faculty members in all disciplines to problems of learning disabled students. Sessions about learning disabilities were held monthly for one year. Experts in the field and learning disabled adults discussed experiences, and faculty members explored ways to teach so that students could use, not lose, their potential.

Since that time, faculty members included in the project have shared insights with their colleagues. A series of pamphlets, written by professors in the HELDS project, describe successful techniques and provide a model for other colleges.

New River Community College

The DSS coordinator at New River Community College (Dublin, VA) spent a summer working with a committee of faculty members to develop ways of identifying and helping learning disabled students. They produced a handbook, *Working with Learning Disabled Students*

at New River Community College, that includes descriptions of learning disabilities and concrete ways to teach learning disabled students specific subjects, such as social sciences, mathematics and data processing, secretarial sciences, drafting, and electronic technologies. For further information or a copy of this handbook, contact Jeananne Dixon, Learning Achievement Program, New River Community College, Dublin, VA 24084, (703) 674-4121.

IN THE CLASSROOM

Classwork techniques described in this chapter come from the repertoires of HELDS participants and faculty members on other campuses who were interviewed for this project.

Course Work Organization

Learning disabled students need structure. They need help distinguishing main and supporting ideas, seeing the relationship of parts to the whole. Other students benefit, too, when organization of course work is clear. Following are suggestions that can help.

Detailed Syllabus. A detailed syllabus helps students plan their time. The syllabus should include course themes and objectives, weekly topics, classroom activities, required reading and writing assignments, and dates of tests, quizzes, and vacations. A complete course calendar of this type increases the learning disabled student's ability to understand the sequence of topics and the relationship of assignments to main themes.

In addition, the syllabus gives students a head start in arranging for taped texts, readers, or test-taking alternatives. HELDS participants and other educators recommend that the syllabus be available by preregistration for learning disabled students.

Leaving a blank space for brief notes in the syllabus, after the outline for each week's work, can be helpful. One professor requires students to fill in the blanks with the key words learned that week—creating a ready-made review sheet for exams.

Rules Clarification. Rules should be clarified in advance: how students will be graded, whether makeup tests or rewrites of papers are allowed, what the conditions are for withdrawing from a course or getting an incomplete. These rules should be listed in the syllabus.

Reviews and Previews. It is extremely helpful if the professor briefly reviews the major points of the previous lecture or class and highlights main points to be covered that day. If possible, reviews and previews should be outlined in more than one way: written on the board or flip chart, presented orally, and/or outlined in a handout.

Study Aids. These aids can include study questions for exams, clarification of content to be covered, and format to be used. Professor Karl E. Zink (Central Washington) gives his freshman English grammar students a pretest before the final exam, with immediate feedback, to permit practice and reduce anxiety.

Classroom Communication

There are many ways that classroom learning can be reinforced. They all involve communication. Following are some ideas that have been used successfully.

Multisensory Teaching. Learning disabled students learn more readily if material is presented in as many modalities as possible (seeing, hearing, speaking, touching). Can a concept be explained in more than one way? Can it be presented visually as well as orally? Can it be demonstrated? Can students move around, participating physically while learning? Can they absorb the information through hands-on practice?

Depending on what is being presented, this concept has exciting possibilities — limited only by imagination and enhanced by trial and experience. Making information available in different modes helps students to be active learners and to use their strongest channel to get information.

Visualization. The more a student can visualize as well as hear what is presented, the better the material will be understood. Professor Ronald Warners at Curry College (Massachusetts) uses a strongly visual approach in his teaching. In his freshman course on music, he explains the structure of a piece of music and has his students draw the patterns they hear in the form of graphs. As a result of visualizing the sounds, he has found that students develop a sophisticated sense of musical composition and are able to read music criticism far beyond their expected reading level.

Visual aids can include overhead projectors, films, carousel slide projectors, chalkboards, flip charts, computer graphics, and illustrations of written text.

Color. The visual impact is even sharper in color, and color coding is an aid to learning. For instance, in teaching respiration technology, everything related to the body's respiratory system might be highlighted in green and the digestive system in orange.

Tactility. Opportunities for touching and handling materials that relate to ideas can strengthen learning. Professor John Herum, who participated in the HELDS project, has his English composition students bring scissors and tape to class, cutting and pasting parts of their compositions to achieve a logical plotting of thoughts.

Motoric Learning. Motor activities and games can be used to learn basic skills. At Ventura Community College (California), Jeffrey Barsch teaches "tennis ball math." Numbers and arithmetic signs

127

are taped to the floor. The student bounces the tennis ball to the correct numbers, signs, and total. This technique fixes multiplication and other facts in the student's memory. Another multiplication trick invented by Barsch is to have students touch, say, and write numbers to the beat of a metronome.

This alternative approach, and others used at the Ventura Learning Skills Program, avoids repeating unsuccessful remedial techniques.

Announcements. Whenever possible, announcements should be in both oral and written form. This is especially true of changes in assignments or exams.

Distinct Speech. An instructor who speaks at an even speed, emphasizing important points with pauses, gestures, and other body language, helps students follow classroom presentations. If there are three points, it helps to say, "my first point is. . ." and "now, the second important point," — to keep the sequence in the student's mind.

Eye Contact. This is important in maintaining attention and encouraging participation.

Demonstrations and Role Plays. These activities can make ideas come alive and are particularly helpful to the student who has to move around in order to learn.

Concrete Teaching. New concepts need to be taught in as concrete a way as possible. A traditional classroom approach is to learn theory first and then practical applications. It is often easier for learning disabled students to learn the theory after its practical application.

Analogies. Analogies to everyday life can make abstract concepts more understandable. For example, the rules of punctuation can be compared to traffic signals: the red light, a period; the blinking yellow light, a comma. Without these signals, a sentence can be as confusing as a traffic jam.

Technical Vocabulary. It is a good idea to limit the teaching of new vocabulary to words used in a specific lecture or exercise. Simple drawings and large print can clarify definitions in handouts. Students also need to know how to spell terms that are used. Tips on introducing new words include:

Breaking words into parts. Long technical words can be better understood if broken into parts: *hyperparathyroidsm — hyper para thyroidism.*

Using the multisensory approach. In teaching technical terminology, Dr. Stanley Steineman, Associate Professor of Dental Hygiene, New York City Technical College, uses these steps: Students write the word, say it aloud, and trace letters of the new terms with their fingers. This method is based on the highly successful Orton-Gillingham multisensory technique for teaching reading to dyslexic children and adults.

Practice. Once a technical term is introduced, it should be used repeatedly in speaking and writing. If two or three terms mean the same thing, the instructor needs to teach the meaning of all of them. The most common of these terms should be used consistently, because inconsistency is a major problem for learning disabled students. Students in an education class, for example, need to know which of the many terms describing learning disabilities will be used. In an auto mechanics class, students need to know that an accelerator can also be called a gas or a foot pedal.

Accessibility of Course Materials

Learning disabled students may need help in using printed course materials. Instructors can do several things to translate text materials into the student's best channel for learning or to compensate for difficulties in coping with print.

Advance Copies of Textbooks. For students who must get printed materials taped, professors can have the bookstore order texts sufficiently ahead of time to allow taping before the semester begins. In some cases, students will have to purchase two copies of the book for taping purposes (required by Recording For The Blind).

Well-Organized Texts. If professors are selecting a new text for a course, and two copies are comparable, it helps to be aware that some texts are better organized than others. Learning disabled students, as well as other students, benefit from texts that include final chapter summaries, subheadings, effective use of graphics, glossaries explaining technical language in plain English, and good indexes.

Cues for Reading Comprehension. Tips for comprehension can help students find the main ideas and supporting details in difficult reading passages. Some instructors prepare handouts that outline a chapter and show students how to identify the author's key points. Study guides, with questions for students to answer, can help students practice unlocking the meaning of heavy reading assignments. (See chapter, "Reading Comprehension.")

Use of Large Type. Instructors can let the coordinator know when it might help to have specific passages retyped in large type or put on tape.

OTHER TIPS

- Allow time for students to work in small groups to practice, to solve problems and to review work.

- Break down teaching into small units. Short daily reading assignments will help the learning disabled student learn how to budget and organize study time. Build up to longer units.

- Teach students memory tricks and acronyms as study aids. Use examples from current course work, and encourage students to create their own tricks.

- Encourage learning disabled students to sit in the front of the classroom where they can hear well and have a clear view of the chalkboard.

- Give learning disabled students the chance to repeat verbally what they have learned — as a check for accuracy. This can take place during class discussion time or after class.

- Be aware that some learning disabled students are particularly self-conscious about talking in front of groups. Ask these students questions with short answers, or start the answer, trying not to interrupt once the student begins to respond.

- Give feedback. Errors need to be corrected as quickly as possible. If the student does well, praise is important to build confidence.

SPECIAL TIPS FOR VOCATIONAL INSTRUCTORS

- Label machinery, equipment, tools, and other workplace materials to help students read technical terms. Also label sizes, such as a two-quart pan or a size five drill bit.

- Use half-pint, quart, and gallon containers to develop understanding of volume measurements.

- Have students use devices such as pedometers, optical tape measures, or other remote measuring devices.

Catalogs of equipment that might be helpful for learning disabled people are

Tools, Equipment and Machinery Adapted for the Vocational Education and Employment of Handicapped People. (For details, see reading list at end of the chapter.)

The American Foundation for the Blind Catalog of Adapted Equipment. This free catalog, which describes tools designed for blind students or workers, can be useful for learning disabled students. Tools include measurement devices with tactile markings and liquid level indicators that sound a tone when the liquid being poured reaches a specific level. For a copy of this catalog, write to The American Foundation for the Blind, 15 West 16th Street, New York, New York 10011.

IDENTIFYING AND HELPING STUDENTS

No matter how much preparation a faculty member does to make his or her classroom accessible, there are often students in need of additional help. Some are reluctant to identify themselves; others do not know they are learning disabled. An instructor who can spot a student with learning disabilities may be able to avert a crisis. (Figure 17 is an example of a checklist used for identifying learning disabled students. In using it, remember that it is not a complete list of characteristics nor does it necessarily indicate presence of a learning disability.)

What Can Be Done?

Whether it is a crisis or a chronic problem, many instructors find it hard to bring up a suspected learning disability with an individual student or know what suggestions to make. What can be done?

Announcements. It is a good idea to make written and oral announcements to the entire class at the beginning of each semester, stating that help is available for learning disabled students. One instructor uses the following message.

"Please let me know right away if you have a documented learning disability that requires special arrangements to be made, such as seating, adjustments in testing situations, providing copies of notes, or other accommodations. Talk to me as soon as possible, after class or during my office hours."

Any announcement to the class about accommodations should include the name, address, and telephone number of the campus office that coordinates services for learning disabled students. Students should be made aware of what that office does, and whom to contact.

Availability. The more available an instructor is just before or after class, or during office hours, the more chance there is to raise concerns in a nonthreatening way. The better the communication, the easier it is to make a referral, if needed.

Use of Campus Resources. Instructors who need advice regarding a student's problems or who want to refer students for extra help can contact disabled student services offices (DSS) or other academic support services to get advice and suggestions. Diagnostic information can be shared either by the student or by DSS, with the student's consent. As instructors become familiar with individual strengths and weaknesses, they can reach agreement with their students on the best way to deal with classroom difficulties.

A Two-Way Street. Creating an accessible classroom is not a one-way street. Students need to remember that it is not necessarily easy for the instructor to make accommodations. The instructor may not understand the problems of a learning disabled student. As discussed more fully in the chapter, "The Art of Coordination," students themselves must take the initiative in giving the instructor a clear idea of the kinds of compensatory strategies they need.

FACULTY RESPONSE

Faculty members who work with learning disabled students have reported with pleasure that the experience heightened their awareness of individual learning styles and increased their ability to communicate with all of their students. Ronald Warners, Professor of Fine Arts and Music at Curry, said it this way:

Attending to the special needs of LD students has actually been the primary source of my development as a teaching professional, and the result has been greater effectiveness as a teacher of persons of all characteristics.

LEARNING DISABILITY CHECKLIST

A learning disabled person may exhibit several or many of the following behaviors:

☐ Demonstrates marked difficulty in reading, writing, spelling and/or using numerical concepts in contrast with average to superior skills in other areas.

☐ Has poorly formed handwriting — may print instead of using script; write with inconsistent slant; have difficulty with certain letters; space words unevenly.

☐ Has trouble listening to a lecture and taking notes at the same time.

☐ Is easily distracted by background noise or visual stimulation; unable to pay attention; may appear to be hurried and anxious in one-to-one meetings.

☐ Has trouble understanding or following directions; is easily overwhelmed by a multiplicity of directions or overstimulation; may not understand information the first time it is given and may need to have it repeated.

☐ Confuses similar letters such as *"b"* and *"d,"* or *"p"* and *"q"*; confuses the order of letters in words repeating *was* for *saw*, *teh* for *the*; may misspell the same word several different ways in the same composition.

☐ Omits or adds words, particularly when reading aloud.

☐ Confuses similar numbers such as 3 and 8, or 6 and 9, or changes the sequence of numbers such as 14 and 41; has difficulty copying numbers accurately and working with numbers in columns.

☐ Exhibits an inability to stick to simple schedules; repeatedly forgets things; loses or leaves possessions; and generally seems "personally disorganized."

☐ Appears clumsy or poorly coordinated.

☐ Seems disorganized in space — confuses up and down, right and left; gets lost in buildings; is disoriented when familiar environment is rearranged.

☐ Seems disoriented in time, i.e. is often late to class, unusually early for appointments, or unable to finish assignments in the standard time period.

☐ Displays excessive anxiety, anger, or depression because of the inability to cope with school or social situations.

☐ Misinterprets the subtleties in language, tone of voice, or social situations.

This checklist was developed by Linda Donnels and Karen Franklin, George Washington University.

FIGURE 17

Additional Reading About Classroom Techniques

A Talking Mouth Speaks, by Barbara M. Chesler. (For copy, write to A Song, P.O. Box 22206, Sacramento, California 95822.) (32 pages, $3.00 prepaid) 1980

Classroom Adaptations and Instructional Strategies for Handicapped Students in Vocational Education Programs, by Sandra Dupuis, Special Needs/Interagency Coordinator. Career Education Resources Center, Erickson Hall, Michigan State University, East Lansing, Michigan 48824. (172 pages, $7.00) 1984

Classroom Strategies to Aid the Disabled Learner, by Jean Abbott. Educators Publishing Service, 75 Moulton Street, Cambridge, Massachusetts 02238. (71 pages, $7.05) 1978

HELDS Booklet Series, by Myrtle C. Snyder. Educational Opportunities Program, Central Washington University, Ellinsburg, Washington 98926. (17 booklets in series, $20.00) 1982

Promoting Successful Mainstreaming: Reasonable Classroom Accommodations for Learning Disabled Students, by Stanley Fagin, Donna L. Graves, and Diane Tessler-Switlick. In-Service Training Unit, Montgomery County Public Schools, Lynnbrook Center, 8001 Lynnbrook Drive, Bethesda, Maryland 20814. (75 pages, $1.95) 1984

Puzzled About Educating Special Needs Students? A Handbook on Modifying Vocational Curricula for Handicapped Students, by Lloyd Tindall, John Gugerty, and others. The Vocational Studies Center, University of Wisconsin-Madison, Publications Unit, 265 Educational Sciences Building, 1025 West Johnson Street, Madison, Wisconsin 53706. (486 pages, $30.00) 1980
User's Guide for Puzzled About Educating Special Needs Students? Available at the same address. (83 pages, $8.00) 1980

The 4 Mat System, Teaching to Learning Styles with Right/Left Brain Techniques, by Bernice McCarthy. Excel, Inc. 200 W Station, Barrington, Illinois 60010. (220 pages, $25.95) 1984

Tools, Equipment, and Machinery Adapted for the Vocational Education and Employment of Handicapped People, by John Gugerty and Lloyd Tindall. The Vocational Studies Center, University of Wisconsin-Madison, Publications Unit, 265 Educational Sciences Building, 1025 West Johnson Street, Madison, Wisconsin 53706. (787 pages, $32.00) 1981
Supplement for **Tools, Equipment, and Machinery** available at same address. (671 pages, $32.00) 1983

Working With Special Needs Students: A Handbook for Vocational Education Teachers, by Douglas H. Gill. The Division of Program Development, Office of Vocational Education, Georgia Department of Education, Atlanta, Georgia 30334. (100 pages, $5.00) 1982

Film Strips

Whatever It Takes, by Lloyd Tindall, John Gugerty, Jeffrey Hamm, and Elizabeth Carlson. A series of three sound film strips on modifying vocational programs through the experiences of an automotive instructor. (45 minutes for the series, $90.00) 1980

A Wider Circle, by Lloyd Tindall, John Gugerty, Jeffrey Hamm, and Elizabeth Carlson. A film strip sequel to **Whatever It Takes,** on cooperation between educators, vocational rehabilitators, and parents. (45 minutes, $90.00) 1983

Both film strips can be ordered from The Vocational Studies Center, University of Wisconsin-Madison, Publications Unit, 265 Educational Sciences Building, 1025 West Johnson Street, Madison, Wisconsin 53706.

7

A BAG OF TRICKS: STUDY SKILLS

OVERVIEW: STUDY SKILLS

John knows his history course material. He can argue points in class with the professor and discuss the subject in detail with other students; yet he cannot get his thoughts on paper in the essay exams. Betsy's restlessness and distractibility make it hard for her to sit through a lecture, much less take notes. Cynthia never has enough time to study for her exams.

Cramming for exams, staring at the same page for hours without understanding a word, not knowing how to write an assignment even though the ideas are there, and never having enough time to complete an assignment, are experiences common to everyone. For most people, the panic can be overcome; but for some, this is a consistent reaction every time an exam is scheduled or an assignment is due. Students who are willing to seek help in developing better ways to study will find that the extra time required is well spent.

STUDY SKILLS COURSES

Many colleges now have study skills courses that are available to all students. Study skills can mean teaching strategies to read for comprehension, to write essays and exams, to take notes, and to listen effectively. Study skills can also mean learning to manage time, set priorities, and improve daily living and social skills. The content can be given as part of one course, such as an English composition class; it can be presented in a separate course or in workshops; or it can be taught in tutorial sessions.

Study skills programs can usually be found in English, psychology, or education departments, in learning centers, or through the disabled student services office. Learning disabled students are frequently referred to these programs if no special courses exist for them. But too often, this is not enough for students like John, Betsy, or Cynthia, who need more specialized help.

How and where these students who learn differently can get study skills help depend on the campus and the student. On many campuses, teachers, advisors, coordinators of services for disabled students, or learning disability specialists are working very hard to devise ways to help these students.

THE AMERICAN UNIVERSITY: ONE SCHOOL'S ANSWER

The American University in Washington, D.C., is an example of how one school is reaching out to help students who need to learn more effective ways to study. Through an academic department, American University is offering a for-credit course, College Reading, with special sections for students who have learning disabilities. The special sections were developed by Faith Leonard, director of the Learning Services program at American University. These sections are taught by learning disabilities specialists, with the participation of a clinical psychologist. Depending on condition of admission, some students are required to take this full-year course; others are strongly encouraged to do so.

The course is a combination of classroom instruction (six to eight students), labs considered necessary for individualized help, and tutorial sessions. The second semester consists of tutorial sessions and labs, as needed.

Skills covered include time management, reading comprehension, textbook survey skills, supervised library usage for research projects, organization of research papers, notetaking, and exam preparation. Students who are having difficulty in the freshman writing course receive additional help in the lab sessions.

CURRY COLLEGE

Some campuses, like Curry, have summer sessions for incoming learning disabled students. Curry, in addition to its special Program for Advancement of Learning (PAL), has a three-week credit session for entering freshman who are in PAL. The purpose of this summer session is to help learning disabled students identify their unique strengths; understand the relationship between their weaknesses and academic difficulties; and acquire strategies to overcome problems in time management, language skills, and study skills. Students also learn how to manage stress, become self-assertive, and develop self-disclosure techniques. Under the skilled direction of Gertrude Webb, who founded the PAL program, ideas and techniques are being tested and applied, and materials are being shared with other campuses and among professionals.

HELPFUL SUGGESTIONS

The skill areas included in this section are time management, organization, reading comprehension, notetaking and listening, exam preparation, personal strategies, memory, and writing. From our interviews with learning disabled students and those who work with them, we have collected many valuable and helpful ideas on these topics. Some of the tips are standard study skills techniques; others have evolved out of personal experiences of learning disabled students, their teachers, and advisors; and others are derived from study skills books as well as from handouts thoughtfully prepared by college faculty members. (One very good resource recommended by several instructors is *How to Study in College* by Walter Pauk. This and other general study skills resources are listed at the end of this chapter.)

Remember, there is no one right way to study. Each person will experiment, use, and adapt techniques until he or she finds the approach or approaches that are appropriate — his or her own bag of tricks.

Note. Although these chapters are addressed to students, anyone who is teaching, tutoring, or advising learning disabled students will find this section useful.

Additional Reading About General Study Skills

College Reading and Study Skills, by Kathleen T. McWhorter. Little, Brown and Company. 200 West Street, Waltham, Massachusetts 02254. (375 pages, $14.95) 1983

College Study Skills Program Level III, by Elaine M. Fitzpatrick, National Association of Secondary School Principals, Reston, Virginia 22091. ($4.50 for the *Student's Guide;* $3.50 for the *Instructor's Guide)* 1982

How to Study in College (third edition), by Walter Pauk. Houghton Mifflin Company, Wayside Road, Burlington, Massachusetts 01803. (410 pages, $12.20) 1983

Learning Strategies Curriculum, developed by Donald Deshler and colleagues at the Institute for Research in Learning Disabilities, Lawrence, Kansas. Inquiries about training and use of this program should be addressed to Dr. Frances L. Clark, Coordinator of Training, Institute for Research in Learning Disabilities, The University of Kansas, Lawrence, Kansas 66045-2342. 1986

Problem Solving and Comprehension, by Arthur Whimbey and Jack Lockhead. Lawrence Erlbaum, Associates. 365 Broadway, Hillsdale, New Jersey 07642. (343 pages, $10.95) 1982

S.O.S. (Strengthening of Skills), a curriculum for teaching study skills in listening, notetaking, memory, time management, and test taking, by Lynn O'Brien. Available from Specific Diagnostics, Inc., 11600 Nebel Street, Suite 130, Rockville, Maryland 20852. 1985

Study Smarts: How to Learn More in Less Time, by Judi Kesselman-Turkel and Franklynn Peterson. Contemporary Books, Inc., 180 North Michigan Avenue, Chicago, Illinois 60601. (85 pages, $3.50) 1981

Teaching the Learning Disabled Adolescent: Strategies and Methods, by Gordon Alley and Donald Deshler. Love Publishing Company, 1777 South Bellaire Street, Denver, Colorado 80222. (360 pages, $21.95) 1979

TIME MANAGEMENT

"Overorganize, always be willing to work thirty-one percent harder, start your papers early in the semester, and give yourself plenty of time to prepare for exams and assignments."

This advice from a learning disabled adult who made it through college underscores the value of learning how to manage time.

Managing time is often the hardest thing learning disabled students have to do. Some may never have used a calendar. Others may not know how long it takes to complete an assignment, may get involved in too many activities, or be unable to set priorities. In addition, learning disabled students must allow extra time to read, to listen to taped notes, or to complete written assignments. Faced with conflicting demands and distractions, students can end up with impossible deadlines and commitments.

Learning a system for managing time can be the single most important step a learning disabled student can take. However, for some students, the pressure of creating and sticking to a schedule can in itself be extremely stressful. It may take much effort and practice before a student finds a system that works.

Following is one way to set up a schedule, based on the approach used at American University. Variations are used by many learning disabled students. The materials needed for planning are the syllabus provided by the instructor of each course, a calendar showing all the months of the semester, and a worksheet dividing the seven days of

139

the week into one-hour segments.

This may not be the perfect system for everyone. Give it a try — or use the parts of it that make sense for you. See how you can best develop a time-management plan that can help you get control of your life.

HOW TO SCHEDULE YOUR TIME

The more observant you are about yourself, the easier it will be to work out a schedule that includes all of your academic and nonacademic activities. Pay careful attention to your lifestyle and your academic obligations. Do you live off campus? Do you attend night school? What time of the day are you most efficient? One hyperactive student could only sit still for fifteen minutes at a time, so he broke his studying into these segments. Another student, who described herself as a "spur of the moment person," knew she had to plan her time very carefully. Keep these clues about yourself in mind as you develop your own calendar.

Use Calendars for Planning

Step One. The beginning of the semester is the time to make up your schedule. Get a *monthly calendar.* Look at every course syllabus to check for deadlines throughout the semester. Then pencil in, on the calendar, all due dates for assignments, papers, and exams. Add holidays and personal obligations, such as an anniversary party or your cousin's wedding. Put the calendar on the wall where you will easily be able to check it (Figure 18a).

Step Two. Make out a *sample weekly calendar,* with slots for each hour. Fill in the times of all classes, lectures, labs, and other things in your life that will *not* change during the semester (jobs, tutoring sessions, appointments, chores). Don't forget to fill in the times for sleeping, meals, social life, sports, and recreation (see Figure 18b).

After you have entered all the activities on this sample weekly calendar, look at the slots that are empty. These are the hours each day that you know you can use for studying.

Keep this sample weekly calendar (your "master schedule") where you will always see it. Make an extra copy for your notebook.

Step Three. Use a daily calendar or notebook to make up a list of things to do each day (see Figure 18c). Take a few minutes before you go to bed to write down what you have to study the next day — and when you will do it. Check your syllabus for reading assignments and your monthly calendar for due dates of exams, quizzes, and papers. Is it time to start studying for an exam, or to do a first draft of a paper? Leave enough time — even more than enough time — to meet deadlines.

This is when to make decisions about how to use those empty slots. Be honest with yourself. Are you allowing enough time to complete the reading for your history course, to go over your lecture notes, to work in the biology lab? Are you trying to get too much done at once? Write down what you expect to do in each available time period, and then see how your plan is working. If it isn't, what can you do about it?

PETE'S SCHEDULE

Pete takes four courses (English composition, history, biology, and art, plus physical education). He also has two tutoring sessions per week, works full time on Saturdays, and saves Saturday nights for his social life. He tries to get to bed by 10 p.m. on most week nights. His large blocks of free time are between dinner and bedtime, most afternoons from 3 p.m. to dinner, and Sundays. He also has an hour before each biology and history class, which he uses for last-minute review of notes, vocabulary, and terminology.

To organize his time efficiently, Pete first makes up a monthly calendar based on semester assignments, quizzes, exams, and special occasions, such as holidays. He then fills out a weekly calendar that includes all classes, tutorial sessions, work schedule, and daily routines, such as meals, exercise, and so forth. From the weekly calendar, he can then draw up a list for each day's schedule and note what he needs to take with him (notebooks, pencils, keys, money for lunch).

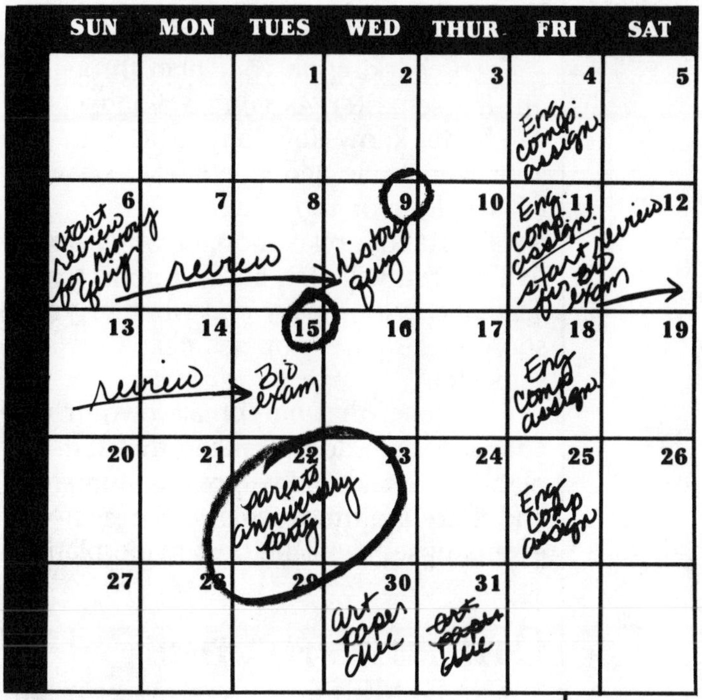

FIGURE 18a
MONTHLY CALENDAR

TIME	SUN	MON	TUES	WED	THUR	FRI	SAT
8-9	BREAKFAST	BREAKFAST	BREAKFAST	BREAKFAST	BREAKFAST	BREAKFAST	BREAKFAST
9-10		Eng. Comp		Eng. Comp		Eng. Comp.	
10-11			Biology		Biology		chores
11-12		History		History		History	Job
12-1	LUNCH	LUNCH	LUNCH	LUNCH	LUNCH	LUNCH	
1-2			Art		Art		
2-3			Gym	Bio Lab	Gym		
3-4		Tutoring				TUTORING	
4-5						run	
5-6	RUN	RUN	RUN	RUN	RUN	SWIM	
6-7	DINNER	DINNER	DINNER	DINNER	DINNER	DINNER	DINNER
7-8						evening out	
8-9							
9-10	SLEEP	SLEEP	SLEEP	SLEEP	SLEEP		
10-11							

FIGURE 18b
SAMPLE WEEKLY CALENDAR

Monday
review history notes
review history lecture
read 3 chapters
textbook/history
read biology
assignment
start preparing for
English Composition
review Art notes
remember
· take notebook, pencil
· take keys
· take money for
lunch & bus
· call Janet for
date Saturday
· do laundry

FIGURE 18c
SAMPLE DAILY LIST

Keep Checking

Keep checking on your plan throughout the semester. As you go along, you will better know how long it takes to get your work done and whether you have left too little or too much time for transportation, relaxation, or other activities. You will also know if your schedule is too heavy and whether you should take fewer courses next semester.

Remember that one breakdown in your schedule doesn't mean that the plan isn't working. Everyone is human, and there are times when unforeseen events upset even the best made plans.

OTHER TIPS FOR TIME MANAGEMENT

■ Know when your high- and low-energy times are, and use your high-energy times to study your more difficult subjects.

■ Study in tolerable doses, and reward yourself after completing a predetermined amount of reading, writing, or reviewing. This is also a good way to do chores. Instead of using chores to avoid studying, use them as a reward. A walk to the post office may be a welcome break after a long study session.

■ Maintain, if possible, a regular time and place to study.

■ Use different colored markers to highlight due dates for exams and papers in each course.

■ Use index cards and wall calendars. They can be helpful tools in getting control over your time. A large monthly wall calendar that you can easily see each day is very useful. Use index cards for copies of your schedule. These can be taped on your desk, near your bed, or on your closet door, or they can be kept in your wallet or the front of your notebook.

■ Make it a habit to check your calendars and daily lists each morning.

■ To figure out time to set aside for long-term projects, count backward from the due date and estimate how much time will be needed. Always allow more time than you think you will need.

■ Keep the syllabus for each course in a place where it won't get lost. Some students paste the syllabus inside the front cover of a course notebook.

■ Schedule a time before a lecture, discussion, or recitation class to review notes so that classroom time is relevant.

■ Grab a few minutes after class to review notes. The more immediate your review, the better the chance for remembering.

■ Think of unscheduled time — and use it. Summarize lecture or reading notes on index cards or tapes. Review material while you are eating, walking, doing chores, jogging, or traveling.

■ When there are conflicting demands for time, learn to ask yourself what is most important to you. Is it more important to go to a career-planning seminar than to do an extra hour of studying? Will one paper that is due have a greater effect on your grade than another? If you go to the movies, will you be able to catch up on your reading? Learn to set priorities.

ORGANIZING ALL THOSE THINGS

"Don't stuff all of your papers in your briefcase" is a comment that one DSS coordinator is always making to her learning disabled students. She says: "So many of my students just gather up their papers, handouts, syllabi, and notes that they have either taken or have had taken by a notetaker and shove them all together into their briefcases or backpacks. The result is that they can never put their finger on what they need without having to go through every piece of paper."

For the learning disabled student, organizing "things" (papers, tapes notebooks, tools, handouts) is hard. Disorganization for anyone is uncomfortable; for the learning disabled student it can mean disaster. To misplace an assignment or a syllabus, to lose handouts, and to have notes from many subjects jumbled together, make it impossible to function effectively.

Students will ultimately have to individualize their own way of organizing things. Some students will want to have a notebook for each subject (each in a different color); others will use a large notebook for all their subjects. Some students will keep everything in a backpack; others will take only what they need for the day. Excellent tips and suggestions have come from learning disabled students and adults. These ideas can be used or modified, depending on need.

TIPS FOR ORGANIZING

▪ Separate your subjects. Every time you get a handout or an assignment, put it in the appropriate section of your notebook. Be sure to use dividers, preferably different colors for each subject.

▪ Figure out a system for keeping papers, books, and other possessions. Find a way that makes sense for you. One student got a cardboard box that was large enough for file folders. She then made a folder for each subject, and every time she got a handout that could not fit into her notebook, she put it in the appropriate file. When she had to get all of the material together for an exam or a paper, she could easily find what she needed.

▪ If you have a notetaker or if you order tapes, be sure to put the notes you receive and the tapes with the other material for that course. Date all your notes and tapes immediately.

▪ Always have a place for each thing. If you use a calculator, keep it in one place and return it to that place. You can apply this to organizing your clothes, books, and school supplies.

▪ Keep keys on a big ring that you can easily spot.

▪ Make sure that you have extra coins for laundry machines, parking meters, buses, and vending machines.

▪ Each day, remember to write down everything you have to take with you for classes, labs, or meetings. Include reminders for money, transportation, and food. Check the list in the morning before you leave your room — so nothing is forgotten.

READING COMPREHENSION

Understanding course content is crucial to succeeding in a postsecondary setting. When you cannot understand the words you are looking at or listening to, you tune out. It is distressing to spend hours and even days reading and rereading assignments and realize that nothing has stuck or that pieces of information are scattered and disorganized.

To read with understanding requires recognizing letters and words; knowing the meaning of words by themselves and in the context in which they are used; and spotting and identifying the author's purpose and structure. What does the author want to tell you? How is the author presenting the material? What do you think about it? Does it confirm an opinion you already have, or does it make you think of other ideas and concepts? Can you use the information in your work, your studies, your daily life?

Each person who teaches reading comprehension has developed techniques and strategies that work. Many courses are given and books written about ways to overcome barriers to comprehension. Some basic themes in teaching comprehension include finding major ideas, relating them to the reader's experience, and using a multisensory approach.

SQ3R (SURVEY, QUESTION, READ, RECITE, REVIEW)

A strategy frequently used to teach reading comprehension is SQ3R, which stands for Survey, Question, Read, Recite, Review. Many students have used this method successfully, often modifying it to suit their own needs. No method is perfect for all students; but because this one is referred to in many study skills courses and books, the major steps are highlighted here.

Survey

Surveying gives you an overview of what the book or chapter is about. First read the title and the introduction. Then skim the book or chapter for main ideas by looking at headings. As you go through the book, pay attention to graphs, tables, picture captions, and italicized words. Finish by reading the summary or concluding paragraph.

Some books are more difficult to survey. Each author has a different way of organizing key ideas and supporting details. If, for example, a book does not have many subheads, then you might look at the first sentence of each paragraph to see if it contains the main ideas and/or check the introduction and summary statement of each chapter.

To get an idea of how SQ3R works, read the title and the introduction to this book. Skim the chapter heads and the main subheads. Does this tell you what the book covers? Now take the chapter, "Time Management." Look at the heads, subheads, and graphics. Can you get a sense of what this chapter is about?

Question

Questioning is the next step. Again using the chapter, "Time Management," look at the main heads and turn them into questions, using the same words or your own words. By doing this, you can gain a sense of purpose for your reading, become more involved in the content, and begin to select the important ideas.

Suggested questions: How can you schedule your time? How can you use calendars for planning? What are three steps to take in making a calendar? What are some other ideas or tips on managing time?

Read

This is the time fo find answers to the questions. One instructor suggests that students read a subsection, make small check marks in pencil next to main ideas or other details, and then go back and underline *only* key words and phrases. Too much underlining makes a paragraph look like a Christmas tree and buries the main ideas.

Now turn to the chapter, "Time Management." Read the paragraph under the heading, How to Schedule Your Time. Check for the main idea and supporting details. Then underline key words and phrases. The following paragraph shows how this might be done.

The more underlined observant you are underlined about yourself, the underlined easier it will be to underlined work out a underlined schedule that underlined includes all of underlined your academic and underlined nonacademic activities. Pay careful attention to your lifestyle and your academic obligations. Do you underlined live off campus? Do you attend underlined night school? What underlined time of the day are you most underlined efficient? One hyperactive student could only sit still for fifteen minutes at a time, so he broke his studying into these segments. Another student, who described herself as a "spur of the moment person," knew she had to plan her time very carefully. Keep these clues about yourself in mind as you develop your own calendar.

Recite

Recite, recite, recite. Whatever method you use, reciting is an excellent way to develop concentration, reinforce understanding, and assure remembering. Cover up paragraphs but not headings or subheadings. The headings become the questions that you answer to yourself in your own words. In this way, you can listen to what you know and check on what you still need to know.

Try this recital technique with the part of the chapter on "Time Management" that lists other tips. Counting the number of tips will help you to recall all of them.

Review

Review is the time to look over the assignments and make sure that you understand the material under the major headings. If there are review or study questions at the end of a section or chapter, see if you know the answers. Go over the ones that you missed.

MORE TIPS FOR READING

- Go back to the troublesome paragraphs — the ones that you do not understand. Find the topic sentence and see if this can help you to identify the main ideas.

- Look at each sentence and isolate the simple subject, verb, and object from modifiers such as adjectives, adverbs, clauses, and phrases. By doing this, you can isolate the primary thought of the sentence.

- Learn to read for different purposes: finding facts, selecting main ideas, looking for inferences, evaluating critically.

- Discover what works best for you. You might have to try several methods. Knowing that you have techniques to master your reading assignments will help remove the barriers to understanding that have been so paralyzing in the past.

LISTENING AND NOTETAKING

Notetaking is hard work for all students. For students with learning difficulties, it can be overwhelming. To make sure that their notes are complete, they usually must spend much more time than nonlearning disabled students in rewriting, consolidating, listening to tapes of lectures, and seeking help from advisors and classmates. They also must be creative and imaginative in figuring out ways to emphasize major points. The rewards come when material is recalled more easily and when exam preparation is not a last-minute scramble.

One way to learn how to take effective notes is to be an effective listener. Donald Deshler and his associates at the University of Kansas have been working for several years on ways to teach learning disabled students many learning strategies, including listening. The techniques they recommend for teaching listening skills (prelistening, listening, and postlistening) also apply to notetaking skills.

PRELISTENING: GETTING SET TO LISTEN

- Before going to class, review your lecture notes from the last class and your reading notes on the topics that will be covered. Preview (in syllabus) any assignments relating to the class.

- Be familiar with spelling and meaning of key terms likely to be used in class. Keep a list of all new words for easy reference.

LISTENING: BEING THERE

- Sit in front of the room so that you can concentrate on the instructor and not be distracted.

- Write down any brief outline that is on the board. If you have a notetaker, be sure he or she makes a copy of the outline for you.

- Date your notes, record the course name, and number each page.

- Use regular looseleaf notepaper. The left-hand margin is a good place to write down key words and phrases.

- Use only one side of the paper.

- Listen for organizational clues, such as "following are three major topics," or "these are the steps," or "in summary."

- Put main thoughts in your own words.

- Jot down essential points. Listen critically and be discriminating about what to include in your notes.

- Use short phrases and key words and leave plenty of white space on each page.

- Put large question marks in the margin when you miss a point or do not understand it. Be sure to get your questions answered.

- Develop and use your own shorthand method (see Figure 19 for suggested abbreviations).

- Make doodles in the margin to emphasize major points.

- Draw boxes around key ideas.

- Color code your notes; for example, red for facts to memorize, yellow for theory, and so forth.

- Use any other visual techniques that help make ideas stand out. One student uses purple ink for outlines and draws pink stars for major points.

POSTLISTENING

- Fill in any information you have from other sources about the topic discussed in class.

- Clarify with your instructor anything that you did not understand.

- Cluster and categorize points in the lecture. If necessary, or if it is helpful, rewrite your notes.

- Ask another student, your counselor, or DSS advisor to go over your notes. In some study skills classes, this review is part of the curriculum.

- Review your notes or notes taken by your notetaker no later than eight hours after the class.

- Keep your notes and your notetaker's notes with all of the other material about that course. Keep your notes in chronological order.

Notetaking symbols and abbreviations

This list is not intended to be exhaustive but will give you some ideas upon which you can build your own list. Be creative!

p.	page	~	about
#	number	>	greater than
b/c	because	<	less than
b/4	before	∴	therefore
wd	word	→	means
w/	with	x, □	important passage, word
w/o	without		
2	to, too, two	T	information that could be used as a test question
ie.	that is	✓	check later
eg.	for example	S	summary
re.	concerning	cont'd	continued
etc.	in addition	—	dashes for words if the speaker is too fast (come back later and use the context to fill in the missing words)
vs.	versus		

Write only the beginning of a word. Examples:

ref	reference	comp	compare, comparison
diff	difference, different	ex	example
def	definition		

Write only consonants and omit vowels. Examples:

impt.	important	lk	like

Use g to indicate "ing" Examples:

writg   meetg   answerg

Don't erase or blank out a mistake; draw a thin line instead.

This list of notetaking symbols and abbreviations is included in a course given by Faith Leonard, Director, Learning Services, The American University, Washington, D.C.

FIGURE 19

The Cornell note-taking system

Try the Cornell Notetaking System. (This is fully described in Walter Pauk's book.) Briefly, this method makes it easier to highlight and recall major ideas in a lecture or a textbook.

Divide your paper into two columns — the left one (the recall column margin) for key words and phrases, the right for the bulk of the information. The left one is filled in *after* the lecture. In reviewing for exams, cover the right column — the bulk of the material — and use the left column words to recall the content (see example, Figure 20).

Diagrams and flow charts

Diagrams and flow charts are highly visual ways of summarizing notes. Some students use these techniques for reviewing or consolidating textbook or lecture notes for exams. One example, the concept diagram, is taught at Curry College (Massachusetts). If it were used to diagram a discussion of learning styles, it might look like Figure 21.

Effective notetaking will give you a summary of the course when preparing for exams. It will also help you understand the organization of the topic, theme and major ideas, and purpose of the course.

NOTETAKING

RECALL COLUMN	INFORMATION COLUMN
Purpose of Book	Book is about campus access for learning disabled students
Who is book for?	Book written for students, high school counselors, parents, college faculty, vocational educators, DSS Coordinators
What topics are included? (list 8)	Organization of Book ① Legislative basis for serving LD students in postsecondary settings ② Background information on learning disabilities, including diagnosis ③ How parents and their sons & daughters can begin to make choices for postsecondary years ④ Types of options, how to narrow decisions, and how to get into a program ⑤ Accomodations and how to obtain them ⑥ Study skills ⑦ Personal adjustment ⑧ How to start a program on campus

FIGURE 20

Based on Cornell Notetaking Method.

CONCEPT DIAGRAM

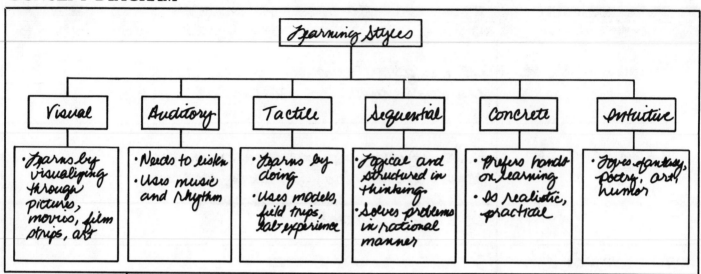

FIGURE 21

Additional Reading About Listening and Notetaking Skills

Educational Tele-Curricula (Video Tapes) Developing Notetaking Skills; Writing Paragraphs and Essays, by Barbara Cordoni and Marshall Welch. Educational Tele-Curricula, P.O. Box 434, Carbondale, Illinois 62903. (Rental $75.00; purchase $250.00)

The Tutor/Notetaker: Providing Academic Support to Mainstreamed Deaf Students, by Russell T. Osguthorpe. Alexander Graham Bell Association, 3401 Volta Place, N.W., Washington, D.C. 20007 (104 pages, $7.50, $2.00 handling charge per order) 1980

PREPARING FOR EXAMS

"How will I ever get through next week? I have three final exams and a paper due, and I haven't even started on my paper."

Anyone who has ever gone to college knows the anxiety in those words. But semesters do not have to end this way.

Many colleges are giving guidance to students who need help in studying for exams. Learning centers, counseling and guidance services, and some academic departments are good places to check for handouts and other materials on test taking. Walter Pauk's book, *How to Study in College,* has several chapters on how to prepare for and take exams. Some strategies are obvious; others can be acquired. Students who have learned effective study skills, including time management, reading, writing, and notetaking, find that they can get through exam time with minimum frustration.

Taking exams can be difficult for learning disabled students; giving and grading exams can be difficult for their instructors. For learning disabled students, exams present mechanical as well as study problems. For faculty members, exams can present a need for special arrangements. Should an instructor make allowances for students who know the content of the course but are unable to write effectively, spell or punctuate correctly, or use the rules of grammar appropriately? There are no simple answers, but there are suggestions, some of which are discussed in the chapters "Alternative Ways to Learn" and "Writing."

153

This chapter outlines ways to prepare for and take exams and quizzes and gives suggestions for taking different types of exams. Learning disabled students who need further help should check with DSS advisors, faculty advisors, and instructors.

PREPARING FOR EXAMS

Gather information about your exams. Find out what the test will cover and what types of questions will be asked (essay, objective, multiple choice, or true/false). There are strategies for taking each of these kinds of tests.

Talk to your instructor, especially if you are not clear about some aspect of the course. Find out what the instructor is looking for. Are there themes that have been stressed throughout the course?

Try and locate previous years' exams. Maybe your instructor will give you a back copy. Talk to students who have taken the course. Think about an essay that you might write on, or answer some sample true/false or multiple choice questions.

Review throughout the semester. Look at your textbook and lecture notes periodically. Make and use summaries on cards or tapes that you can have with you when you are doing other things, such as traveling to and from school. You will remember more when you review and recite throughout the semester than when you cram the night before.

Consolidate lecture and textbook notes into summary sheets and recite them. Pauk thinks that this is the most effective strategy for test preparation. By summarizing lecture and textbook notes, he believes that you can achieve three things. You can review your notes and add other information; you can pull material together by category, which makes it easier to recall during an exam; and you can have a concise summary (approximately ten pages) to study just before the exam.

To do this summarizing, Pauk recommends using the Cornell system, described in the chapter, "Listening and Notetaking." This technique combines use of cue words and recitation. Make columns, with the left column containing key words (see Figure 20), or organize material in outline form. Either way, you can cover up the information and recite the appropriate material to check on what you know and what you have missed.

Memorize terms. By memorizing the spelling and meaning of terms throughout the semester, you will not have to worry about them in the exam.

Review material with other students. Talk about the exam with other students, especially students who are knowledgeable about the course content. Organize study groups, or study with a group of successful students.

TAKING THE EXAM

Your studying is completed, and it's time to take the exam. Arrive early and sit in a seat where the light is good, the blackboard is easy to see, and distraction is minimal. If you are tense, use relaxation techniques before the exam starts. Don't sit next to worriers or anxiety carriers.

Understand the directions. Read and listen to all instructions. Make sure you know what is required for each question. Are you being asked to compare, summarize, enumerate, review, trace, or justify? If in doubt, raise your hand and ask the proctor.

Skim the exam. Look at each question to determine points. This helps you decide how to plan your time and where to put your greatest effort. It also gives you an opportunity to note whether the exam has a theme or a main idea.

Answer easy questions first. When you get to a question you think you can't answer, go on to the other questions. When you go back to the difficult questions, make an outline or notes, and try to develop some reasonable answer. A little credit is better than no credit.

Use the full time. Check to see that you did not miss any questions or that you did not misinterpret any directions. Research indicates that students who use the full time to review questions can often improve their answers.

DIFFERENT TYPES OF EXAMS

Essay Exams

Use the essay question in your first sentence. This helps make the first sentence a clear, strong statement about the topic. It announces what the essay is about and makes it easier to organize facts, ideas, and details.

Make your reasoning as logical as possible. Use transition words such as *for example, accordingly, nevertheless, following are, similarly, finally.*

If you were taking an essay test on the material in this chapter, the following might be a question that you would have to answer.

Q What are four steps to use when you are taking an exam? (20 Points)

A (Opening sentence): Following are four steps to use when taking an exam.

Did you notice how many steps to list? Did you notice the point value?

True/False, Multiple Choice, and Matching Exams

Although all answers are given and can be recognized, the process of finding the answer differs for each type of question. Campus study skills courses and study skills books, such as Pauk's, give excellent ideas on how to prepare for each of these kinds of questions.

• In taking tests that require marking boxes or circles for answers, use a ruler, a file card, or paper to help you keep an eye on the correct lines.

• In true/false tests, watch words such as *all, most, some, none, always, usually, sometimes, never, good, bad, more, equal, less.* Be wary of those words that overstate or understate, such as *all* or *never.* For example,

Q All colleges give guidance to students who need help in studying for exams. True or false?

A False

(Did you notice the word *all?* The use of a word that overstates can be a tip that the answer is false.)

• In multiple choice questions, read all of the options; eliminate the ones that are foolish or that seem to overstate or understate. Often an option that is long and detailed is appropriate. Use your knowledge of prefixes, *(hyper, under)* and suffixes, *(able, ology).* Look for subject and verb agreement and for article ending — if a stem statement ends in *an,* then the answer will start with a vowel.

Try this multiple choice question:

Q **In preparing for exams,**
   (a) Wait until the night before to study.
   (b) Get as much information as possible about the exam, including types of questions.
   (c) Read the book from cover to cover.

A **(b)**

Did any of these answers seem foolish? Did the more detailed answer seem appropriate?

• In matching questions, look over both columns. Start by matching those that you are sure of.

Sentence-Completion and Short-Answer Exams.

Read sentences carefully. Think about the context of each question. As in all other tests, go through the exam and answer those questions you know. When you tackle the ones you are unsure of, jot down anything that comes to your mind about the question.

REVIEWING EXAMS

When you get your exams back, spend some time going over them. A careful review can be very helpful in preparing for other exams. Learn what you missed and why. Was your organization poor? Did you spend too much time on one question? Did you overlook main points and get sidetracked by details? Did you misread the question? It is also important to know what questions you did well on and why.

SUMMARY

Exam time is tense for all students. Fortunately, there are many techniques and strategies for studying and taking exams. You might have to try out several to see which one fits your learning style. Above all, don't be afraid to seek help from counselors, instructors, and other students.

Additional Reading About Test Taking

Test-Taking Strategies, by Judi Kesselman-Turkel and Franklynn Peterson. Contemporary Books, Inc., 180 North Michigan Avenue, Chicago, Illinois 60601. (120 pages, $3.95) 1981

CHEWING APPLES AND OTHER QUIRKS

Many of the strategies learning disabled people use are personal ones. They may not fall under the category of study skills or even have anything to do with academia. However, once discovered, personal strategies become part of the learning disabled adult's self-knowledge and can be used whenever needed. Some strategies, once dismissed as quirks, are proving to be good, solid techniques.

STUDY STRATEGIES

Lynn O'Brien, director of Specific Diagnostics, Inc. (Rockville, Maryland), works with learning disabled adults, as well as with other students of all ages, and has a large repertoire of strategies to stimulate learning and enhance studying. The ideas that follow combine her experiences and those of students who shared some of their own strategies.

The Sound of Music

Although a quiet, nondistracting place is helpful to most students, others study best while listening to music or watching TV. Contrary to respected dogma, having the radio or TV on *can* be an aid to concentration for some students. The sound of music can block out other distracting noises and thoughts, enabling the mind to focus on the visual task at hand. Interesting recent studies have shown that a background of Baroque music can provide a structure for the mind when reading or writing. One successful student turns on TV re-runs while studying. When her mind wanders, she looks at the screen and this helps her re-focus.

Peak Energy Time

Efficiency varies with the time of day for most people. Being aware of your peak times contributes to self-management; lower energy periods can be used for less demanding, more routine activities.

Relaxation

Relaxation is the key to storing information efficiently. One simple tip: Take three deep breaths before starting a learning task.

Color

Color can be a great stimulus for learning and an aid for memorizing. Educators are finding that reading rate and comprehension actually improve when a color transparency is placed over a white page with black print. Also, a large sheet of colored paper placed under a book on a table or desk can help the mind focus on reading. A little experimenting can tell which colors are best. Color is also helpful in organizing notes.

Physical Activity

Physical or motor activity can be an important part of an individual's learning style. A person with a strong need to move around and be active might stifle learning by trying to study for hours at a time. Studying in small chunks of time is recommended, with short exercise breaks. Some learning disabled adults take walks while reviewing exam questions. One student reads while riding her exercise bike. Another practices juggling before getting down to work or during study breaks. O'Brien points out that motor techniques get the brain fired chemically and electrically and involve the entire person in learning.

Doing It Your Way

Most of us have a feel for what makes us comfortable while we work, but we haven't given these idiosyncracies any particular honor. If we do our best thinking lying down, or need to crunch apples and nuts while we read or write, we tend to shrug away such traits as weaknesses. But the truth is, these personal styles are assets. It can be a relief and a strength to know it's okay to do things your way.

MEMORY TRICKS OF THE TRADE

Many learning disabled adults told of their difficulties in remembering words, names, dates, and other facts. There are some basic rules and tricks that help.

• **Decide to remember.** Memory experts say that if you don't remember something, it's probably because you didn't try to remember it in the first place. You may have been daydreaming while listening to a speech or reading a chapter. Deciding to remember takes extra concentration, motivation, and interest.

• **Make sure you understand what you're memorizing.** If material is complicated or technical, ask questions until it's clear. When reading or taking notes, put information you want to remember into your own words.

• **Don't try to remember everything.** Key ideas or main points are what's important. The cues for reading (SQ3R), notetaking, and exam preparation provide good background for remembering.

• **Organize in clusters.** Cluster information into categories. Categories for causes of the American Revolution might be issues, people, events — with major facts under each one. Keep categories to a manageable number, and don't overstuff each one with too much detail.

• **Say it aloud.** After you have read and thought about information you want to remember, close your eyes or cover the page and say it out loud in a conversational tone. Writing it down will help, too.

• **Visualize.** We've talked about visualizing in various parts of this book. It is practically a surefire way to store and recall information. Drawing a time line, a simple diagram, or a silly cartoon helps to fix ideas in the mind and bring them back when you want them.

• **Use associations.** Association is a powerful tool for memorizing, especially if the association is visual. To be even more effective, the experts say, the association should be to something absurd and exaggerated. *The Memory Book,* by Harry Lorayne and Jerry Lucas, has a wealth of ideas for using visual associations to increase memory. Other kinds of associations can also strengthen memory. Some people put key words to the tune of a familiar song. Others remember by using their hands. Putting a machine together, step by step, combines tactile associations with visual memory.

• **Make up Mnemonics.** These clever inventions for organizing and remembering information can help learning disabled students improve their spelling. Mnemonics often use first letters of key words, terms, or names to form a word. For example, H O M E S stands for the names of the Great Lakes: **H**uron, **O**ntario, **M**ichigan, **E**rie, **S**uperior.

Many learning disabled students found that by making lists of their own mnemonic tricks and reviewing them frequently, their confidence went up and they made fewer errors. One favorite trick is spelling *piece* by thinking of a piece of pie.

The Achieve program teaches mnemonics, giving nongraded pre- and post-tests to measure ability to remember commonly misspelled words.

Additional Reading About Memory Tricks

The Memory Book, by Harry Lorayne and Jerry Lucas. Ballantine Books, 201 E. 50th Street, New York, New York 10022. (206 pages, $2.50) 1974

WRITING

"Fear of writing is my biggest obstacle."

"Getting the thought out — that's the hardest part."

"I can say it, but I can't write it."

Writing is a complex task. Ideas that float in the brain must be translated onto paper. Points must be selected, organized, and put into logical order. Sentences must be woven together with correct grammar, punctuation, capitalization, syntax, and spelling. The task requires integration of many skills — including memory, sequencing, organizing, language structure, motor skills, and visual-motor integration.

For many learning disabled students, writing is painful. Problems with mechanics constantly get in the way. Spelling errors, erasures, and crossed out words may mar the appearance of any paper. Thoughts get stuck, and content may be limited. Frustrated by the entire process, students frequently have what they call "writing phobia." They fear that any writing they do will make them look stupid.

160

IMPORTANT OF WRITING

The need for help with writing is critical. English composition is required for graduation by almost all colleges. Writing papers and exams is essential for mastery of most postsecondary courses. In the working world, written communication takes place every day. Writing is the face of literacy one shows the world.

Until recently, little was done to teach writing skills. High school resource rooms have tended to concentrate on drill of grammatical rules, and most learning disabled students graduate without experience in written composition. Only a limited number of campuses have created writing programs for learning disabled students.

But some models do exist. They can include courses, labs, and tutoring in written composition; intensive, small group instruction in writing skills, such as vocabulary, sentence structure, and punctuation; and compensatory strategies to bypass difficulties with spelling and grammar.

The National Writing Project

The National Writing Project is an excellent source of assistance. There are National Writing Project sites throughout the country. Most have skilled writing specialists with a special education background who can help develop plans for teaching writing to students with learning difficulties. For a list of sites, write to National Writing Project, School of Education, 5635 Tolman Building, University of California at Berkeley, California 94720.

Focus of the Chapter

This chapter focuses on techniques that can be learned for dealing successfully with the writing process. Many of the ideas are basic tips for writing and can be used by all students. For the learning disabled student, it is essential to learn these or similar approaches for overcoming writing blocks, gathering and organizing ideas, writing and revising drafts, and editing and polishing the final product. Students and their instructors can use the ideas as a beginning and explore further on their own.

OVERCOMING A WRITING BLOCK

The best way to learn to write is by doing it. Improvement comes by tackling the task. Without practice, it gets harder and harder to overcome mental blocks about writing.

Write Without Stopping

Try to write steadily for about ten minutes every day, without stopping, correcting, or worrying about quality. Any everyday subject like "what I had for breakfast" could start this kind of activity. If it's easier, say it into a tape recorder.

Keep a Journal

Keeping a daily journal helps many people get into a writing habit. Again, it is important to write without worrying about mistakes or feeling that someone is looking over your shoulder. Whatever gets put down is part of the act of capturing thoughts in written form.

Avoid Self-Criticism

Learning disabled learners, like others who have had little experience with writing, frequently think that everyone else writes easily. They feel that a first draft should be perfect, and they edit every word as they write. Self-criticism can keep the process from even getting started. It helps to realize that good writers throw many drafts into the wastebasket.

Use Personal Experiences

Learning disabled adults who have struggled through the writing process stress the importance of using one's own experiences in developing ideas. Personal experiences with your family, jobs, schools, friends — all the big and little things in life — are powerful sources for writing.

Break Writing into Tasks

Whatever the writing assignment is, it helps to divide it into tasks. These can be four stages: (1) prewriting, (2) drafting, (3) reviewing and revising, and (4) editing and polishing. Although prewriting — getting ideas together — is the biggest part of writing, none of these activities is totally separate. The following paragraphs describe the activities in each of these stages.

PREWRITING

Prewriting is a time to gather ideas and to ask questions that can bring ideas into focus. English teachers have found that during this period students benefit greatly from talking over their topics with peers, instructors, and others. Here are some questions that can get the process started.

Questions

Topic. A topic may already have been assigned. If so, what is the purpose of the assignment? Is it to take a closer look at one aspect of the course? To present a point of view on a topic? If no topic is assigned, the first task is to pick one. Is there an aspect of the course that is especially interesting? Do you have an opinion you want to share? Is there a historical character you particularly admire?

Point of View. What do you want to say about the topic? What is the main point you want to make? How can you narrow it down so it's not too broad?

Audience. Who is the audience you are writing for? Students? Teachers? The community? What do you want to tell your readers about the topic?

Purpose. Why are you going to write this piece? Is it to tell about a personal experience? To persuade others that your stand on an issue is the right one? To explain an idea or describe how to do something?

Form. Questions about form may already be decided by the teacher. Is this to be an essay, an article, a narrative? How long should it be?

Talk to your instructor and to other students about these questions. The clearer the answers, the easier writing will be.

Gathering Ideas

Instead of staring in panic at a blank page, try techniques such as brainstorming, interviewing, role playing, and mapping to clarify your point of view or identify main ideas.

If this is a research paper, this is a good time to learn and practice skills in using the library and organizing research. Reference librarians are there to help you. Don't hestitate to ask them for help in locating materials that you need.

Brainstorming. Brainstorming can be done in a large group, in small groups of two or three, or by individuals working alone. The first step is to list whatever ideas you think of, whether they come out as single words or phrases. Let them flow. Don't try to organize or be selective at this point. If possible, put up a large sheet of paper and list ideas with a colored marking pen.

The second step is to cluster ideas into categories. On a new sheet of paper, write headings that describe each category. List the ideas that fit. The result is a loose outline of main and supporting ideas.

Interviewing. Find out what other people on campus or in the community think about the topic. What do they see as most important? Why? The number of people you interview depends on how much time you have. If you want to quote a person in your paper, ask for permission and be sure to get the correct spelling of names. Keep notes of ideas or use a tape recorder.

Role Playing. In role playing or dramatic improvisation, students play a part in a situation. Ideas come out as they act out their point of view. (This might be appropriate as a classroom technique but harder to do on your own.)

Mapping. Mapping is a way to make friends with your mind and the way it thinks. Instead of starting with a sequential outline in an orderly one-two-three approach, mapping lets you follow your train of thought. As you draw a map, you will probably find that a natural organization of ideas begins to take place. Many students find that mapping frees their minds and allows them to see the most important ideas. Also called webbing, clustering, or drawing a mind map,

mapping is especially helpful for visual learners and for students who have difficulty with sequential outlining. It is used successfully at Curry College, where English instructors work individually with students on mapping and then follow up by helping to prioritize ideas.

To see how mapping works, pick any topic and write it down in the center of a piece of paper. An example might be "styles in food." To start mapping, you would draw a circle around the topic, like this:

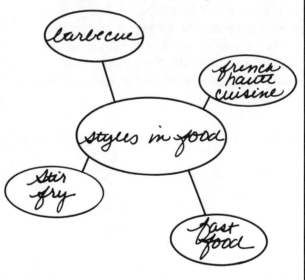

What does the topic make you think of? Write down one or two words for each thought, draw circles around them, and connect them to the topic like this:

Write down the next thoughts as quickly as possible.

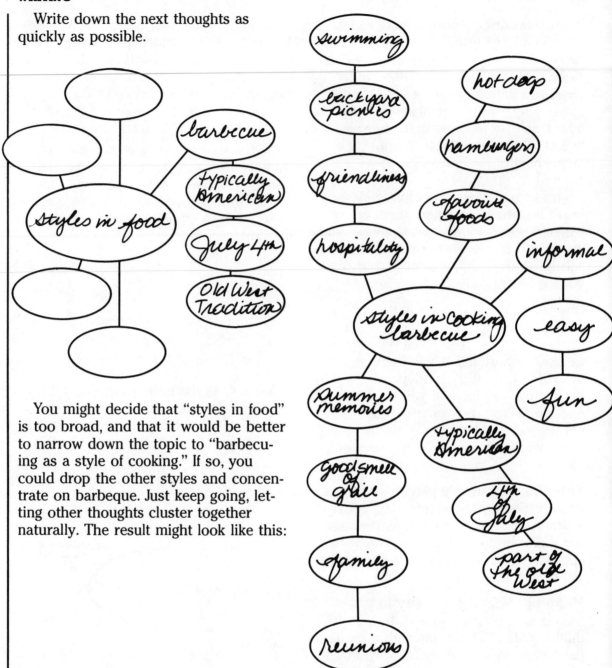

You might decide that "styles in food" is too broad, and that it would be better to narrow down the topic to "barbecuing as a style of cooking." If so, you could drop the other styles and concentrate on barbeque. Just keep going, letting other thoughts cluster together naturally. The result might look like this:

164

The clusters of thoughts that have tumbled out of your mind can be translated into a point of view and an outline of main points, with supporting ideas. For instance:

Point of view: Barbecuing is a typically American style of cooking, combining American informality, friendliness, and love of family with favorite, easy-to-prepare food.

Main Points.
1. Reflects American informality
   - backyard entertainment of neighbors and friends
   - poolside parties
   - picnics
2. Shows American knack for doing things efficiently, easily, and having fun at the same time.
   - typical menu is easy to cook and delicious
3. Connected to American history
   - Old West steak barbecues
   - July Fourth celebrations
4. Part of American home life
   - summer reunions
   - smell of charcoal brings back summer memories

There isn't only one way to map or cluster thoughts. Experiment with ways that work for you. No matter what the topic, mapping can be a good way to get started.

DRAFTING

After gathering your thoughts, it's time to write a draft. You need to tell the reader what you intend to say and say it as clearly as possible. You need to select a logical order to present ideas. You need to decide what details to include and what sentences and words to use. Your objective is to put it all together in a unified structure.

Thesis Statement

Writing a thesis statement helps to organize your thinking. This statement expresses your point of view about the topic simply and clearly. It announces your main idea and what the paper will document.

The thesis statement should *not* be an observable fact or a personal opinion. For example:

Observable fact: Writing research papers is a requirement of many courses.

Personal opinion: I hate writing research papers.

Point of view (a good thesis statement): Writing research papers is relatively *easy* as long as the writer follows certain specific, sequential tasks.

In many cases, the controlling idea of a thesis statement is expressed by an adjective, like the word *easy*. By developing your statements, you can also become more adept at spotting other writers' thesis statements.

Putting it on Paper

A first draft does not have to be perfect. It can be written many times. Writing teachers recommend that students experiment with different ways of expressing ideas. If one approach doesn't work, try another. You may have to discard or change several attempts before coming up with a first draft.

While writing a first draft, continue to ask questions. Why is the paper being written? Who is it being written for? What is the main point? As you write, check back to your original intention and to the thesis statement. Do your ideas develop that intention? Do they prove your thesis? Do they hold together? These questions can help you develop a structure for your paper.

Achieve Program

The Achieve Program at Southern Illinois University has created a writing lesson that vividly describes how to construct a written draft. The lesson compares writing to the construction of a bologna sandwich. The main idea — a slice of bologna — needs supporting points such as relish and mustard to be interesting and enjoyable. Details like spaghetti or oatmeal would be irrelevant and spoil the taste. Finally, there must be a top and bottom piece of bread, an introduction and a conclusion, to hold the sandwich together.

This lesson, based on the ideas of Don Link, Utah Learning Resource Center, is available on video cassette from the Achieve Program. (For information, see end of this chapter.)

REVIEWING AND REVISING

Feedback on a first draft is important. Peers and instructors can make suggestions for improvement. Students should check to see if they have said what they wanted to say. Does the introduction give the reader a picture of the subject? Is the point of view clearly stated in an opening or thesis statement? Do ideas prove the point of view? Professor John Herum of Central Washington University describes the opening as "a promise" and teaches students to evaluate their work by asking, "Did you keep your promise to the reader?" Revision fills in the gaps.

EDITING AND POLISHING

Before beginning to edit and polish, let the draft cool for about twenty-four hours. Then, do two readings — first, for content, organization, and transitions; then, for spelling, punctuation, and grammar. Some specialists suggest checking for errors by reading the paper backward. Start with the last word. Put your pencil on the word, and say it out loud. This way, spelling errors are easier to catch. To check for sentence structure, read the entire last sentence out loud, then the next-to-last, and so on. Backward reading takes time and patience, but it is a good way to focus on mechanics.

This is a time for instructors to work with students on rules of grammar. By learning in the context of a real assignment, not in a vacuum, there is far greater opportunity for teaching to take hold.

COMPENSATING FOR MECHANICAL PROBLEMS

For some learning disabled students, problems with spelling, handwriting, capitalization, and punctuation persist despite all efforts to proof their work. For some instructors, these mechanical problems create conflicts about grading. Should they mark down for these errors even if content quality is high? Some instructors have decided to grade papers and exams on the student's grasp of subject matter and give additional time to make corrections in spelling, grammar, and punctuation.

Following are some compensatory strategies recommended by instructors and students:

Typing. Submit all papers in typed form. A carefully proofed, typed paper can be the perfect solution to handwriting disabilities. If typing is impossible, try to find someone who will type for pay.

Consider dictating. Students who dictate exams and papers usually outline or write a first draft ahead of time. They dictate it to a scribe, or read it into a tape recorder or dictaphone and have the tape transcribed. Dictating itself is a skill to be mastered. Some students recommend taking a short course in dictation.

Create a personal speller. Use a notebook to write down every difficult word you learn to spell correctly. Keep it on hand, and request permission to bring it to exams as an accommodation.

Use spelling aids. Examples of spelling aides are *Spellex,* a guide to spelling words in all forms, and *Hominex,* a list of all homonyms (their, there, they're), with examples of correct usage. (For information about these and other aids, see list at end of this chapter or check bookstores and libraries.)

Try using a word processor, with a spelling check. (See chapter, "Using Technology.")

Use colored file cards. Write each new word, technical term, or proper name in large black letters. Check cards during free minutes.

Use mnemonic tricks. (See chapter, "Chewing Apples and Other Quirks.")

INDIVIDUAL ASSISTANCE

The learning disabled student, in many cases, needs individualized assistance in all steps of writing. The person who provides the assistance may be a classroom instructor, a tutor, a learning disability specialist, a graduate assistant, or a peer.

One talented and intelligent learning disabled student spoke of freezing when a writing assignment was due. She was unable to "get thoughts unstuck." With the help of a learning disability coordinator, she finally overcame her writing block. The coordinator listened to her talk; took down the ideas as they came out; and together, they began to put them in order. They went over the final draft carefully, looking at flow of sentences, vocabulary, and grammar. Working in this way, the student's panic about writing subsided. Her anxiety went down and her skills went up.

At Brown University (Rhode Island), dyslexic students are encouraged to team up with writing fellows. These fellows are students who are specially selected and trained to help other students who are having writing difficulties.

Extra time spent focusing on individual needs can help remove blocks and set the stage for effective expression of ideas.

Additional Reading About Writing

"English and the Learning-Disabled Student: A Survey of Research," by Gerald Siegel. Pennsylvania English (Volume 9, Fall 1982). (Write to Pennsylvania College English Association, c/o Ben McKulick, Treasurer, York College of Pennsylvania, York, Pennsylvania. ERIC Document # ED 222034.)

English Skills (third edition), by John Langan. McGraw Hill, Princeton Road, Hightstown, New Jersey 08520. (418 pages, $15.95) 1985

Enhancing Written Expression of The Learning Disabled: An Instructor's Guide to Promoting Written Competency at The Postsecondary Level, by Diane Perreira. Office of Special Services, Marist College, Poughkeepsie, New York 12601. (52 pages, $6.00) 1984

Hominex, by Joyce Scinto. Curriculum Associates, 5 Esquire Road, North Billerica, Massachusetts 01862. (Catalogue #278.1, 72 pages, $5.25) 1977

6 Minutes a Day to Perfect Spelling, by Harry Shefter. Pocket Books, 1230 Avenue of the Americas, New York, New York 10020. (262 pages, $2.95) 1976

Spellex, by George Moore, Richard Talbot, Willard Woodruff. Curriculum Associates, 5 Esquire Road, North Billerica, Massachusetts 08162. (Catalogue # 133.1, 128 pages, $3.75) 1975

"Syntactic Complexity in Written Expression of Learning Disabled Writers," by Susan Vogel. Annals of Dyslexia. Orton-Dyslexia Society, 724 York Road, Baltimore, Maryland 21204. ($11.00 includes postage and handling) 1985

Webster's New World Misspeller's Dictionary. Simon and Schuster, New York, New York. ($3.95, available at most book stores) 1983

Writing the Natural Way, by Gabriele Lusser Rico. J.P. Tarcher Inc., Los Angeles. Distributed by Houghton Mifflin Co., Boston, Massachusetts 01803. (280 pages, $9.95) 1983

"GO THE ROAD":
COUNSELING
AND SUPPORT

"GO THE ROAD": COUNSELING AND SUPPORT

"If I had to sum it up, I would say that a learning disabled student's life is filled with frustration and terrible anxiety. You are always anxious about everything from whether your professor will give you extended time on a test, to whether you will understand the lecture, to whether you will say something foolish or irrelevant in class or to a friend."

"I am always afraid that I will be excluded from a group and that I won't have anyone to talk with or do things with. It reminds me of how hurt I used to get when no one played with me. I was so clumsy that I was always the last one chosen on a team or kids would call me dummy because I had trouble reading."

"I was so angry growing up. I knew there was some reason why I could not read very well even though I always got good grades in school. When I got to college, everything got more difficult. I could not keep up with my work. I finally got myself tested and found out that I was dyslexic."

"My bitterness and anger made me very demanding of my instructors, and they just turned off. Finally, after much counseling, I was able to let go of this fury and could approach my instructors in such a way that they listened to my explanations about my problems and trusted my assurance that any accommodations I might request would not diminish the quality of my work."

171

These quotes from interviews with learning disabled students reflect the common denominators of frustration, anger, anxiety, and loneliness that accompany so many as they enter postsecondary schools or programs.

Some learning disabled students will weather the transition storms by themselves or with help and guidance from a teacher or a friend. Others may find support in peer groups or through a buddy system, and others may need more formalized help from a counselor. This chapter on personal adjustment describes not only the needs of these students, but also resources and suggestions for resolving some of their problems.

SOMEONE WHO CAN LISTEN

A successful college experience often depends on friendship. Joys, sorrows, and achievements all need to be shared. But how difficult this can be for many learning disabled students. Susan Vogel, founder of the learning disabilities program at Barat College (Illinois), put it this way: "It is so important for learning disabled students to have an emotional support system — a home base, someone who can listen to the hurts and frustrations, and who can say, 'I know you can get it together again, I have faith in you'."

These words are echoed by many people who work with learning disabled students. They are also the silent wish or prayer of parents as their learning disabled children leave the shelter of home. Most of all they are the spoken and unspoken hope of learning disabled students who so often need a friend or mentor as they try to handle not only the major crises but the daily problems of academic and social life.

"Go the Road"

Some students will find friendship and support from a faculty member. Katherine Garnett, a professor of special education at Hunter College (New York), urges all faculty members who have contact with learning disabled students to think of themselves as their partners. "Go the road," she says, "Help them find out what they can and cannot do. Help them discover their talents and their best learning styles."

Garnett thinks of faculty and administrative staff as being in a square dance with each student. As students go down the line, they reach out to one partner, then the next, and so forth, But there must always be the next partner.

Where to Look

A support system — formal or informal — can be found in many campus corners. Campuses that already have a special learning disability program always have advisors who are available not only for academic help but for emotional support. Most campuses have counseling centers where students can talk with a counselor about a problem.

Other people who can be resources for support are coordinators of disabled student services; resident counselors in dormitories, who are usually graduate students selected because of their interest in helping students; or chaplains on campus, who are skilled in working with college students. A college or community hotline might also provide suggestions. And last but not least, other learning disabled students can provide valuable help because they know what it is like.

172

Types of Support

Campus support can include a buddy system in which two students with similar problems are put in touch with one another by a disabled student service (DSS) coordinator or a learning disabilities advisor. It can be an ad hoc group in which students who are entering a special program within a university or college spend a week or more together during the summer or just before registration. This group might not stay together during the school year, but at least the students know each other. Or it can be a formal group that meets on a regular basis, with or without faculty involvement.

COUNSELING

If a student needs more than a support system or caring advice to cope with problems, then counseling should be considered. Although many students have already had some form of therapy when they were younger, it may not have been helpful at that point in their lives. However, older students are frequently more receptive to counseling. It becomes their choice, not their parents'. Because they are at an age when they are more introspective, or at least more interested in understanding themselves, they can become partners in the counseling process.

Making the Diagnosis

Counseling adults with learning disabilities requires a knowledge of learning disabilities. Whether counseling is done by a therapist (privately or in a counseling center), a disabled student services advisor, or a faculty member, an understanding of how learning disabilities can affect academic, social, and emotional development is crucial.

The therapeutic goals and directions may need to be different from the more traditional forms of therapy. The origins of symptoms, such as depression and anxiety, must be looked at from a broader perspective. In a learning disabled individual, these symptoms may be purely emotional in origin, they may be a result of the learning disability, or they may be a combination of both.

A good starting point in differentiating the causes of symptoms is a thorough case history. A developmental background, including early school experiences, can frequently indicate the presence of a learning disability. Whenever a counselor suspects that there might be a learning disability, testing should be given high priority. (For a discussion of testing, see chapter, "Diagnosis: Now What?")

Using the Diagnosis

An accurate diagnosis can provide several pieces of information. It can help to identify neurological and emotional causes, and it can indicate the realistic limitations of the disability. It can also give the counselor clues about what should be remediated, what should be left alone, and what compensations are possible. Finally, it can reveal strengths and suggest directions for academic and vocational goals.

Steven Schulman, a Washington, D.C., psychologist who works with learning disabled students, uses the diagnostic assessment as a basis for exploring with the student how learning disabilities have affected all aspects of his or her life. For many students, this is the first time they have realized that their actions and thoughts are not a result of being crazy or weird. The relief is often enormous, and in the therapeutic process, it can be a time of energy and exhilaration.

The Work of Therapy

However, the hard work is still ahead. Dr. Schulman feels that if progress is to be made, patients ultimately need to look at the defenses they have built up over the many years of trying to cope with their learning disabilities. Some have used their disability as a crutch and an excuse; others have compensated by exerting tremendous efforts of time and self-control; others have used it to avoid undertaking risks.

For each positive strategy, there is often a negative consequence. A student who spends many more hours than most students on assignments may give up a social life. A student who works so hard on controlling impulses because of fear of embarrassment may lose all spontaneity.

Establishing Trust

Whatever the defense mechanism, change can come if the therapist's credibility has first been established through a groundwork of supportive and empathic listening as well as involvement in helping to solve the student's everyday problems

Many students need assistance with basic living skills, such as getting along with roommates, dating, and managing time and money. Teaching these skills takes patience. But the reward can be the establishment of trust between counselor and student. It can also be the turning point in a student's growth toward responsible adulthood.

One counselor "saved" a very despondent student who had gone to the bottom after many failures. Not only did she help him understand his disabilities, but she taught him how to behave appropriately, even going with him to restaurants or other settings that were hard for him to manage. She helped him analyze his study skills and handle his extreme restlessness through the use of exercise breaks and short study times.

By working with him on practical problems, the counselor enhanced the student's self-esteem and earned his trust. She could then help him face his deep anger, especially toward his father whose disappointment was a controlling force in this young man's life. As this student's anger receded, he was able to make and keep friends — for the first time.

Other Techniques

Counselors often use a variety of techniques. In some settings, videotape is used to call attention to a student's restlessness, lack of eye contact, and body language. Thorne Wiggers, a counselor at George Washington University, works with learning disabled students on issues of time management, procrastination, stress, and socialization. He teaches students relaxation techniques and has also used art therapy as a means of reaching students.

Even when counseling is limited by time and money, the same goals and objectives are important. The counselor needs to refer the student for testing if a learning disability is suspected; help the student understand what the learning problems are and how they can be circumvented; and work out strategies and options so that strengths and talents can be developed.

174

DEVELOPING SOCIAL SKILLS

Many learning disabled persons have strong interpersonal skills. However, others find that their perceptual difficulties, which cause academic problems, also cause problems with personal relationships. Reading facial expressions, sensing whether a conversation is going well, understanding the point of a joke are all part of getting along with others. These supposedly easy responses for most people are major barriers for learning disabled people, who may never even know that their inappropriate reactions lost them a friend or a job.

Through counseling, many learning disabled students learn to enhance their social skills. However, developing social skills can also occur in other ways.

Self-awareness can be the first step in trying to overcome interpersonal difficulties. An older student, who has dealt with many of these problems, has worked hard to learn how to monitor herself in social and group situations. She now recognizes when her mind is racing, when she is turning someone off, or when she is making irrelevant comments. By being aware, she is often able to alter the situation. Role play is one technique she uses to improve her social skills.

Feedback

To improve interpersonal relations often takes not only self-awareness but sensitive feedback from someone who can talk directly about what needs to be changed in a person's behavior. Myrtle Snyder, of Central Washington University, uses every opportunity to work with her students on improving their social skills. Mixing her comments with humor and love, she does not hesitate to point out a student's inappropriate behavior, such as interruptions, coming late, or lack of eye contact. She too uses role playing to help students rehearse difficult real-life situations.

Psychodrama

The staff at the learning disability center at Philadelphia Community College has developed a three-day summer program for learning disabled students. Staff members have successfully used psychodrama to help students learn alternative ways of responding in difficult situations, such as reacting to a negative comment by an instructor, asking an unsympathetic professor to repeat a point, or dealing with peers who don't understand.

By taking each role in a situation, students learn to see other points of view and to understand how another person might feel. One student told the learning disabilities coordinator that he now has a "different set in my mind, and now I can respond in more positive ways."

SUPPORT GROUPS

Another approach to working out personal problems is to share them with others who have similar experiences. Whether studying in college or working and living in a community, learning disabled adults are linking up with one another to talk about common problems, to get practical help, and to build a social life.

175

Groups are cropping up in many parts of the country. Some are self-help, others are organized by professionals. Some have formal programs on topics of concern to members. Others stress rap sessions and personal development. It is in these groups that learning disabled adults can unburden themselves, exchange tips and strategies about how to handle course material, instructors, or job situations, and learn daily living skills. Groups are also a safe place to practice social skills and to heal and renew. For some, it is the first step away from families and into independent living.

Brown University

An exciting self-help story comes from Brown University (Rhode Island), where dyslexic students have become crusaders and outreach workers. These students have an official campus organization. They meet every two weeks to discuss common difficulties about places to study, how to handle problems with certain professors, what courses to select, and special accommodations that might be helpful. They are always on the lookout for students who might be dyslexic. They encourage these students to be tested so that they can learn about their areas of strength and weakness.

Another goal of this group is to educate the academic community about dyslexia. To do this, they have written a handbook, *Dyslexics at Brown, A Student's Perspective,* that describes what it is like to be dyslexic as well as alternatives on how to deal with it. This handbook is distributed to faculty members and advisers at the beginning of each year. The group is also helping other colleges start support groups.

The Marin Puzzle People

One of the most innovative and successful community self-help groups is the Marin Puzzle People. Jo Ann Haseltine, the founder of the Puzzle People, knows first hand how desolate and alone learning disabled people can feel. Out of her own struggles, she has developed this self-help group in the San Francisco Bay area.

Through well-planned social and educational activities, many members are learning how to socialize comfortably, how to share their problems and "war stories," how to discuss their legal rights, and how to develop independent living skills. Counseling sessions are offered to group members, and anyone can drop in to the office when they have a need to talk over a problem. The Puzzle People group works informally on social skills by providing immediate feedback or more formally through minicourses on assertiveness training, job hunting, and interpersonal relationships.

Setting up Support Groups

Whether on the campus or in the community, the first step in setting up a self-help group is to plan a gathering of learning disabled people. Announcements placed in school or local newspapers and on radio stations, posted on campus or community bulletin boards, or given to counseling and diagnostic centers are ways of spreading the word. Finding a time to meet is always difficult, but on a campus, possibilities include a dean's hour or club period.

Community groups might find it most convenient to meet at night or on weekends. A comfortable, private setting can encourage people to relax and feel at ease about talking and sharing.

Pitfalls

Not all efforts to start self-help groups have succeeded. No matter how well-organized and planned, no matter how flexible the meeting times or how ingenious the activity, the response is sometimes disappointing. Different explanations have been given. Students do not have enough time or prefer to be in mainstream campus activities; other learning disabled people do not necessarily share common interests; and many others do not want to be labeled as having a disability.

National Organizations

Despite organizational problems, self-help groups for learning disabled people are spreading. Two national organizations are committed to the growth of this movement and are encouraging and helping groups get started.

The Association for Children and Adults with Learning Disabilities (ACLD) has incorporated the needs of adults into its organization. The Youth and Adult section provides guidelines and assistance for setting up support groups and has published a booklet, *How to Start an LD Youth and Adult Group.*

The National Network of Learning Disabled Adults is an expanding, umbrella organization founded by men and women with learning disabilities. Over twenty communities have groups that are affiliated with the Network. Each one develops its own programs, based on the needs of its membership. (For addresses of local self-help groups, see the list of organizations at the end of the book.)

THE OTHER SIDE OF THE STORY

Although this chapter has concentrated on problems of personal adjustment, the other side of the story is the quiet heroism of so many learning disabled people. The disabilities are very real, but so are the talents, strengths, and abilities. Anyone who has worked with these adults has also made a personal adjustment in recognizing, admiring, and respecting their extraordinary efforts and accomplishments.

Additional Reading About Counseling and Support Groups

"A Psychological Consultation Program for Learning Disabled Adults," by R. Craig Lefebre, Journal of College Student Personnel (Volume 25, No. 4, July 1984, pages 361–362). (For reprints, write to Dr. Lefebre, The Counseling Center, University of Virginia, Charlottesville, Virginia 22903.)

Counseling and Accommodating the Student with Learning Disabilities, by Dale Brown. President's Committee on Employment of the Handicapped, Washington, D.C. 20210. (7 pages, free) 1980.

"Dyslexia," by Katherine Hinds. Brown Alumni Monthly (December 1984/January 1985). Box 1854, Brown University, Providence, Rhode Island 02912.

Dyslexics at Brown, A Student's Perspective. Available from the Office of the Dean of The College, Brown University, Providence, Rhode Island 02912.

"Learning Disabilities and Adolescents: Developmental Considerations," by Jonathan Cohen, Adolescent Psychiatry: Developmental and Clinical Studies (Volume 12, pages 177–196, edited by Sherman Feinstein). University of Chicago Press. (583 pages, $25.00) 1985

"Learning Disabilities and the College Student: Identification and Diagnosis," by Jonathan Cohen, Adolescent Psychiatry: Developmental and Clinical Studies (Volume 11, pages 177–198, edited by Max Sugar). University of Chicago Press. (239 pages, $22.00) 1983

"Psychotherapeutic Issues for the Learning Disabled Adult," by Steven S. Schulman. Professional Psychology: Research and Practice (Volume 15, Number 6), 1984. (Reprints available from Steven S. Schulman, 4400 East-West Highway, Suite 1104, Bethesda, Maryland 20814.)

Social Development of Learning Disabled Persons, by Doreen Kronick. Jossey-Bass Publishers, 433 California Street, San Francisco, California 94104. (222 pages, $22.95; also available in paperback) 1981

Social Solutions: A Curriculum for Young Adults, by American Institutes for Research. Professional Associated Resources, 2917 Adeline Drive, Burlingame, California 94010. ($200.00) 1983

Socialization of Learning Disabled Adults: Why and How to Organize a Group, by Jo Ann Haseltine. (Available from the Marin Puzzle People, Inc., 1368 Lincoln Avenue, Suite 106, San Rafael, California 94901, $3.00.)

The Life Skills Training, A Program for Parents and Their Learning Disabled Teenagers, by Suzanne Harmon and Marjorie Kramer. Closer Look, 1201 16th Street, N.W., Washington, D.C. 20036. (64 pages, $30.00) 1983

ACCESS

ORGANIZATIONS THAT
CAN HELP

INTERVIEWS

ACCESS

With this final chapter, we come full circle, back to the beginning, back to questions about the need for access to postsecondary education for learning disabled students, back to questions about ways that campuses can make accessibility work. This chapter describes how services for learning disabled students can get started. It draws on the experiences of campus leaders who have brought about changes in attitudes, policies, and programs. By looking at these beginnings, we can prepare to meet the growing imperative for action.

The learning disabled population is the fastest growing group of disabled students on American campuses. The American Council on Education reports that the percentage of learning disabled students grew from 4.7% in 1978 (the first year that statistics on disabled students were gathered) to 14.3% in 1985.

The demand for higher education for learning disabled students raises urgent issues. Campus administrators and faculty members are asking how they can serve a new population of students in a period of rising costs. High school staff members are asking how to develop stronger links to postsecondary schools and programs so that choices made by learning disabled students are appropriate. Parents are asking what to do to prepare their sons and daughters for education beyond high school. Parents, professionals, and learning disabled adults are asking how existing options can be expanded.

IGNITING THE SPARK

Many of the concerns felt by administrators, faculty, students, and parents are addressed in earlier chapters of this book. Innovative ideas have been tested and proven on campuses throughout the country, and practical solutions are already making a difference in the lives of learning disabled students.

How can these practical ideas take root on other campuses? How can we spread knowledge about learning disabilities and accommodations that permit learning disabled students to use their strengths? How does change begin?

In our interviews for this book, stories repeatedly told of how change occurs through individual acts of courage or compassion. A student who takes the step of explaining his or her learning disability to a professor ignites a spark of understanding that starts the process of change. An instructor who takes the time to discover how a student learns advances the process of change. Conviction and insight that come from small human interactions pave the way to broader action.

Educational Pioneers

At the core of institutional change are remarkable individuals — dedicated and imaginative educational pioneers. They come from backgrounds that include special education, counseling, speech therapy, or rehabilitation. Some are administrators; others are professors often motivated by personal experience with a learning disabled child or inspired by the determination of a learning disabled student. All could have taken safe and conventional paths but chose to work in a new and uncharted field. It is from these leaders that we have learned the most about change.

WINNING COMMITMENT

Whoever takes the lead and wherever action starts, ideas need to be shared, information gathered, and plans made. There is no particular order for getting started. But possibly, the most important way to begin is by winning the commitment of administrators and faculty members. Their support is essential if a major effort on behalf of learning disabled students is to succeed.

Knowing the Facts

Knowledge of learning disabilities is still new. Many faculty members and administrators question the abilities of learning disabled students, view accommodations with skepticism, and need proof that new expenditures are justified. They need to know the facts. They need to know the record of learning disabled students. On several campuses, for example, learning disabled students, who had appropriate accommodations, achieved higher grade point averages than other students.

At Adelphi College (New York), Fred Barbaro, director of the program for learning disabled students, analyzed the grades of the entire student body and found that learning disabled students in the Adelphi program had their share of A's and less than half as many D's, incompletes, and withdrawals as nonlearning disabled students.

These and other facts about learning disabled students can be disseminated through personal interviews, workshops, seminars, conferences, and informal meetings. On many campuses, films, fact sheets, and reprints of articles and newsletters are used to explain what learning disabilities are and what they aren't, and how they can affect a student's life. As communication is established, as knowledge grows and spreads, commitment evolves.

182

ASSESSING NEEDS

Commitment must also be based on the reality of needs that exist on each campus. When faculty members at the University of New England became aware of learning disabled students on campus, Barbara Berkovich, consultant and learning disabilities specialist, was asked to evaluate the problems and recommend ways to help instructors meet the needs of these students. She spent several months interviewing the staff, and when she developed the Individual Learning Program, she had full faculty commitment.

Each campus has its own way to assess needs, but some concerns are common to all. What students will be served? How many? How will students be identified? What services should be provided? Who will provide them? Are there campus centers that can be tapped for diagnostic or other services? How will the need for special instruction be handled? How will the cost of services be met?

INTERDISCIPLINARY PLANNING TEAMS

To assess needs and make plans, many campuses set up interdisciplinary planning teams that include key administrators and members of faculty departments. The planning committee at Miami-Dade Community College illustrates how a planning team brings together many campus services.

The committee, convened by the associate deans for Student Development and Learning Support Services, met ten times between June 1979 and December 1980 to develop a highly successful, intensive program for learning disabled students. Members included representatives of disabled student services, student activities, financial aid services, developmental studies (reading, writing, and study skills programs), behavioral

studies, counseling, the English Language Institute, psychological services, and the Speech, Language, and Learning Clinic. The learning disability specialist acted as a consultant to the committee. The integration of so many services in the planning period has had a major, positive effect on the Miami-Dade program.

COSTS AND BENEFITS

During the planning process, information about costs — and benefits — must be carefully evaluated.

Retention Rates

In this period of cost constraints, it is important to note that several studies have found that the rate of retention for learning disabled students is higher than for other students. Records at one university showed that learning disabled students have a seventy-five percent retention rate, compared with an average of fifty percent for other students.

Enrollment Changes

Another aspect of cost effectiveness relates to shifts in college enrollments. During the next decade, a significant drop in enrollment is expected. Institutions are alarmed about the loss; some fear for their survival. In response to this fear, leading educators point out that qualified learning disabled students can, with appropriate accommodations, fill spaces that soon will be empty or already are.

Types of Expenses

High retention figures and potentially high student enrollment are expected benefits from serving learning disabled students. But what about actual costs? Costs that need to be investigated include salaries for a program director or coordinator who is a specialist in learning disabilities and for other staff mem-

183

bers who can provide diagnostic and instructional services. Other costs are for auxiliary aids such as taping equipment, support services of tutors and readers, and administrative expenses.

Some campuses absorb the entire cost of services; others, as discussed earlier, only charge for certain services, such as tutoring and diagnosis. A fee is charged by a number of private colleges that provide intensive support.

USE OF EXISTING RESOURCES

In developing new programs, there is no need to reinvent the wheel. Program developers on most campuses have found that costs can be contained through intelligent use of available resources. Some of these resources are writing and math labs, developmental or reading courses, psychological services, and peer tutor programs. These services are not necessarily designed for learning disabled students. But on some campuses, learning disability specialists work with staff members to sensitize them to specific needs of learning disabled students.

Another cost-effective strategy is to use services already in place for other disabled groups. Notetakers for deaf students and readers for blind students are examples of services that can be of help to learning disabled students.

In addition, development of compensatory strategies and accommodations is not costly. Changes in ways of teaching, stimulated by a new awareness of differences in styles of learning, can create an accessible environment without large outlays of funds.

The Greatest Resource

Campuses have given special recognition to those faculty members who extend an extra measure of understanding and help to learning disabled students. At Marist College (New York), an annual Awareness Recognition Day applauds the consistent support of its faculty. At Towson State College (Maryland), an "Aw Shucks" award is given yearly to the faculty member who has contributed most to the success of a learning disabled student. These acts of appreciation reflect awareness that a receptive instructor is the greatest resource available to learning disabled students.

ALLIES AND INFORMATION PROVIDERS

Outstanding organizations are allies in the effort to create greater postsecondary accessibility for learning disabled students. Operating on national and local levels, these groups are excellent sources of information, literature, ideas, and practical advice. They include

• The Association for Children and Adults with Learning Disabilities (ACLD)

• The Association on Handicapped Student Service Programs in Postsecondary Education (AHSSPPE)

• The Council for Exceptional Children

• HEATH Resource Center, The National Clearinghouse on Postsecondary Education for Handicapped Individuals

• National Network of Learning Disabled Adults (NNLDA)

• The Orton Dyslexia Society

Each of these organizations is in touch with dedicated and knowledgeable people in different parts of the country, who can give valuable suggestions for program development. Addresses and descriptions of the work of these organizations are listed under "Organizations That Can Help."

National Data Bank

Another source of information is the National Data Bank for Disabled Student Services, which conducts an annual survey on campuses throughout the country. The survey includes data on services to learning disabled students, such as assistance in ordering taped texts, counseling, editing and notetaking, priority registration, remedial services, support groups, and test administration. For information about the Data Bank, write to William Scales, Director, Disabled Student Services, Shoemaker Hall, University of Maryland, College Park, Maryland 20742.

Learn from Models

Each campus can learn from the work of others. There is no one "best" model, but there are many successful approaches developed by schools that have long served learning disabled students. Curry College, The American International College (both in Massachusetts), Wright State University in Ohio, Barat College in Illinois, Achieve Program at Southern Illinois University, Westminster College in Missouri, Columbus Technical Institute in Ohio, and Ventura, De Anza, and Cypress Community Colleges in California, and the University of California, Berkeley are among the schools that have had years of successful experience.

For descriptions of these and other programs, check *Guides to Postsecondary Programs for Learning Disabled Students* (Figure 13, in chapter "Matchmaking: Selection and Admission"). In addition, the people interviewed for this book are excellent sources of ideas and information. (For names, see "Interviews".)

SOURCES OF FUNDING AND TECHNICAL ASSISTANCE

Federal grants have made funds available for start-up costs of programs, demonstration or model projects, and development of materials and services. These grants are competitive and usually limited from one to three years. Time must be spent on careful investigation of the requirements of grant-making agencies; learning disabilities is only one of many possible areas these agencies might select for support. Even if federal funds are awarded, programs for learning disabled students must have institutional backing if they are to survive and flourish.

For further information about submitting grant proposals, get in touch with the following offices:

Dr. Joseph Rosenstein, Division of Innovation and Development, U.S. Department of Education, Third and C Streets, S.W., Washington, D.C. 20202, (202) 732-1176.

Diana Hayman, Program Officer, Fund for the Improvement of Postsecondary Education, Room 3100 ROB 3, U.S. Department of Education, 400 Maryland Avenue, S.W., Washington, D.C. 20202, (202) 245-8091.

Carole Smith, Division of Student Services, Office of Postsecondary Education, Room 3066 ROB 3, U.S. Department of Education, 400 Maryland Avenue, S.W., Washington, D.C. 20202, (202) 245-2165.

Technical Assistance

The federal government, through the Office for Civil Rights, U.S. Department of Education, offers technical assistance on accommodations covered by Section 504. A 504 technical assistance staff is available at ten regional offices to respond to inquiries. (See "Organizations That Can Help," for a list of regional offices.)

A free pamphlet, *Section 504 of the Rehabilitation Act of 1973: Handicapped Persons' Rights Under Federal Law,* can be obtained from the U.S. Department of Education, Office for Civil Rights, Washington, D.C. 20202. The pamphlet explains the provisions of the law and gives information on how the technical assistance staff can help.

Support for Vocational Education

It is important to remember that the Perkins Act makes federal funds available to the states for postsecondary vocational education programs for handicapped students. Community-based programs (public or private) can apply to states for use of these special set-aside funds.

State Funding

In California, the costs of services for disabled postsecondary students, including those who are learning disabled, must be covered by state funds. In 1976, the state legislature passed the Lanerman Act (AB-77), mandating support services for all disabled students on postsecondary campuses. At the present time, 106 community colleges in California offer a wide range of state-sponsored services. Services are also provided at state colleges and universities.

EXAMPLES OF CHANGE

There are many exciting stories about the ways in which different campuses have created services for learning disabled students. The following are examples of how different programs got started and how they solved common problems. The HELDS Program, the Learning Efficiency Program at Johnson County Community College (Kansas), and the Ohio Consortium have each made an unusual contribution to the state of a new art.

The HELDS Project: Student and Faculty Involvement

The idea for the HELDS Project grew out of the Educational Opportunity Program to provide tutoring for students at Central Washington University, an institution with 7,000 students. The tutoring program coordinator, Myrtle Snyder, was a reading specialist and special educator. Her experience with learning disabled students alerted her to the fact that a large number of students applying for tutoring were actually learning disabled. Snyder, with the Assistant Dean for Minority Affairs and Educational Opportunity and a group of faculty members, submitted a grant proposal to the U.S. Department of Education (Fund for the Improvement of Postsecondary Education) to provide academic support services for learning disabled students and train a corps of professors to develop new techniques for teaching learning disabled students in mainstream classrooms.

The project started in 1980. To find professors with whom to work, Snyder used an innovative approach. She went to the students and asked them to identify faculty members in each department who were known to be sympathetic to student problems. These faculty members became the nucleus of a successful effort to raise awareness of learning disabilities throughout the university community. (See chapter, "How to Keep the Glare Off the Chalkboard.")

Johnson County Community College: Reaching High-Risk Students

At Johnson County Community College (Kansas), the administration's concern about declining enrollment and the vision of the Special Services Director have combined to produce an innovative program for high-risk students.

The program, Strategies to Improve Learning Efficiency, offers special classes in conjunction with the regular curriculum. Developed by Edward Franklin, Director of Special Services, these "learning efficiency" classes are given for students enrolled in a specific course, such as psychology or history. Working on class assignments, students are taught strategies for skimming and scanning textbooks, paraphrasing, expanding vocabulary, improving memory, and taking tests. In addition, students are taught to generalize and to apply learning strategies to their other courses.

The program is voluntary. Students sign up for various reasons. Some are getting good grades but are under stress because of inefficient learning habits. Others are learning disabled but do not have to be identified in order to enroll.

A light assessment is done to find out the learning needs of each student in the program. If indicated, more thorough diagnostic testing is arranged. Students who require accommodations may obtain them, often with the help of a special instructor who sits in on a class to see what is needed.

The program is growing, and the college is finding that students who might otherwise drop out of school are learning tools not only for survival but success.

Ohio State University: Consortium for Equal Access

Collaborative planning and pooling of resources can make it possible to provide special services for disabled students despite limited financial resources. The recently developed consortium for serving learning disabled students in Ohio is an example.

For several years, the Office of Disability Services at Ohio State University in Columbus has provided accommodations and support services to a steadily increasing number of learning disabled students. Lydia Block, Coordinator of Counseling and Learning Disabilities Services, saw the need to create equal access for learning disabled students on the five other Ohio State campuses. These small, two-year campuses, all of which offer Associate degrees, had a valuable contribution to make to learning disabled students. But none of them had the resources to undertake a new program on its own.

The idea for the consortium was born. Under Lydia Block's leadership, plans were made for joint financing of shared personnel; and in September 1984, the consortium got started with a one-year grant from the U.S. Department of Education.

During its first successful year, 100 students received help from two itinerant learning disabled specialists and a psychologist, in addition to other psychologists available on an as-needed basis. On-campus supervisors, trained on Ohio State's Columbus campus, coordinated services at each school. Faculty members have been extremely responsive.

Ohio's learning disabled students now have the opportunity to attend a campus close to home, prepare for work, or get the start they need to transfer to the four-year university program.

THE BROADER PICTURE

Building programs requires community as well as campus support. Local conferences on postsecondary opportunities for learning disabled students can bring parents, high school and college professionals, and students together to assess the need for new services and plan action based on knowledge. Concerned groups can let the public know the value of accommodations in education and in employment. They can write to the editors of their local papers, call the attention of city desks to local success stories, and inform editors and broadcasters about the issues. They can talk at meetings of citizen groups, sensitizing members to learning disabilities and paving the way for acceptance of learning disabled men and women in all of society.

UNLOCKING POTENTIAL

Campus access for learning disabled students goes beyond an immediate goal. It has far-reaching implications for all students and for all teaching and learning.

For learning disabled men and women, access to learning opportunities means access to hopes and aspirations, to talents and abilities, to dreams that might otherwise fade but can now flower.

For others, too, the ideas inherent in accessibility are liberating. Basic to these ideas is the recognition of differences in the ways that people learn, think, and create. As we acknowledge differences and respect their worth, we give everyone the opportunity to use strengths that may lie hidden. Each of us is *disabled* when life is limited by narrow definitions of potential. Each of us is *enabled* when we see potential through a wide lens, encompassing the brightness of the many different gifts and abilities of humankind.

ORGANIZATIONS THAT CAN HELP

The Association for Children and Adults with Learning Disabilities (ACLD), **4156 Library Road, Pittsburgh, Pennsylvania 15234, (412) 341-1515. Jean Petersen, Executive Director.**

The ACLD is an international membership organization of parents of learning disabled children, adults with learning disabilities, and professionals who are devoted to finding solutions to problems associated with learning disabilities. Approximately 800 state and local affiliates are active in areas including education, legislation, and research.

The national office refers inquirers to local chapters; sends a free packet of information; disseminates more than 500 publications, including a listing of postsecondary programs; and publishes a bimonthly newsletter, *ACLD Newsbriefs.* ACLD's annual conference is a major forum for exchange of ideas and information.

The Association on Handicapped Student Service Programs in Postsecondary Education (AHSSPPE). **P.O. Box 21192, Columbus, Ohio 43221, (614) 488-4972. Jane Jarrow, Executive Director.**

AHSSPPE consists of 600 members in 400 institutions of higher education. They are dedicated to helping people with disabilities participate fully in the mainstream of campus life.

The national office shares information about postsecondary opportunities and puts inquirers in touch with its campus network of disabled student service providers throughout the country.

The organization sponsors a national Special Interest Group on learning disabilities, which publishes its own newsletter on campus services and programs. AHSSPPE's publications include a quarterly newsletter, a journal, and published proceedings of its annual conferences.

Council for Exceptional Children (CEC). **1920 Association Drive, Reston, Virginia 22091, (703) 620-3660 (TTY). Jeptha V. Greer, Executive Director.**

CEC is a major national organization that serves special educators and others dedicated to the education of exceptional children and youth. The CEC Division for Learning Disabilities is involved in improving the quality of services to learning disabled children, youth, and adults. The Division publishes two journals, *Learning Disabilities Focus* and *LD Research.* CEC publishes two journals, *Exceptional Children* and *Teaching Exceptional Children,* and holds numerous conferences on significant issues.

HEATH Resource Center, The National Clearinghouse on Postsecondary Education for Handicapped Individuals. **One Dupont Circle, Suite 670, Washington, D.C. 20036. Toll-free number 1-800-54-HEATH. Washington, D.C. area (202) 939-9320 Voice/TDD. Rhona Hartman, Director.**

The staff of this national, federally funded center gathers and disseminates information about postsecondary educational support services, policies, procedures, adaptations, and oportunities on American campuses, vocational-technical schools, adult education programs, and independent living centers. The center publishes a newsletter three times a year, disseminates an excellent series of fact sheets on topical issues, publishes a resource directory, and responds to mail or phone requests for information.

National Network of Learning Disabled Adults (NNLDA). **808 West 82nd Street, F-2, Scottsdale, Arizona 85257. William Butler, Steering Committee.**

The National Network of Learning Disabled Adults (NNLDA) was formed in 1980 to provide mutual support and to improve understanding and communication among learning disabled adults, self-help groups, national organizations, and the general public. NNLDA also encourages institutions and employers to provide accommodations for the learning disabled adult. A quarterly newsletter and annual convention are part of the Network's national activities.

The following is a list of self-help groups compiled by NNLDA (information updated in January 1985). Information about changes in address or about new self-help groups should be forwarded to Dale Brown, ALDA, P.O. Box 9722, Friendship Station, Washington, D.C. 20016.

Alaska
Cable Starling
Alaska Association of
Learning Disabled Adults
4300 Lois
Anchorage, Alaska 99503
(907) 562-5301 or
(907) 272-9162

Arkansas
Calvin Johnson
Adult Group of ACLD
Dept. Curriculum & Instruction
Univ. of Arkansas-Little Rock
33rd & University Avenue
Little Rock, Arkansas 72204
(501) 535-1075 (h)
(501) 569-3124 (w)

Arizona
Wayne French
Phoenix Chapter of Adults with
Learning Disabilities
1901 E. Osborne
Phoenix, Arizona 86016
(602) 265-5085 (h)

California
Joanne Haseltine, Ex. Director
Marin County Puzzle People
1368 Lincoln Avenue, Suite 105
San Rafael, California 94901
(415) 453-4006 (w)

Colorado
Kathy Knight, Director
Association of Adults with
Learning Disabilities
2645 Chestnut Drive
Grand Junction, Colorado 81501
(303) 245-4471 (h)
(303) 244-6191 (w)

Connecticut
Paul Seigel
New Horizons
17 Willard Street
New Haven, Connecticut 06516
(203) 389-8330

Georgia
Richard Kaplan
Georgia Association of Adults
with Learning Disabilities
475 Burgandy Court
Stone Mountain, Georgia 30087
(404) 498-1606 (h)

Iowa
Joyce Suchsland, President
Iowa Youth and Adult Section
1137 1/2 Sixth Street
Nevada, Iowa
(515) 382-5915 (h)

Maryland
Gale Bell
Association of Learning
Disabled Adults
P.O. Box 9722
Friendship Station
Washington, D.C. 20016
(301) 593-1035 (h)

Massachusetts
John Namber
P.O. Box 636
Prudential Station
Boston, Massachusetts 02188
(617) 232-2737

Michigan
Brian Gbur
Michigan ACLD Young Adult
Support Team
1510 North Blair
Royal Oak, Michigan 48067
(313) 544-4561

Minnesota
Connie Firminger
Southwest State Support Group
c/o Marilyn Leach, Director
Learning Resources, CAB 109
Southwest State University
Marshall, Minnesota 56258
(507) 537-6169 (w)

New Jersey
Mary Ann Riccitelli
Advocates for LD Adults
70 Freemont Street, EI
Bloomfield, New Jersey 07003
(201) 429-0113

New York
Nonnie Star
Adelphi LD Group
Adelphi University
Garden City, Long Island, NY
11630
(516) 228-7409 (w)
(516) 374-9285 (h)

Allan Fine
Bronx Organization of the
Learning Disabled
2300 Olinville Avenue
Bronx, New York 10467
(212) 798-3475 (h)

Delos Smith
New York Branch, Orton Dyslexia
Society Adult Group
80 Fifth Avenue, Room 903
New York, New York 10011
(212) 691-1930

Ohio
Dave Saunders
ACLD Youth and Adult Section
of Clark and Champaign Counties
237 South Houston Pike
South Vienna, Ohio 45369
(513) 568-4167 (h)

Pennsylvania
Richard Cooper
Pennsylvania Network of LD Adults
P.O. Box 716
Bryn Mawr, Pennsylvania 19010
(215) 895-8596 (h)

Jere Miller
ACLD Youth and Adult Section
154 N. Laurel Street
Manheim, Pennsylvania 17545
(717) 665-5065 (h)

Texas
John Moss
LAUNCH, Inc.
Dept. of Special Education
East Texas State University
Commerce, Texas 75428
(214) 886-5940 (w)

Virginia
Susan Opal
Northern Virginia Support Group for
Adults with Learning Disabilities
49 Mount Vernon Avenue
Alexandria, Virginia 22301
(703) 548-8691 (h)

Washington
Deborah Dishman
LD Adults, Seattle and
Surrounding Areas
4051 S.W. Concord
Seattle, Washington 98136
(206) 932-5507 (h)

190

Orton Dyslexia Society, Inc., **724 York Road, Baltimore, Maryland 21204, (301) 296-0232. Eleanor Hartwig, Administrative Director.**

The Orton Dyslexia Society is an international organization concerned with specific language difficulty or developmental dyslexia. The goals of the society are to improve understanding and knowledge about dyslexia and to promote research and appropriate teaching techniques. In addition, national and branch offices respond to requests for information about postsecondary education and related resources.

The society holds national and state conferences and publishes a yearly journal and a quarterly newsletter, along with a wealth of materials on various aspects and treatment of dyslexia. There are 33 branches of the society.

Parent Training and Information Centers. Federation for Children with Special Needs. **312 Stuart Street, Boston, Massachusetts 02116. (617) 482-2915. Contact Martha Ziegler.**

This is a national network of federally funded local and regional centers dedicated to providing services to parents of handicapped children and youth. Members are knowledgeable about community resources and programs contributing to successful transition to employment and independence. Approximately sixty local centers and five regional centers are coordinated under a federal program, Technical Assistance to Parent Projects (TAPP), administered by the Federation for Children with Special Needs. The Federation can make referrals to the nearest parent center.

U.S. Department of Education, Office for Civil Rights, Washington, D.C. 20202. **Regional Civil Rights Offices.**

Region I
Connecticut, Maine, Massachusetts, New Hampshire, Rhode Island, Vermont
Regional Civil Rights Director
Office for Civil Rights, Region I
U.S. Department of Education
John W. McCormack Post Office and
Court House-Room 222
Post Office Square
Boston, Massachusetts 02109
(617) 223-1154, TTY (617) 223-1111

Region II
New Jersey, New York, Puerto Rico, Virgin Islands
Regional Civil Rights Director
Office for Civil Rights, Region II
U.S. Department of Education
26 Federal Plaza, R33-130
New York, New York 10278
(212) 264-5180, TTY (212) 264-9464

Region III
Delaware, District of Columbia, Maryland, Pennsylvania, Virginia, West Virginia
Regional Civil Rights Director
Office for Civil Rights, Region III
U.S. Department of Education
Gateway Building, 3535 Market Street
Post Office Box 13716
Philadelphia, Pennsylvania 19101
(215) 596-6772, TTY (215) 596-6794

Region IV
Alabama, Florida, Georgia, Kentucky, Mississippi, North Carolina, South Carolina, Tennessee
Regional Civil Rights Director
Office for Civil Rights, Region IV
U.S. Department of Education
101 Marietta Tower, Room 2702
Atlanta, Georgia 30323
(404) 221-2954, TTY (404) 221-2010

Region V

Illinois, Indiana, Minnesota, Michigan, Ohio, Wisconsin
Regional Civil Rights Director
Office for Civil Rights, Region V
U.S. Department of Education
300 South Wacker Drive, 8th Floor
Chicago, Illinois 60606
(312) 353-2520, TTY (312) 353-2540

Region VI

Arkansas, Louisiana, New Mexico, Oklahoma, Texas
Regional Civil Rights Director
Office for Civil Rights, Region VI
U.S. Department of Education
1200 Main Tower Building, Room 1935
Dallas, Texas 75202
(214) 767-3951, TTY (214) 767-6599

Region VII

Iowa, Kansas, Missouri, Nebraska
Regional Civil Rights Director
Office for Civil Rights, Region VII
U.S. Department of Education
324 E. 11th Street, 24th Floor
Kansas City, Missouri 64106
(816) 374-2223, TTY (816) 374-7264

Region VIII

Colorado, Montana, North Dakota, South Dakota, Utah, Wyoming
Regional Civil Rights Director
Office for Civil Rights, Region VIII
U.S. Department of Education
Federal Office Building
1961 Stout Street, Room 1185
Denver, Colorado 80294
(303) 844-5695, TTY (303) 844-3417

Region IX

Arizona, California, Hawaii, Nevada, Guam, Trust Territory of the Pacific Islands, American Samoa
Regional Civil Rights Director
Office for Civil Rights, Region IX
U.S. Department of Education
1275 Market Street, 14th Floor
San Francisco, California 94103
(415) 556-9894, TTY (415) 556-1933

Region X

Alaska, Idaho, Oregon, Washington
Regional Civil Rights Director
Office for Civil Rights, Region X
U.S. Department of Education
2901 3rd Avenue, Mail Stop 106
Seattle, Washington 98121
(206) 442-1636, TTY (206) 442-4542

INTERVIEWS

The information used in this book was gathered primarily through extensive interviewing of people with first-hand experiences — campus professionals, parents of learning disabled high school and postsecondary students, and learning disabled students who were currently enrolled in or had graduated from a postsecondary program. Additional interviews were conducted with counselors, diagnosticians, vocational rehabilitation professionals, and other specialists.

A series of on-campus interviews was conducted to learn about practical strategies currently in use for accommodating learning disabled students in many different postsecondary settings. Selection of sites for these interviews was made in consultation with the Advisory Board of the CALD project listed below. The criteria for selection of campuses set by the Advisory Board required that campuses be representative of each of the ten federal regions; four-year and two-year institutions; public and private institutions; liberal arts, vocational, and adult education programs; campuses at which learning disabled students were mainstreamed; and campuses that offered intensive specialized learning disabilities programs.

We received invaluable assistance from the Association on Handicapped Student Service Programs in Postsecondary Education (AHSSPPE), which helped in making the final selection of campuses, based on Advisory Board recommendations, and in recruiting college professionals to conduct on-site interviews.

In addition, the Association for Children and Adults with Learning Disabilities (ACLD) arranged interviews with parents; the National Network for Learning Disabled Adults assisted in interviewing learning disabled adults; and the National Capital Area Disabled Student Services Coalition made it possible to carry out interviews on campuses in the Washington, D.C., area.

Advisory Board

The Advisory Board for the CALD (Campus Access for the Learning Disabled) project consisted of the following leaders in the fields of education, disabled student services, diagnosis, rehabilitation, psychology, and government: Hazel Benn, Associate Executive Director, Association of Collegiate Registrars and Admissions Officers (Retired) • Sharon Bonney, Director, Disabled Student Program, University of California-Berkeley • Dale Brown, Program Manager, President's Committee for Employment of the Handicapped • Dorothy Crawford, Past President, Association for Children and Adults with Learning Disabilities • Linda Donnels, Assistant Dean for Educational Services, The George Washington University.

• Anne Fleming, President, Association for Children and Adults with Learning Disabilities • Rhona Hartman, Director, HEATH Resource Center, The National Clearinghouse on Postsecondary Education for Handicapped Individuals.

• Eleanor Hartwig, Administrative Director, Orton Dyslexia Society • Pamela J. Leconte, Coordinator, Collaborative Vocational Education Program, The George Washington University • Lynn Harrison Martin, former coordinator, Special Student Services, Montgomery College (Maryland) • Lynn O'Brien, Director, Specific Diagnostic Studies, Rockville, Maryland • Marlene Pinton, Past President, American School Counselor Association • William Scales, Director, Disabled Student Services, University of Maryland • Steven Schulman, Clinical Psychologist • Gerald Siegel, York College of Pennsylvania • Myrtle Snyder, Director, The HELDS Project, Central Washington University • Martin Spickler, Rehabilitation Services Administration • David W. Stewart, American Council on Education.

• Nancy Stout, Assistant Executive Director, Independent Living Services, San Antonio, Texas • Dorothy Stump, Learning Disability Specialist, University of California-Berkeley • Michael McMullen, graduate of Central Washington University • Eleanor Westhead, Director, Learning Needs and Evaluation Center, University of Virginia.

Campus Interviews

The following educators, disabled student service coordinators, faculty and other campus professionals provided an immense fund of knowledge: • Barbara A. Bernhardt, Catholic University (Washington, D.C.) • Constance Bohns, 916 Vocational Center, Minnesota • Davis Burrell, De Kalb Area Vocational-Technical School (Georgia) • Barbara Cordoni and Gary Phillips, Achieve Program, Southern Illinois University • Fred Barbaro and Nonnie Starr, Adelphi University (New York) • Jonathan Blum-Feshback, psychiatrist, Georgetown University Counseling Center (Washington, D.C.) • Lynne Dowell, Towson State University (Maryland) • Linda Donnels, The George Washington University (Washington, D.C.) • Johanna Fisher, Bowie State College • Douglas Gill, Division of Vocational Technical Education, State of Washington • Lillian Hursaker, Community College of Denver • Todd Hutton and Audrey T. Edwards, Frostburg State College (Maryland) • Carrie R. Johnson, Prince Georges Community College (Maryland) •

Warren King, Ohio State University • Marilyn Leach, Southwest State University (Minnesota) • Faith Leonard, The American University (Washington, D.C.) • John F. Locker, Hocking Technical College (Ohio) • Charlotte Loveless, Catonsville Community College (Maryland) • Lynne Harrison Martin, Montgomery College (Maryland) • Bernice Munsey, Educational Specialist (Washington, D.C.) • Hank F. Ottinger, Westminster College (Missouri) • Dianne Perreira, Marist College (New York) • Betty S. Robinson, College of the Ozarks (Arkansas) • Dianne Rossman, Miami-Dade Community College (Florida) • Joan Sedita, Landmark School (Massachusetts) • William Scales, University of Maryland • Myrtle Snyder, Central Washington University (State of Washington) •

Dorothy Stump, University of California, Berkeley • Pat Giannini, Project A.B.L.E. (Norwalk, Connecticut) • Susan Vogel, Barat College (Illinois) • Gertrude Webb and Ronald Warners, Curry College (Massachusetts) • Virginia Westhead, University of Virginia • Henry Wilcox, University of the District of Columbia • Linda Wetters, Columbus Technical Institute • Barbara Greenfeld, Howard Community College (Maryland) • Dr. Stanley Antonoff, New York University College of Dentistry • Jeffrey Barsch, Ventura Community College (California) • Laurel Best, Cypress College (California) •

Nancy Dworkin, Center for Unique Learners (Maryland) • Barbara Given, George Mason University (Virginia) • Edward Franklin, Johnson County Community College (Missouri) • Margaret Glad, St. Louis Community College (Missouri) • Eleanor Harner, University of Arizona • John Herum, Central Washington University • Shushila Kapur, Vocational Rehabilitation (Washington, D.C.) • John Moss, East Texas State University • Robert Nash, University of Wisconsin-Oshkosh • Margaret M. Policastro, Roosevelt University (Chicago) • Lisa Schell, Southern Vermont University • Janet Schrock, Lab School of Washington (Washington, D.C.) • Nancy Smith, University of Wisconsin-Madison • Robert Shaw, Brown University (Rhode Island) • Arlene Silverstein, LEAP (Maryland) • Carol Sullivan, Northern Virginia Community College • Janet Way, Springfield School District (Pennsylvania) • Thorne Wiggers, The George Washington University (Washington, D.C.) • Sandy Webb, Capital Area Career Center (Michigan) • and Ann Winters, Marietta Kobb Technical School (Georgia).

194

Campus Interviewers

On-campus interviews were carried out by Maria Bacigalupo, Curry College; Lydia Block, Ohio State University; Sally Dedecker, Achieve Program, Southern Illinois; Barbara Greenfeld, Howard Community College; James Hemauer, University of Arkansas; Barbara Irwin, Miami-Dade Community College; Kathleen Desmond Knight, The George Washington University; Dr. Victor H. Margolis, Nassau Community College; Lynn Monge, Southwest State University; Elizabeth K. Nelson, Prince Georges Community College; Donna H. Phillips, University of Missouri; Anne Thompson, Central Washington University; Suzanne Tucker, Connecticut State University; and Bradley T. Webber, Marist College.

Interviews with other professionals, parents, students, and learning disabled adults were carried out by the authors, the CALD Project staff, and the Closer Look staff and interns, including Roberta McFarland and Rachel Rockenmacher.

Learning Disabled Students

The many students who told us about their personal experiences included the following: Richard Biby, The George Washington University; Tom Blatnik, Curry College; Rhoda Lee Berchuck, The George Washington University; William F. Clare, Catholic University; Brian Cohen, The American University; Meg Hunter, The American University; David Johnson, Central Washington University; Lynn Leeper, Bowie State College; Felicia Meyer, Central Washington University; Elizabeth K. Nelson, Prince George's Community College; Deborah Ragan, University of Maryland, and Joan Young, University of the District of Columbia.

Parents

Although the parents who were interviewed are not mentioned here by name, their experiences are an important part of this book. They — and hundreds of other parents — deserve special honor for their long, hard battles to open up opportunities for their learning disabled sons and daughters.

Index

Index

Index

ABOUT THE MAKING OF THIS BOOK

This book was set in
Cheltenham by American
Printing Company, Inc., of
Cheverly, Maryland. It was
printed and bound by Edwards
Brothers of Ann Arbor,
Michigan.